From Commandant to Captive

The Memoirs of Stalag Luft III Commandant Col. Friedrich Wilhelm von Lindeiner genannt von Wildau With Postwar Interviews, Letters, and Testimony

MARILYN JEFFERS WALTON
AND
MICHAEL C. EBERHARDT

Copyright © 2015 Marilyn Walton and Michael Eberhardt.

All rights reserved. No part of this book may be reproduced, stored, or transmitted by any means—whether auditory, graphic, mechanical, or electronic—without written permission of both publisher and author, except in the case of brief excerpts used in critical articles and reviews. Unauthorized reproduction of any part of this work is illegal and is punishable by law.

ISBN: 978-1-4834-2539-9 (sc)
ISBN: 978-1-4834-3157-4 (e)

Because of the dynamic nature of the Internet, any web addresses or links contained in this book may have changed since publication and may no longer be valid. The views expressed in this work are solely those of the author and do not necessarily reflect the views of the publisher, and the publisher hereby disclaims any responsibility for them.

All photos without credits are in the possession of the authors.

Any people depicted in stock imagery provided by Thinkstock are models, and such images are being used for illustrative purposes only. Certain stock imagery © Thinkstock.

Lulu Publishing Services rev. date: 05/13/2015

Although every effort has been made to recreate the original authentic translation of the memoirs, we reserved the right to make a few minor changes for the sake of clarity, formatting, consistency, and for ease of understanding by the reader. In many cases, particularly in the von Lindeiner letters written at Stalag Luft III and the postwar letters between Col. von Lindeiner and Col., later Maj. Gen. Delmar T. Spivey, a former POW, non-traditional or unconventional word usage, spelling, paragraphing, grammar, and punctuation have been retained to preserve the authenticity of the original translated documents exactly as they were originally typed. Some of the aging documents, many over seventy years old, proved to be too delicate and could not be brought up to good book-printing resolution, so we re-typed them "as is" in order to more clearly share their content. Trial testimony pages were typed exactly as they were from the original transcriptions of the court recorder over sixty years ago. When the recorder could not decipher notes, those areas are shown as dashes or blank underlined spaces. Since many of the documents came from different sources, the original typing reflects whether the typists chose to use the German umlaut when dropping a vowel in names such as Göring or Müller, so both forms have been retained. Any material in brackets to facilitate understanding of the text was inserted by the authors.

Bracketed sections marked [sic] in the actual memoir do not necessarily reflect errors made by Col. von Lindeiner, but in many cases reflect transcription errors from the original when it was first transcribed many years ago.

Contents

Prologue...xi
Acknowledgements..xxi
Introduction..xxiii

Chapter 1   Military Career 1
Chapter 2   The Memoirs of Colonel Friedrich-Wilhelm
                   von Lindeiner-Wildau, Commandant Stalag Luft III 5
Chapter 3   Von Lindeiner Correspondence with POW
                   Senior Officers – Stalag Luft III....................................... 175
Chapter 4   Interrogation/Interview Summaries - Col.
                   von Lindeiner Regarding the Killing of 50
                   POWs from Stalag Luft III London Cage –
                   August, 1945 189
Chapter 5   Goering Testimony Regarding Great Escape
                   and von Lindeiner 222
Chapter 6   Trial Transcripts - War Crimes Trials -
                   Hamburg, Germany - 1947 242
Chapter 7   Mutual Respect - Postwar Correspondence -
                   Col. Friedrich von Lindeiner and Maj.
                   General Delmar T. Spivey 277
Chapter 8   Final Thoughts 339

Appendix: Lisa Knüppel – Friedrich von Lindeiner's Secretary
         "A Young Woman's Life in Wartime Germany".......................343
Authors' Biographies 367

Special Acknowledgement

The extensive research for this book involved the German Archive in Freiberg, the Air Force Academy McDermott Library Stalag Luft III Collections, the Imperial War Museum, the RAF Museum, the British National Archives, and the POW Camps Museum in Zagan, Poland. In addition, Mike corresponded with the descendents of the von Lindeiner family in Germany as part of our efforts to collect material and information. Air Commodore Charles Clarke, OBE and President of the RAF Ex-POW Association, once again was instrumental in developing a project that allows us to donate all proceeds from the book's sale to benefit POW institutions that preserve the prisoners' memories, especially the POW Camps Museum in Zagan, Poland, and we are grateful to him for providing us with some of the photos as well as his wisdom. The cooperation of all of these rich sources, providing information, photos, and guidance allowed us to document the story of an intriguing man who experienced firsthand the tragedy of the Great Escape and the difficulties of running the Allied airmen's camp. To all we are deeply grateful.

Note: The word genannt, used in Col. von Lindeiner's formal name, differentiates the von Wildau branch of the von Lindeiner family from other von Lindeiners. Genannt means "named" or "called" and reflects the merging of families.

Prologue

By November 2010, after two years of researching the identity and location of any members of my father's crew, downed near Munich in March 1944, when their B-17 was hit by an incendiary bomb dropped from an American plane flying above it, I had launched my next project to see if any of his roommates from Stalag Luft III were still alive. My father had passed away in 1986 with little revelation of his World War II experience, including over a year as a POW. Buoyed by the fact that I had found that two of his crewmembers were still alive (and I became friends with both who shared extraordinary details with me), I thought my chances were good that I could meet some of his roommates from Stalag Luft III. That turned out to be a disappointment. By 2010, all were deceased except Charles Woodworth, who shared barrack 138 in South Compound with my father, but whom I would never meet since he passed away shortly after I discovered his whereabouts. However, his son, Mike, and I developed a friendship, and we would later travel together to Zagan, Poland, and stand in what was left of room 12 of that barrack where our fathers had lived during their captivity.

Preparations for the trip to Zagan began in November 2010. At that same time, I happened to be having lunch in Washington, D.C. with two old colleagues from my U.S. Department of Justice days when all of us served as prosecutors in its Organized Crime and Racketeering Section. Kurt Muellenberg and Howard "Buck" O'Leary had joined me for a casual lunch just to catch up. Kurt had been the Chief of the Organized Crime and Racketeering Section and one of my first bosses; Buck had worked with Kurt as a prosecutor in their early days in Detroit.

I knew Kurt's background fairly well---conscripted Hitler Youth with a dangerous escape from East Germany after the war--subsequent service in the U.S. Air Force in the 1950s, and eventual work as a federal prosecutor. So, I thought Kurt might be interested to know a little about my research and the fact that I was planning a visit to Stalag Luft III in the following months. As I explained what I had found, and revealed some of the history of Stalag Luft III, Buck listened intently and then towards the end of my description, he matter-of-factly interjected, "My wife's mother was a secretary at Stalag Luft III during the war." Quite stunned and astounded by this fact, particularly since I had known Buck for twenty years, I remarked that as a "secretary" she would have also served as a multi-lingual censor of the POW mail to and from Stalag Luft III. I speculated that perhaps his wife's mother may have even read the mail between my mother and father during his incarceration.

A short time later, I met Buck's wife, Andrea Hatfield, and we began a long dialogue that continues to this day about her mother, whose name was Lisa Knüppel.

Even more interesting was the fact that Lisa not only served as a censor, but she was the "personal" secretary to the Stalag Luft III Camp Commandant, Friedrich von Lindeiner, and as such, had been summoned to his court martial in 1944, following the Nazi inquiry into his accountability for allowing the 1944 massive prison break later known as the Great Escape. The two of them maintained a postwar relationship, including correspondence between Lisa and von Lindeiner and his wife after Lisa moved to the United States and married American attorney, Weston Hatfield, whom she had met in postwar Germany.

Lisa Knüppel
Courtesy Andrea Hatfield

I tucked this "small world" story in the back of my brain, and in 2013 Marilyn Walton and I conceived the idea for our first book entitled, *From Interrogation to Liberation, A Photographic*

Journey - Stalag Luft III - The Road to Freedom, which was published in early 2014, and reflects a photographic history of life in Stalag Luft III and Stalag VIIA from 1942-1945. A small portion of that book deals with Commandant von Lindeiner.

In doing the research on that first book, Marilyn told me of the existence of von Lindeiner's postwar memoirs, which had been largely overlooked for thirty years and were housed in the German Archive in Freiberg, Germany, and discovered there by Col. Art Durand who had taught at the U.S. Air Force Academy. Col. Durand's book, *Stalag Luft III, the Secret Story*, was published in 1988. After meticulous research, and without benefit of a computer, Col. Durand published the classic history of the famous camp with the encouragement of the late Lt. Gen. A.P. Clark, Superintendent of the Air Force Academy, a former prisoner of war at Stalag Luft III, who created the Stalag Luft III Collections at the Academy.

One aspect of Col. Durand's research was the exploration of the life of Col. Friedrich-Wilhelm von Lindeiner-Wildau who was court martialed after the Great Escape. Fortunately, Col. von Lindeiner wrote his memoirs fourteen years after he left Stalag Luft III in disgrace. Their discovery and translation by Col. Durand gave a little visibility to the memoirs, but they otherwise remained as part of the obscure and often hidden materials that relate to the history of WWII.

The irony and coincidence of Buck's original comment about his wife's mother and her service as von Lindeiner's personal secretary prompted me to obtain a copy of the von Lindeiner memoirs. Few were aware that the memoirs existed, and only a handful of people had an actual copy of them. I was added to the small list of those who possessed the memoirs, besides the Freiberg Archive and the U.S. Air Force Academy, where Col. Durand donated his research materials.

Von Lindeiner's memoirs are clearly not as historically revealing as the memoirs of men like Albert Speer, *(Inside the Third Reich)* or those of Walter Schellenberg, Hitler's Chief of Counterintelligence *(The Labyrinth)*. However, the von Lindeiner memoirs clearly provide an interesting look from inside the Third Reich by a man with torn allegiances, whose recollections describe the challenges for a gentleman of the old guard and an avowed anti-Nazi forced to please the Nazi High Command while abiding by the Geneva Conventions—a man adhering to his convictions of integrity and duty to prisoners of war while under the auspices of a madman. "Intelligent and bitter" might best describe the characterization of von Lindeiner that unfolds from his memoirs. But the unique perspective of the memoirs and the additional research that Marilyn and I have done for this book are clearly worth sharing for those who want to learn more about life at Stalag Luft III and the distinctive character of the man chosen to oversee the officers' camp until his removal in 1944.

So, while I picked up the tab for that lunch with Kurt and Buck in November, 2010, Marilyn and I still owe much to both of them---to Buck, and certainly Andrea, for all they have shared, and to Kurt for his encouragement in putting this book together, as well as his translation assistance.

Mike Eberhardt

§ § §

As the daughter of a Stalag Luft III POW, my interest in the history of the camp has been intense. While I was researching for a book I was writing in 2007, Col. Art Durand became a dear friend of mine as well as a mentor. Many hours were spent on the phone discussing "all things Stalag Luft III," including the memoirs of Col. von Lindeiner that he found in Germany while researching his classic book. It was with great sorrow that I lost my friend, Art, and in our final conversations just weeks before he died in 2012 Art told me that he would like the von Lindeiner memoirs made available to the public. He had expressed that interest to several other of his close friends in the Stalag Luft III community as well.

It is only with the enthusiasm and cooperation of many that projects like this one are developed. European researchers, Alan Bowgen, (England) Finn Bunch, (Denmark) Edouard Renière (Belgium) and Axel Wittenberg (Germany) were four such enthusiastic and knowledgeable people. Claudius Scharff, Kurt Muellenberg, Wolfgang Klaws, Ed Zander,

Ernie Hasenclever, and Heinz Schneider were quick with translations so crucial to the understanding of the old German records. The book required author visits to the Imperial War Museum in London and the British Archives to dig through reams of paper held there to discover and examine many documents that had not seen the light of day for decades.

It took a coalition of many other people, all dedicated to granting Art's wish, including Dr. Mary Ruwell, archivist at the Air Force Academy, Trudy Pollok of the Air Force Academy, the Durand family, Duane Reed, the former archivist at the Air Force Academy, the Archive in Freiberg, Germany, and above all, my co-author, Mike Eberhardt, who handled the legal release, to make the memoirs accessible to anyone wanting to read or use them. Without his expert assistance, the memoirs would still remain for the most part shut away and closed to the public. Art Durand's discovery of the memoirs, and Mike's release of them now make it possible for researchers and those interested in the German perspective to learn Col. von Lindeiner's thoughts during the cataclysmic years of World War II when Allied forces took the war to the enemy's heartland. We learn his state of mind before and after the Great Escape, his feelings for the High Command, Gestapo administrators, and the Allied POWs in his care. He shares his thoughts on the Battle of Britain, as well as other decisive battles of the war and reveals the inner-workings of the German military. Finally, we learn his plight after the war, an inevitable fall from grace resulting in lasting repercussions. We are gratified that Col. von Lindeiner's story can now be told as he wished it to be, in his own words, and simultaneously that a final promise to Art has now been fulfilled.

Marilyn Walton

This book is dedicated to the late Col. Art Durand—
Promise kept.

U.S. Ambassador John E. Dolibois
Courtesy The Kent State University Press – Ron Stevens Photographer

In Memoriam

John E. Dolibois
Former U.S. Ambassador to Luxembourg

Just prior to the publication of this book, the Stalag Luft III community lost a valued friend, former U.S. Ambassador to Luxembourg John E. Dolibois. He passed away at the age of 95 after a full and rich life. He was probably one of the last Americans who actually knew the Nazi High Command, having interrogated them at a secret Luxembourg location at the war's end in preparation for the Nuremberg War Crimes Trials that followed. John was probably most familiar with Reichsmarshall Hermann Göring, whose trial testimony appears in this book.

John was a born story teller and attended a Stalag Luft III reunion at the age of 93, captivating attendees with his stories and charm. He was a walking history book, yet a humble and accomplished man who came to this country from Luxembourg as a very young boy, later to become a citizen, an Eagle Scout, and to serve in the U.S. Army in World War II. He took great pride in serving his country. John did not live to see this book's publication, which he highly encouraged, but his undeniable enthusiasm brought it to fruition. His beloved *"Ons Heemecht,"* the National Anthem of Luxembourg, was played at his funeral, but *"American the Beautiful"* was deeply engrained in his heart.

Acknowledgements

Bowgen, Alan
Bunch, Finn
Clarke, Air Commodore Charles
Consolmagno, Joe
Dement, Ed
Dolibois, John
Durand, Col. Art
Edy, Barb
Green, Colin-Kirby
Hasenclever, Ernie
Hatfield, Andrea
Klaws, Wolfgang
Lazarz, Marek
Langlois, Pippa
Muellenberg, Kurt

O'Leary, Howard "Buck"
Pollok, Trudy
Reed, Duane
Renière, Edouard
Ruwell, Dr. Mary
Scharff, Claudius
Schneider, Heinz
Spivey, Scott
Swiatek, Marian
Talbert, Stephanie
Waller, Chelsea
Walton, Julie
Wilson, Tom
Wittenberg, Axel
Zander, Ed

Introduction

Heavy was the burden that fell to the men chosen to perform the tasks of commandant of Stalag Luft III. Lt. Col. A.P. Clark, one of the very early American prisoners at the camp, was in a unique position to assess three successive men who held that job during his time in the camp. According to Clark, Friedrich von Lindeiner was an elderly, old-school, aristocrat who was more generous with promises for better conditions than he was with actual improvements.

Col. Friedrich von Lindeiner
Courtesy USAFA McDermott
Library, Stalag Luft III Collections

Upon reflection, in a secret War Department document, now declassified, recorded when Clark returned to the United States after the war, when he was debriefed in Washington D.C. May 25, 1945, he remembered von Lindeiner as possessing a violent temper which he seemed unable to control whenever anything unexpected occurred. Upon one occasion, he leveled a pistol threateningly at American POW and perpetual escaper, Jerry Sage, when the latter was in the cooler following escape activities. Clark also remembered that von Lindeiner often launched into long tirades during official meetings, and he claimed that von Lindeiner took at face value all statements of his subordinates about given situations, although some of these reports were not correct.

When von Lindeiner was removed from the camp after the British Great Escape in 1944, he was succeeded by Major Erich Cordes, who was a temporary appointee and was not in charge long enough to be accurately characterized. He had served as commandant for only a few months when the Gestapo found he was involved in the black market, and he was removed from the camp and court martialed. It was during his tenure of office that American POW Cpl. C.C. Miles's death occurred from a shooting for which Clark believed Cordes should have been held responsible. He never was. Cordes was replaced by Oberst (Colonel) Franz Braune.

Braune was much more definite in his decisions than von Lindeiner and rather strict in general policy. He was easier to deal with than Oberst von Lindeiner, according to Clark, in that he gave definite answers to requests and usually acted upon his statements, although he also was somewhat inclined to meaningless promises.

It is not known if any definitive records exist regarding the latter two commandants, but, fortunately, von Lindeiner left a long and rich document detailing all facets of life in the camp. His remembrances were written when his memories of events were not quite as fresh as Lt. Col. Clark's were only weeks after the war ended, but at the same time, the former commandant's memoirs bear reading and evaluating as a view of an historic time for which many official German records were quickly destroyed leaving a void for comparative analysis. After reading his memoirs, the reader can more fully judge his tenure as commandant and draw individual conclusions about this colorful figure from the war who was an integral part of Stalag Luft III and the lives of those who were in his care.

Lt. Colonel Clark's critical characterizations of von Lindeiner are somewhat contrasted by the views of others who knew Commandant von Lindeiner. The quotes on the following pages, as well as the post-war correspondence between von Lindeiner and USAF Major General Spivey found in Chapter 7, are particularly insightful.

Relevant Quotes

"I suppose I had more to do with him than any other POW. In all my dealings with him--either stormy or calm--he always behaved with the greatest courtesy. In my opinion, though an enemy, he was an 'officer & a gentleman' in the best sense of the expression."

       Wing Commander Harry "Wings" Day – RAF - Senior
       British Officer North Compound - Stalag Luft III

"Closing this long letter, I repeat my best wishes for a very good year for yourself and your family. And if you ever come to Germany, please do not forget us, but do not wait too long, as I am growing old."

       Col. Friedrich von Lindeiner to
       Major Gen. Delmar Spivey – postwar letter

"I shall never forget the three Christmases I spent in Germany as a prisoner of war. To my great surprise and happiness, I found that there existed a common understanding of the spirit of Christmas between the German people and ourselves. I hope this understanding continues in the future."

       Major Gen. Delmar Spivey to
       Col. Friedrich von Lindeiner – postwar letter

"In many respects, von Lindeiner was an anachronism. His beliefs and practices represented the moral code of an earlier age, making him especially vulnerable in a period of Nazi decadence and modern warfare."

       Col. Art Durand – Author – *Stalag Luft III – The Secret Story*

"A little bit remote from the people he dealt with, perhaps because of his aristocratic upbringing, von Lindeiner was nevertheless very kind. Von Lindeiner had a distaste for the political gang on top in Germany, even if he never said it directly."

Henry Soderberg – International YMCA
Representative - Stalag Luft III

Chapter 1

Military Career

Friedrich Wilhelm von Lindeiner genannt von Wildau was born in Glatz, Germany, (now Klodzko in west Poland) in 1880. He entered the 3. Garde-Regiment zu Fuß as a Second Lieutenant upon graduating from the Corps of Cadets on 15 March 1898. On 1 May 1902, he left the Prussian Army and the following day entered the Schutztruppe [Protection Force] for German East Africa. Von Lindeiner served as the Adjutant of Gustav Adolf von Götzen, the Governor of German East Africa, from 20 June to 13 September 1905 and as the Headquarters Adjutant of the Schutztruppe for German East Africa from 7 September to 11 October 1906, taking part in the Maji Maji Rebellion, for which he received the Pour le Mérite and the Prussian Order of the Crown 4th Class with Swords. He left Schutztruppe service on 31 July 1908 and rejoined the Prussian Army on 1 August 1908 with a simultaneous promotion to oberleutnant [1st lieutenant] and was assigned to the 4. Garde-Regiment zu Fuß.

On 20 July 1912, after promotion to hauptmann, [captain] von Lindeiner was assigned as the Commander of the 11th company of 1. Garde-Regiment zu Fuß. [1st Foot Guard--an infantry regiment of the Royal Prussian Army] On 10 August 1914, he was assigned as the Commander of the Infanterie-Stabswache ["Infantry Staff Guard"] at the Kaiser's General Field Headquarters, returning to his regiment as Commander of the 11th company on 19 September, where he was wounded during the First Battle of Ypres on 17 November 1914. Returning to duty on 13 April 1915, he assumed command of the regiment's 5th company and later of its second battalion on 27 May 1915. He was again wounded during a pursuit between the Bug River and Jasiolda on 29 August 1915. After returning to duty, von Lindeiner assumed command of the Füsilier Battalion of 1. Garde-Regiment zu Fuß and was again severely wounded on 5 December 1915 in fighting around Roye-Noyon.

On 24 September 1914, von Lindeiner was assigned to Etappen-Inspektion 5 [Lines of Communication Inspectorate] and on 4 October 1916, he was assigned as the Personal Adjutant of Prince Joachim of Prussia, the youngest son of Wilhelm II, the German Emperor. After von Lindeiner's return to his regiment on 30 October 1917, he became the Adjutant to the Governor of Riga-Dünamünde. Appointed as Adjutant to the Garde-Reserve-Korps on 23 April 1918, von Lindeiner was promoted to major on 15 July 1918. His final wartime appointment was as Adjutant of the 4th Army, a post he assumed on 8 November 1918.

Following the Armistice, von Lindeiner was leader of the collecting point in Potsdam of the Volunteer Border Protection Unit East and Upper East (Grenzschutz Ost/Oberost) from 18 January 1919, retiring on 20 September 1919 with permission to wear the uniform of the 1. Garde-Regiment zu Fuß. He then worked in several civilian posts and married a member of the Dutch aristocracy, Baronesse Henriette van der Goes.

In 1937, von Lindeiner joined the Luftwaffe as one of Hermann Göring's personal staff. Since he was promoted to oberst [colonel], he was refused the retirement that he sought, and he was instead made the Commandant of Stalag Luft III. He and his wife lived in Sagan. Following the massive prisoner escape in 1944, he was court martialed, but he feigned mental illness to avoid imprisonment. After his release from a sanitarium, he was later wounded by Russian troops advancing towards Berlin while acting as second in command of an infantry unit. Von Lindeiner later surrendered to advancing British forces as the war ended and was taken for interrogation to the British interrogation center known as the "London Cage." He later testified during the British SIB [Special Investigations Branch] investigation concerning the Stalag Luft III prisoner of war murders. Von Lindeiner was later held as a prisoner of war at several British facilities before eventually being released and making his way back to Berlin, where he was eventually reunited with his impoverished wife.

WWI Military Decorations

Friedrich von Lindeiner-Wildau received the Pour le Mérite and the Prussian Order of the Crown 4th Class with Swords for the brutal fighting in the German East Africa campaign of 1905-07. He was also awarded the Colonial Medal with that bar. During World War I, he was also awarded the Saxe-Ernestine House Order - Knight 1st Class with Swords (1 May 1918) as Hauptmann and 1st Adjutant of the Government of Riga and the Mouth of the Düna, and the House Order of Hohenzollern Honor Cross 3b with Swords on 5 February 1915. Additionally, he was awarded the Iron Cross First and Second Class.

Table of Contents for Memoirs

The original memoirs are fairly unstructured, so the following table provides a guide to sections of the memoirs:

Introduction – Col. Art Durand
Preface – Lt. General Albert P. Clark

Introduction – Colonel Friedrich von Lindeiner
The General Staff of the AF (AF Operational Staff)
Structure of the POW System of the Air Force in Germany during WWII
POW Camp of the AF Nr. 3 (Stalag Luft 3)
The German Camp Organization of Stalag Luft 3
    Group 1 – Commandant and Court Officer
    Group 2 – Administration of the Various Compounds
    Group 3 – Counterintelligence
    Group 4 – Administration
    Group 5 – Medical Branch
    Group 6 – Mail Service and Censorship
    Group 7 – Guard Unit
    Group 8 – Military Officer of the Barrack
The Great Escape of 24-25 March 1944
    Construction of the Tunnel
    The Escape Proper and First German Countermeasures
    Court Martial Investigation and Actual Court Martial
    Back in Sagan
My Own POW Captivity
My Return Home and Final Words
Poems from German POWs
    Evening Prayer of a POW
    Spring 1946 (The Realist)
    A Returnee from 1947

Chapter 2

The Memoirs of Colonel Friedrich-Wilhelm von Lindeiner-Wildau, Commandant Stalag Luft III

Translated into English by Mr. Berthold Geiss
Edited by Col. Arthur A. Durand
Re-edited by Marilyn Jeffers Walton and Michael C. Eberhardt

Introduction

Stalag Luft III, a World War II German prison camp designed to hold captured Allied flyers from the West, has become one of the most widely-studied and best known prison camps in the annals of history. It acquired notoriety already during the war as a result of the widely-publicized, cold-blooded murder by the Gestapo and SS of fifty of its former inmates who participated in the Great Escape of 24-25 March 1944. Ironically, the murders that drew attention to the camp were conducted outside of its jurisdiction and were far different in nature from the daily conditions and events that made up the history of Stalag Luft III. While every prisoner of war lives in fear and misery, there is widespread agreement among those who were incarcerated in Stalag Luft III that the camp was very well managed and offered a modicum of safety and humane treatment that seems almost incredible in light of what is now known about the concentration and death camps operated by the Reich.

Because conditions in a prisoner of war camp are greatly affected by the personality of its commandant, we are fortunate to have access to the memoirs of the man who served as commandant of Stalag Luft III throughout most of the camp's history. Colonel Friedrich-Wilhelm von Lindeiner Wildau, Commandant from March 1942 until late March 1944, contributed immeasurably to the prisoners' safety and well-being. He was a proud and capable businessman and officer from the old school of German soldiers. When von Lindeiner assumed command of the camp, he was sixty-one years old, had a distinguished military career with two Iron Crosses to his credit, and had clearly indicated his displeasure with the recent turn of events in his beloved Germany. Severely wounded three times in World War I, he was never able to return to active combat. He served as aide-de-camp to Prince Joachim, the Emperor's youngest son, and became head of the guards at court. After the war, he went into business and nourished an interest in politics, inspired in part by his brother who was a respected member of parliament in Germany. He lived in the Netherlands from 1919 to 1932, and after his return to Germany, became a prominent member of the firm, Schenker and Company, which was swallowed up by the German government in 1937. At that point he left the company. Feeling the Luftwaffe was the least Nazi oriented of the three services, he joined Göring's personal staff in the Air Ministry. When he became Commandant of Stalag Luft III, he brought with him his Dutch baroness wife, who settled in Sagan.

Most observers have rated von Lindeiner very highly as a camp commander. He was well educated and spoke fluent English. One report states that he was a man with whom "a shouting match was out of the question." Perhaps the most telling comment on the man came from the prisoner who wrote, "No Commandant, to a prisoner, is a good man, but I think von Lindeiner was."

Von Lindeiner died on 22 May 1963, having lived to the age of 82. Before his death, he noted that five prominent books had been written about Stalag Luft III between 1946 and 1953, namely:

> *Escape to Danger* by Paul Brickhill and Conrad Norton
> *The Great Escape* by Paul Brickhill
> *The Wooden Horse* by Eric Williams
> *The Tunnel* by Eric Williams
> *Reach for the Sky* by Douglas Bader [sic] – [Paul Brickhill]

He sympathized with the indignation expressed in these books over the deaths of the fifty prisoners, who were killed by the Gestapo and SS, after the Great Escape of 24-25 March 1944. But he also pointed out that the descriptions given in the books were based exclusively on news and observed situations accessible to the incarcerated POWs and that for the most part they disregarded the conditions that prevailed in Germany during the war. He states, "It may seem understandable that the authors of these books misjudged the position and possibilities of action of the members of the German armed forces employed here. Less understandable, however, is the fact that the personalities, who risked the most to ensure the humane treatment of the POWs, were repeatedly described rather unfavorably." Stressing that the first two books, in particular, contained factual errors and misjudged prevailing conditions, Colonel von Lindeiner set out to disclose the German view of what transpired in Stalag Luft III and asserted that his memoirs were intended to be "a search for the truth," so that coming generations could have a factual description of the actions of German men.

Arthur A. Durand
Editor

Preface

POWs in the camp at Sagan respected Colonel von Lindeiner for his genuine efforts to make life bearable and to abide by the Geneva Accords. The camp was regularly inspected by representatives of the Protecting Power (Switzerland), and we had frequent and uninhibited communication with them. While prisoners of war can never be expected to be satisfied with their lot, the significance of the standards, which the Luftwaffe and von Lindeiner sought to maintain, can be grasped when one realizes that Russian prisoners were being allowed to die of neglect by the millions, and masses of political prisoners were being exterminated elsewhere in Germany.

In some respects, Colonel von Lindeiner's efforts to improve living conditions in the camp were a matter of self-interest. His theory was that supporting cultural, athletic, and educational activities in a clean and relatively livable environment would discourage escape attempts and lessen the danger of a takeover of the camp by the SS or Gestapo, which was a very real and serious threat. Unfortunately, in the officer camps the logic of this view was lost amid the ceaseless and inspired struggle of a high percentage of the prisoners to continue the war by all available means – intelligence, blackmail, sabotage, and escape. One element of the prisoner psychology involved ridicule of the Germans and everything they did. Thus, most of von Lindeiner's efforts went unacknowledged by all except the most responsible of the senior prisoner leadership.

Von Lindeiner's efforts to prevent his garrison personnel from creating emotional incidents in their relationships with the prisoners were a never ending challenge. Prisoners constantly badgered and ridiculed the ferrets and the guards, many of whom were disabled combat veterans or had lost their families and homes in the bombing. It is not surprising that we had a few pot shots into our crowded camp.

Colonel von Lindeiner was sacked and court martialed in late 1944 after the Great Escape. Only the confusion inherent in the collapse of

Germany and the intervention of a psychiatrist and friend, who consigned him to an asylum to ensure his safety, prevented his incarceration. Colonel von Lindeiner was then held prisoner by the English for almost two years after the war in spite of his non-involvement in the execution of the fifty RAF escapees from the tunnel at Sagan. By any standards, he was shabbily treated, and this is reflected in the bitterness displayed in his account. He was an officer of the old school, and his disgust for Hitler and the Nazi regime is unconcealed. His effort to defend the German armed forces and the Luftwaffe for their honorable treatment of captured Allied flyers is understandable.

As one reads this account, especially a former prisoner at Sagan, one is tempted to rebut some of Colonel von Lindeiner's view of things. This is a subjective account and written by an old soldier and gentleman shortly before death. He has provided for the record a unique view of the Sagan story from the other side of the fence, and I believe it should be protected against nit picking by those of us who have had over thirty years to write and publish our views of the prisoner experience.

Lt. Gen. Albert P. Clark
USAF (Ret)

Friedrich von Lindeiner's Introduction – Start of Memoirs

In April 1944, the free world fighting against Germany received what seemed to be unbelievable yet horrifying news. Born of feelings of inferiority and nurtured by some spectacular pre-1939 successes in foreign affairs, Hitler's Caesar Complex had received a deep and insulting blow when news arrived of the escape of 76 Royal Air Force and American Air Force officers. [sic] [No Americans escaped.] from the German Air Force prisoner of war camp Nr. 3 (Stalag Luft 3) at Sagan during the night of 24-25 March 1944. At a meeting on 26 March 1944 on the Obersalzberg, Hitler, in one of his sick rages, had ordered the immediate shooting of all recaptured prisoners. The military personnel present vehemently protested such unheard of orders. Hermann Göring interjected that such an act would be outright murder; however, as had been the case for the past three years, he was shouted down by the enraged Führer. Attempts to get the madman to change his mind or delay the executions proved unsuccessful, but in the end the military's resistance brought about a reduction in the number to be shot from 76 to 50. Thus, the unheard of happened and young lives were erased, their only crime having been to fulfill their duties as soldiers and try to return to their work.

To the German people, who were suffering more under Hitler's tyranny than those in his occupied foreign territories, this and other evil deeds remained hidden. Yet, where daring souls heard of it on enemy broadcasts, it stirred up deep disgust. The authorities of the German POW organization were told officially that the 50 had fallen while resisting arrest or while trying to evade recapture. Members of the armed forces, in particular, however, knew from experience that escaped Britons normally did not undertake acts of sabotage and gave themselves up voluntarily once they realized there was no way out. Additionally, it was more than strange that of the 50, none were wounded, though all had been shot. In the ranks of the German Armed Forces, the feeling of horror and disgust was augmented by a feeling of shame and the knowledge that their good name had been soiled.

The indignation, which, naturally, was felt the strongest in the British Empire, led to heated discussions which culminated in serious debates in the House of Commons. Retaliatory measures involving the German POWs in British hands were considered but luckily dropped. However, the British authorities pushed forcefully for the apprehension and strict punishment of the culprits in this crime against international law.

The continuing public indignation in the affected countries, primarily among the families and comrades of the dead, brought some who wrote about the German-English air war to talk particularly and in detail about the plight of the flyers in Germany. The discussions centered primarily around the conditions in Stalag Luft 3 at Sagan and the events after the Great Escape of 24-25 March 1944 and their deplorable consequences. Five main books dealing with this subject appeared in the years 1946-1953, to wit:

> *Escape to Danger* by Paul Brickhill and Conrad Norton
> *The Great Escape* by Paul Brickhill
> *The Wooden Horse* by Eric Williams
> *The Tunnel* by Eric Williams
> *Reach for the Sky* by Douglas Bader [sic] [Paul Brickhill]

They sold copies in the hundred thousands, were translated into many foreign tongues, and some were made into movies. The descriptions given in these books are based exclusively on news and observed situations accessible to the incarcerated POWs and, for the most part, disregard the conditions in Germany during the war years. It may seem understandable that the authors of these books misjudged the position and possibilities of action of the members of the German armed forces employed here. Less understandable, however, is the fact that the personalities who risked the most to ensure the humane treatment of the POWs were repeatedly described rather unfavorably.

Primarily, the first two books give particulars which, in part, do not agree with the facts and misjudge the prevailing conditions. It, therefore, seemed desirable to bring up the German standpoint on the questions asked and happenings described, particularly in reference to the prevailing spirit of the German Air Force in general and the development and execution of its Prisoner of War program with special emphasis on the conditions at Stalag Luft 3. We will find that the Germans, stereotyped by the English writers as brutal and uneducated, neither disregarded the international laws of warfare nor committed sadistic acts. They were simply men who were doing their duties in a most honorable fashion under most trying conditions. Quite often they were under grave emotional stress yet did not fear to take on personal risks for others.

Having been in command from fall 1939 to March 1944, and having witnessed firsthand the events described above, I was asked by many to give my point of view. I thought that I could not shirk this task. My decision was influenced primarily by my desire to give thanks to my trusted co-workers for standing by me in trying times. The official German documents are either destroyed or otherwise unobtainable. It was, therefore, necessary to rely on private documentation, the memories of participants, and publications in print since 1945. The purpose of this document is to search for the truth, to hand down to coming generations a factual description of the actions of German men. This appears all the more important since one-sided reporting has brought, even in circles friendly to the Germans, sentiments which harm the image of the armed forces and do not coincide with the facts.

As for myself, I would like to add that I served six years in the colonial service before WWI. In 1919, I got out of the service and worked in economics in positions abroad. Numerous lengthy trips took me to all countries in Western Europe, as well as the three Americas. In early 1932, I was recalled to Germany in my economic capacity but gave it up in 1937 based on the radically changed situation there. In July 1938, I was called into the General Staff of the AF to work on the English situation. In January 1940, I was appointed head of the section, "Foreign Air Forces West." At the beginning of the air war with England, I joined the twelve man "Luftwaffen Fuhrungsstab" (Air Force Operational Staff, Fu-Stab). After Japan entered the war, the Chief of Staff gave me the added duty of liaison to the Japanese military mission in Berlin and consequently the supervision of the East Asian theatre of war.

In spring 1942, the Chief of Staff of the Air Force, in agreement with Admiral Canaris, ordered my appointment as air attaché to the German Embassy in Lisbon. This was rescinded, however, after intervention from higher up. My third request within 3½ years for retirement from the service was again rejected, and I was appointed Commander of the POW camps, AF, with HQs in Sagan and also Commandant of the newly erected POW camp, AF Nr. 3, also situated there. In the first position, there were rather early, sharp discussions with the personnel division of the AF which led to the termination of that position and the creation of the Inspection of the Air Force under the Air Ministry. In the fall of 1943, Adolf Hitler ordered the retirement of all officers married to foreign nationals. My repeated reports, as belonging to that group, were rejected on the grounds that I was needed. The escape of the 76 POWs from Stalag Luft 3 on 24-25 March 1944 gave nonmilitary authorities the opportunity they sought to remove me from office. Heinrich Himmler, during the meeting on 26 March with Adolf Hitler on the Obersalzberg, is alleged to have said, "Finally I got this Lindeiner; for four years now I have been trying in vain to get him." I was suspended from duty, court martialed, and accused of disobedience during wartime, leading to damage to the Reich. After 6½ months of investigations, the court martial convened in October 1944. The prosecution had asked for demotion and 18 months prison. The sentence I received was for 12 months fortress incarceration. Before the sentence could be carried out, a medical commission diagnosed mental fatigue and ordered my transfer to the mental hospital in Görlitz. When this hospital was moved westward towards the end of January 1945, due to the closing in of the Russians, I, being healthy, could not go along and returned to my home near Sagan. I was wounded by the Russians on 12 February 1945, left as dead, and escaped. I was then first in American and then in English captivity, was taken to London for interrogation on 7 August 1945, and remained there until June 1947 at the English POW camp Nr.13 (Shap Wells) and camp Nr.18 (Featherstone Park), respectively.

The General Staff of the AF
(AF Operational Staff)

With the beginning of the war, the operational sections of the General Staff of the AF moved from Berlin to the military academy at Wildpark near Potsdam which had been closed. The staff included representatives of the Italian, and in the first months, also representatives of the Russian AF. With the start of the air offensive in the west, the "Fuhrungsstab des Luftwaffe" (Fu-Stab, Operational Staff) was created within the General Staff. It consisted of about 14 persons including myself. This Ops staff accompanied the Supreme Commander AF, Hermann Göring, on his trips to the Front in his special train. At the end of September 1940, the Ops staff was transferred to its own train (which it occupied until 21 March 1941) and consequently was moved to the Baltic Front. The reasons for these changes were the fact that Hermann Göring was needed more and more somewhere else, and the Ops staff was required on the Western Front.

It should be uncontested that Adolf Hitler, in his foreign policy goals, dreamed for a long time of a close relationship between Germany and England in which Germany controlled the European continent and England represented the interests of both countries overseas. Hitler's apparent love, yes admiration, for Great Britain receded only slowly. As late as the turn of 1941-42, I received a request for a report detailing under what circumstances an accord with England might be possible. This love was then replaced by a hatred which brought forth decisions like that which led to the shooting of the 50 escaped POWs from Stalag Luft 3.

Not until the middle of 1938 did the General Staff concern itself with the geographical, military, and economic situation of the British Empire, with special emphasis on their existing and planned preparations for an air war. These studies were made in close cooperation with the navy department and other Reich authorities like the German economy. I joined Section 5 of the General Staff on 1 August 1938 as a co-worker on the above matters. Any act which could be interpreted as an act of espionage was strictly forbidden. Any requests for information not obtainable within Germany had to be routed through the counterintelligence division of the O.K.W. [The Oberkommando der Wehrmacht - "Supreme Command of the Armed Forces"] All members of the General Staff AF had to sign a declaration to desist from any activities which could be interpreted as espionage if they either were transferred or took leave in England.

Our work was especially in the area special emphasis on the AF. This also included a detailed study of the meteorological conditions in and around the British Isles. Sources of information included not only the regular travel brochures but also publications of the government, parliament, and the press, and especially industrial publications. Their study was especially important since the knowledge of the size of a plant, plus the number of employees, led to certain conclusions as to its production capacities. At that time, there were plans underfoot in England to move all aircraft factories situated in the south toward the northern part of the country. Further sources of information were the publications of the British economic consortiums and individual companies. Also very revealing were brochures on expositions and reports on conferences. A lack of knowledge in this area on the part of the German staff was filled by contacting similar German companies. In the military sector, publications were available from the information offices of the Foreign Armed Forces as well as the personnel and rank lists of the RAF giving location and armament of their units, as well as the publication, *Army Air Force Quarterly*. Further excellent services were provided by air photography reconnaissance and the recording of radio transmissions of British aircraft and their home bases. Pre-requisite for all these duties was an excellent knowledge of the English language which made the compilers independent of a translator. Recommended was the personal knowledge of the country and its inhabitants. This knowledge was rather important, if it was based not on short trips or excursions to the country, but on longer stays with an accompanying feel for the British mentality which is so different from the German in many ways. The wealth of information available from the Reich's office for statistics in Berlin was impressive. It had such information as population density of individual sectors divided into men, women, and children and separated by age and profession, number of industrial plants with production figures and capacities, food production and raw materials, import and export figures, quantitative as well as by country of origin and port of destination, figures on the merchant fleet and inland transportation lanes, production and movement of electricity and many other things for the judgment of industrial capacities. Again, the help of related German industries was very productive. The military and economic potential of the British Empire was rank ordered according to its importance in the following manner:

1. Air bases and their manning
2. Ports and their turnover
3. Aircraft industry
4. Fuel shortage and hydro-electric plants
5. Industrial plants, including power sources, ranked by importance for weapons industry
6. Mills
7. Transportation lanes (railroad and canals)

With the beginning of the war, additional information came from POWs and deserters as well as the listening service. The latter service especially got excellent results. According to my own observations, we had, at least until mid 1942, an accurate picture of enemy air power on European and African soil.

The Commander of the German Air Force, Hermann Göring, pushed for accomplishment of the given tasks with his own energy. When it was reported to him towards the end of 1938, that the goals set by him could not be accomplished in the allotted time, he replied, "If I had looked at the order of Adolf Hitler given to me in 1934 for the construction of an air force within five years as 'impossible,' then we would not be today where we are. Tell me what and how many people, how much money, how many printers and printing plants, or whatever else you might need, and I will get it for you, but I do not want to hear the word impossible ever again."

And so it happened that in less than a year, a wealth of information was readied and distributed to the staffs of the air force.

Beginning in 1939, the General Staff of the Air Force conducted a kind of war game in which an English-German armed conflict was looked at from the English point of view. It was desired to uncover the weak points of the English defenses and, thereby, open up possibilities of aggressive maneuvers on the part of the German Air Force. An English cabinet was created, using members of Section 5 of the General Staff. I received the post of Minister of Supply. With the cooperation of members of the scientific and economic sectors, we came to the following conclusions after many weeks of hard work.

1. England's survival depends on its overseas trade. To prevent an acute shortage of food, the English government has ordered that import companies, wholesalers, mills, retailers, and households stock up for supplies for 3-4 months. It can be assumed that the industry is also stocking up on raw materials. To increase the utilization of the available ship cargo space, it is assumed that England will drop import of unwieldy raw materials for those half or fully processed goods.
2. England's lifeline can be paralyzed or at least considerably impaired by air attacks against port facilities as well as mining of harbors from the air. These actions have to be coordinated with the navy under utilization on U-boats.
3. The defense against enemy air attacks within the German realm can be effectively supported by destroying the enemy's air bases.
4. The destruction of industrial targets within England, especially aircraft production, will be accomplished by specially selected and trained aircraft and crews operating in good weather to prevent too many losses. The use of large closed formations of aircraft would be impractical due to inadequate protection by fighters.
5. The rules of the convention of The Hague are to be enforced. Terrorist attacks, i.e., those against nonmilitary targets and/or key points of civilian life, like sewer systems and water supply, will not

take place since they would violate the articles of war, especially attacks on residential areas of the civilian population.
6. Total control of the air space over England, even considering an expanded radius of action of new aircraft, would appear unfeasible since the enemy air force can rely on more rear area air bases.

These guidelines worked out in March 1939 in regards to an air attack against the British Isles could only be looked upon as a plan of action for future use, since it was not feasible at that time. The radius of action for German aircraft from the closest air base, without violating Dutch or Belgian air space, was restricted to the most southeast corner of the Isles. It was rather surprising in these times when an experienced pilot actually made it to the mouth of the Humber. Not until the construction of better aircraft and the use of the Dutch, Belgian, and French air bases, which took some months to expand into, could the operational plans of the General Staff be brought closer to realization. We should not forget that the newly-formed air force also had to struggle in setting up new guidelines in air warfare. The experiences gained in Spain against an inferior enemy force were only partially of value, even if important improvements had been made. Additionally, the protection of attacking bombers by using short-range fast fighters was rather cumbersome. Attacks on such desirable targets as the ports lying on the Humber, like Firth of Forth, Bristol Channel, as well as on the Messey, [sic] [Mersey] Solway-Firth, and Firth of Clyde could only be undertaken after the night flights had been perfected and only after repeated requests to the highest Reich authorities. An additional burden in such missions was the rather unreliable weather reports the pilots had to put up with. The actual mission order could sometimes only be given two hours in advance, which required longer alert times if full advantage was to be taken of good weather conditions over the target area. Weather reports arriving from Russia, until about June 1941 brought some relief, but they were not sufficient. Night flights of the meteorologists in unprotected fighters became a necessity in the west. Their fearless, valuable service over the Atlantic, mostly at night or in the early morning hours, has not been given the praise it deserves. Heavy losses were the order of the day which became harder and harder to replace.

The increased aircraft production of England and France after 1935 did not escape the attention of the General Staff of the Air Force. After the lifting of the neutrality laws of the U.S.A., both nations tried to increase their production further by awarding contracts to American firms. It was noted that the aircraft and motor industry in the U.S. was rather reluctant at first to take on these contracts, since it meant considerable expansion of existing plant facilities. One reason for their reluctance was the experience gained by American companies after WWI when they were left with huge plants which had been used for war production for their allies that no longer produced a profit and yet tied up an immense amount of capital. It was finally agreed that such expansion was to be financed by the British and French.

The increased production of especially the English Air Force caused the Fu-Stab to issue a memorandum already in 1940 pushing increased production of fighters, especially night fighters. They were considered essential if one wanted to protect the German areas against bomber attacks which were sure to come if the war continued. We sought to create an air barrier made up of fighters, one located on the Atlantic and Baltic coast, the other near the Reich's borders. To this would be added readiness groups stationed within the German borders. Repeated requests of this nature, supported by Hermann Göring, were without success. Approval authority for such plans lay with the Reich's leadership which would have had to authorize such a program. They were rejected on the grounds that Germany was fighting a Blitz war and not a long term engagement. This reasoning was used repeatedly during the war and had regrettable consequences. Similar thoughts must have influenced Adolf Hitler's thinking in the latter part of 1942 when he persisted in the construction of propeller-driven aircraft as bomber attack weapons rather than order the serial construction of the proven jet fighters, the ME 262. Neither Hermann Göring nor the General Staff of the Air Force can be blamed as was maintained by certain factions after the war that this wonder aircraft never saw regular duty. Its use would have made possible the destruction of the bomber forces attacking Germany in 1943 and 1944 despite their fighter protection.

The abundant amounts of information that reached the Reich's leadership made itself felt in a negative and disturbing way. Adolf Hitler leaned toward believing the news that coincided with his own wishful thinking. Aside from reports by the foreign office and the counterintelligence division of the O.K.W., the following authorities submitted reports:

1. The Reich Security HQs under Obergruppen Führer Kaltenbrunner and Müller
2. The Private Information Service of Reichsführer Heinrich Himmler under SS-Brigade Führers Schellenberg and Jost
3. The Propaganda Ministry under Minister Göbbels
4. The East Ministry under Reichsleiter Rosenburg
5. The Foreign Organization of the Party under Reichsleiter Bohle and his district leaders in the various foreign countries

One was trying to outdo the other in its factual reporting, especially the Foreign Office, as well as the counterintelligence section of the O.K. Army under Admiral Canaris. The sharpest confrontation here, as in all other areas, was the quiet but embittered power struggle of Heinrich Himmler against counterintelligence under Admiral Canaris. After an agreement was reached between the two that Canaris was the only one authorized to gather information overseas, Himmler's agents tried to buy all agents working for counterintelligence, thereby drying up that source of information. This was but one act of the struggle between Himmler and Canaris, and yet an outsider could get the impression that the two were the best of friends rather than deadly enemies.

At the start of the fighting in September 1939, the Commander of the Air Force, Hermann Göring, disseminated the following principles of operation to his units, "During the First World War, in which I participated as an active pilot, there reigned between the rival air forces a spirit of chivalry which lasted even after tempers got hotter. I wish and hope that the newly-formed German Air Force makes this chivalry, in the fighting which is about to start, their guiding principle also."

This wish of their commander found full approval among the ranks of the flyers. When around the turn of 1940 and 1941 the German news media, in their reports of enemy activities, started to call the attacking fighters names like "air gangster" and "murder pilots," the German Air Force protested energetically, saying that soldiers who were doing their duties often times did not realize the consequences of their actions and were being judged too harshly. Enemy pilots who had been shot down or made emergency landings were received on German air bases as defeated comrades and sometimes lived there as equals for many days until their transport under humane conditions was possible. A reader of the books of Mr. Brickhill and Douglas Bader [sic] will find to his disappointment that a number of English pilots were harboring different principles, at least during their captivity. Their behavior gave the impression they were trying to provoke German personnel.

The treatment of enemy pilots in the hands of the Air Force will be discussed later on; I would just like to point out here that the German Air Force has always done everything it could to treat downed comrades of the enemy forces according to international laws and tried, where the conditions allowed, to protect the honorable safety and life of the pilots. If enemy flyers ended up in the hands of the German political authorities, the Air Force insisted, sometimes in the face of immense risks, that they be turned over to them. Never has it happened, however, that German pilots were conducting strafing runs at women working in the fields or at children going to school and shooting them like fair game. They have never shot up trains full of women, old people, and children fleeing from the enemy, or vehicles marked with the red cross in such a way that it took hours to clear the roads littered with dead bodies of people and animals and demolished vehicles. Wing Commander Arthur Lee of the RAF says on page 61 of his book, *The German Air Force*, published in 1946, that the German Air Force dropped their bombs in the spring of 1940 on columns of southward fleeing Belgian and French civilians. This statement must be refuted most energetically. Never has the German leadership ever issued such inhumane orders nor have German units ever carried out such orders. If noncombatants in their flight were ever killed by aircraft bombs, then it can only be found in cases where the retreating civilian population was mingling with retreating troops of the enemy. Never has the German Air Force, even in times of absolute air supremacy, dropped their bombs on strictly residential areas far removed from military installations or those of military value or dropped them on isolated farms. Sir Arthur Harris, Marshall of the Royal Air Force and Supreme Commander of the English Bomber Force during the war, however, writes in his book, *Bomber Offensive*, about the surface attacks of the English on Germany: "The destruction of industrial complexes always came as a kind of special bonus; our actual target was always the center of the city." Mr. Winston Churchill, who, since the Boer Wars, hated everything associated with the Germans, published already in 1924 in the *Pall Mall*, an article which contained the sentence, "One should invent a bomb, not bigger than an orange, which could destroy a city without sparing churches, houses, and museums." And the well-renowned military journalist, General J.F.C. Fuller, wrote in his book, *The Second World War*, published in 1948, that the now Prime Minister of England, Mr. Winston Churchill, gave to his minister in charge of aircraft construction the following directions on 8 July 1940:

> "There is something which can throw back and destroy the enemy, and that is in all destructive and all-out exterminating air war with very heavy bombs from England against the German homeland. We must overpower the enemy by these means. I see no other alternative."

On 16 December 1941, the same Mr. Winston Churchill, again according to a report by General J. F.C. Fuller, made the following entry in his own diary:

> "Let us hope that we weaken the production and resistance of the Germans by bombing their cities and harbors more

and more effectively. Great Britain is as of now taking these steps and escalating the English-American bombing of Germany without restrictions, upwards, until the end of the war."

Based on the decision of the English cabinet in May 1940, the air attacks of the western powers began against the German homeland. In area bombings, the houses of nonmilitary wives, children, the old, and the sick were destroyed, and hundreds of thousands were buried under rubble. Peaceful isolated farm homes were destroyed, people in the fields and on country roads, as well as refugees, were shot down, all without being able to defend themselves. Apparently, they sought to drive people living under tyranny to commit mutiny against their rulers. These people had not wanted the war, they had no influence on its end, nor had they committed any atrocities. However, they could hear in the enemy radio broadcasts the words, "We are not waging war against the German people, we are waging war against Hitler."

The exact number of civilians killed in the bombing war of the Second World War may never be known exactly, but a figure of 1,200,000 is surely not too high. Of those who died, 45% were women, 35% children, 23% old or sick people. In answer to the above directives issued by Winston Churchill on 8 July 1940, Adolf Hitler yelled on 4 September 1940, in one of those demagogic speeches, which did little for the prestige of the office he held:

> "If the British air force throws 2,000 or 3,000 or 4,000 kilo, then we will throw now in one night 15,000, 18,000, 20,000, 40,000, and more kilo. And if they declare that they will attack our cities on a large scale, we will erase them!"

These words are often held against Germany. They were an answer to English threats, their actual execution based on the available technology, but in reality, they were impossible. At the time of the air war against England, late summer 1940 until about the end of April 1942, almost all orders of the Fu-Stab went through my hands, and I have never seen one asking for civilian bombings. Even if some young hotheads sometimes cried, "Throw bombs on their heads, and they will raise their hands," this never influenced leadership. The total air war of the enemy brought untold misery to the German people but in no way influenced the outcome of the war. Despite the all out efforts of the western powers in 1943-44, production in Germany increased in 1944, considerably over 1943. This was partly seen because of the move of German production underground and partly because of its move to the eastern areas.

After the end of WWII, the commander of the English bomber squads, the aforementioned Air Marshall A. Harris, called "Bomber Harris," was reprimanded even in English circles because of his ruthlessness in bomber warfare. To preserve the dignity of the country, however, it was done in correct fashion in closed English circles, not in public. In 1946, he was overlooked at the endowment and nobility ceremonies for successful statesmen; he received a good position in South Africa and thus disappeared for a while. In 1953, it was thought that grass had grown over the affair, and he was raised to the rank of nobleman.

Different principles apparently apply in Germany, even though the defamation of our best soldiers let up somewhat after 194. This is apparent when we come to the question of who led the first bomber attack on a free city, namely Freiburg im Breisgau, on 10 May 1940. Rumors circulated pretty soon in Germany that the attack had been ordered by high circles in the German command structure to be executed with German planes, without nationality markers in an effort to create an excuse to fly missions against open cities in enemy territory. A commission of the military looking into the events as to whose nationality had flown the attack remained inconclusive, or if any evidence surfaced it was restricted to a very small group. After the occupation of Paris in June 1940, we found in the ministry of the AF protocols of talks between French and English AF ops staff regarding the joint handling of the air war. With the beginning of the war, English air units had been stationed on the continent in the areas around Calais and Metz, and the British representatives made the suggestion that they, together with the French Air Force, attack Germany's industrial areas. These proposals were always rejected by the French, apparently for fear of retaliatory measures against the French domain. Any more rumors circulating in Germany that the attack was orchestrated by the Germans slowly but surely died, especially after General J. F. C. Fuller reported on a document from the Principal Assistant Secretary in the English Air Ministry, Mr. J. M. Spaigh, [sic] [Spaight] detailing the attack on Freiburg in the following manner:

> "We (the British) had started bombing targets on German soil before the Germans started bombing British soil. But since we were in doubt about the psychological effect of twisting the truth for propaganda purposes, namely, that it was us who started the strategic offensive, we shied away from publicizing our great decision of May 1940."

Then on 4 April 1956, eight years later, German newspapers reported in sensational headlines in big black titles:

> "After Sixteen Years, Finally Proven!"
> "German Pilots Attacked Freiburg!"
> "Göring's Disgrace Covered Up!"

Apparently, certain German circles thought they were doing the public a great favor by digging up a bad deed which their own people had done sixteen years ago. The "Zentral Institute fur Zeitgeschichie" [sic] ["Zentral-Institut für Zeitgeschichte"] (Central Institute for Contemporary History), created in Bavaria after WWII, thought their countrymen had committed a criminal act on 10 May 1940. The actual events could possibly have happened in the following manner:

On 10 May 1940, the great German western offensive started with a simultaneous attack of the German air force units on enemy air bases. It was a smashing success. POWs reported later that for at least 24 hours there was no solid leadership left, and enemy aircraft in the air had to look long and hard to find a place to set down.

Included in this offensive was the attack on the Southern Front of Fighter Squadron 51 (strength, 96 aircraft) against the French air base at Dijon. The flight took place in hazy weather and partly under instrument flying rules. It is entirely possible that a lieutenant, who maybe later fell under honorable conditions, together with his pack (total, three aircraft) lost all sense of direction (lost his bearings), thought Freiburg was the target and dropped his bombs. An order for such an attack was never given, however, and how it is a disgrace for the commander of the air force, if one of his young officers makes a mistake, is not quite clear. To the world, and without foundation, however, the Germans announced after sixteen years how brutally the German Air Force had been waging war.

The elaboration of Air Marshall A. Harris in his book, *Bomber Offensive*, as well as Vol. 2 of the *Official War History of the Royal Air Force*, tell of the air war England fought on directions given by Winston Churchill. Of the total weight of 960,000 tons of explosives, which the RAF dropped on Germany, 435,000 fell on inner cities and only about 145,000 on actual industrial complexes. In the area of today's Federal Republic of Germany alone, 1,062 cities with more than 3,000 inhabitants received heavy damage, 166 of those cities were more than 70% damaged. Over 1,100 historical and cultural structures of irreplaceable value were totally destroyed.

As a comparison of the losses of the German and English populations, resulting from bombings throughout the war, 1,200,000 Germans died while British losses consisted of only the following as derived from English publications from 1946:

Killed:	Men	26,923
	Women	25,399
	Children under 16	7,736
	Not identified	575
	Total	60,633 persons

[Computation error present in original text]

The number of wounded through bombings was given at 86,182; the number of dead and wounded in the British Isles during the whole Second World War, therefore, was 146,815 persons. That's about as many as the number who died from only one attack by the enemy air forces on the city of Dresden and upon the refugees camped on the outskirts of town on the Elb [sic] [Elbe] meadows one night in February, 1945.

The leadership of the German Air Force repeatedly and successfully opposed terror or vengeance acts ordered by Hitler or succeeded in toning them down to a more humane level. Beginning in June 1940, Hitler ordered a concentrated area attack on the city of Paris. It somehow had to be pulled off and was staged under the code name "Paula." The actual target, however, was restricted to the Renault factories situated on one of the Seine Islands. The city of Paris with its irreplaceable treasures was spared entirely. Even the revenge attacks against England, later ordered by Hitler, were code named "Baedecker-attacks" [sic] [Baedeker] in our inner circles and executed in the style of the Paris attack. I would only like to mention York and Cambridge. Hitler's orders were executed by dropping the bombs on the outskirts. Even during the time of the German attacks against English harbor installations, from about November 1940 to April 1941, the attacking units always carried map information, which highlighted the strategic targets exactly to prevent bomb drops on civilian houses.

Two of the attacks of the German Air Force are often used to reproach their activities as violations of the laws of war, namely the attack on Rotterdam on 14 May 1940 and on Coventry on 15 November 1940. Both attacks, it must be said with all decisiveness, were directed towards strictly military targets, and were, therefore, within the confines of the law. On 10 May 1940, German paratroopers had orders to land on the Dutch airfield of Waalhaven, situated on the south bank of the River Maas, and by taking the open city of Rotterdam on the north bank, to break the "Fortress Holland." Some weak forces of the paratroopers had succeeded in crossing the heavily-defended Maas bridge and had gained the northern shore. Here they were trapped in front of heavy fortifications of the supposedly open city of Rotterdam and more or less awaited their deaths. The main body of paratroopers on the south side went without support from the rear for several days and also were threatened by superior forces coming up from a southerly direction. The German commander had ordered the Dutch commander of Rotterdam to surrender on a certain deadline and had not received an answer by the appointed time. In this situation, he requested in the early hours of 14 May air support for his troops situated on the northern shore who were cut off. These aircraft had orders to attack the fortifications in question as a kind of extended artillery. A map of the area to be bombed had been brought to the rear echelons to indicate friendly and enemy positions. At 1500 hours, two groups of 48 bombers each took off. The targets had been exactly specified and comprised, aside from the Dutch positions on the north shore of the Maas, also the Maas train station directly by the river, and a small segment around the northern end of the bridge. Placing such limitations on the targets resulted from humane considerations and the duty of sparing the civilian population. A very somber military fact also needed to be considered, a minimum of craters and house ruins to ensure the roads would be free for a continued advance. It was only necessary to disable the strong fortifications around the bridge. To prevent any kind of terror attacks, the loading of incendiary bombs was not authorized.

Later, after the take-off of the aircraft from their rear bases, a Dutch envoy arrived and declared his commander's willingness to negotiate terms. The German units in the air were immediately notified of this development and rerouted to secondary targets. The most westerly squadron received the information and immediately turned to fly against their secondary targets, in this case the reinforcements arriving from the south. This message, however, was not received by the more easterly squadron. When the German air observers on the Waalhaven airfield saw this, they immediately shot off a great number of red stop flares. They could not be seen by the attacking aircraft, however, due to hazy weather (cloud ceiling 700 m). Thus, they came to their bombing run, but again only on the military targets specified.

Despite all this, a whole section of town was laid in ashes and ruins, not because of carpet bombings, but because of a fire which the local fire department could not control. Their rescue efforts were hampered by the fact that a bomb had hit a water main. Thus the fire ate its way from home to home, and the huge surface fires consumed everything.

The attack on Coventry on 15 November 1940 was flown by 400 German aircraft, which according to their capacities, had no more than 300 tons (300,000 kilos) worth of bombs. With this concentrated attack against an extremely important military target, we deviated for once only from the principal of single attacks, which had been set in early 1939, mainly because of the decided importance of Coventry as a center of the English aircraft motor industry. The auto factories had also been converted to airplane engine factories and their destruction would hamper the continued enlargement of the English Air Force. The individual industrial complexes were not on the outskirts or grouped together, but were distributed all over the city. Thus, if the industrial targets were attacked, the destruction of human habitation could not be avoided. Despite all the above factors, the attack on Coventry, which is being used so much against the German Air Force, resulted in only about 650 dead, or about 35% of the total population of 183,000 souls. The losses inflicted on the civilian population of the militarily unimportant city of Dresden, bursting at the seams with refugees in February 1945, stood according to estimates at 125,000 dead; that's about 19½% of the permanent population figures. Other estimates go as high as 250,000 dead, including the refugees who had camped on the banks of the Elbe. In any case, though a loss of human lives (during that night) of about 20% seems a rather conservative figure, that figure is about 60 times higher than the losses inflicted in Coventry.

Even passionate critics of the missions flown by the German Air Force during World War II will be hard pressed to prove that destruction of nonmilitary targets on the Western Front and Italy took place or was caused by German bombs. The damage inflicted on Warsaw in August and September 1944 was inevitable since the well-organized and trained Polish underground army under the command of General Count Bor-Kowolowski [sic] [Gen. Tadeusz Bor Komorowski,] was threatening to destroy the much weaker German forces. The western Allies were also helping the Poles through drops of weapons, ammunition, and food. The Russian army standing before the gates of Warsaw in the east apparently did not want to intervene because of political motives, even though they had been requested to intervene repeatedly in telegrams from Churchill to Stalin. Apparently, he did not want to strengthen the political clout of the Poles fighting in Warsaw to the detriment of the Polish communists on his staff. The allies also knew that Hitler could have a separate peace with Russia since the summer of 1943 based on the principles of August 1939. When the Poles had to capitulate on 2 October 1944, after 63 days of merciless fighting, there were 17,000 dead on the German side, against 15,000 dead on the Polish side. A greater number of dead in the civilian sector resulted mainly from the house-to-house combat which was not started by the Germans.

If in the area of the Atlantic west coast, human habitations had to be cleared or raised, it did not happen because of a sick desire for destruction, but because a British-American invasion was feared.

During the month of July 1940, the work on the Dutch, Belgian, and French airstrips was completed, and the aircraft industry had progressed to better designed aircraft so that increased action of the air force against targets in England became a possibility. The execution of this plan, however, influenced some rather undesirable circumstances.

The 19 July 1940 attack brought a special session of the so-called German Reichstag in the Kroll Opera House in Berlin, in the course of which Hermann Göring was proclaimed "Reichsmarshall." A traditionally large number of officers were advanced to the rank of "Feldmarschall," and Hitler thought he made peace overtures to the British. During the return from this meeting to the HQs Air Force in Wildpark near Potsdam, my section chief remarked that Hitler must really have meant it with his peace offer. He professed he knew from informed sources that Hitler had studied the text of the speech he had given moments before with special care to ensure he expressed his desire for a peaceful settlement with England. I replied that a speech like the one I had just heard was rather made to bring about the opposite, judging by content and tone of voice.

It was again proof of the total ignorance Hitler and his advisors exhibited when judging the English way of thinking.

The situation stemming from the continuation of the war brought about in Hitler a certain insecurity as to the next steps. It impressed itself on his decisions regarding military operations in the Western Front in the next months. The hope for a more favorable English mood caused Hitler to issue certain orders to his commanders on 24 May 1940 that made it possible for more than 300,000 English and about 30,000 French troops to evade capture at Dunkirk. Certain places have tried to tie this decision to more strategic contemplations, such as the desire to reach Paris rather quickly, reports from Hitler's entourage, however, negate this assumption. The previously mentioned Wing Commander Arthur Lee, considered to be my opponent on the English side, said in his book, *The German Air Force*, on page 58 that the evacuation of about 330,000 trained English and French soldiers, even though heavy armament had to be left behind, was made possible by the intervention of the British Spitfires and Hurricanes. The intervention of enemy flying squadrons here as well as later while protecting the British Isle has always found chivalrous recognition on the part of the Germans. The successful evacuation was only made possible, however, after Hitler had ordered the stopping and rerouting of the German army. This again emphasizes Hitler's desire to make England and especially its prime minister inclined to the idea of an early separate peace treaty. The total lack of any response on the part of England to Hitler's direct and indirect advances dealt him a rather heavy blow. It haunted him now that he had given little or no thought to the idea of how and when he could stop a military skirmish with the western powers once he had broken relations with them.

True to the principle of the English people to "never give up," the heavy blows England had received in the early months of the war intensified their resistance, especially under the new prime minister, Winston Churchill. The troops that escaped from Dunkirk to England, even though they had left all their heavy armament, made the creation of a new army rather easy. It is an open question what influence on the morale of England the capture of that army would have had in general and specifically what impact it would have had on the position of the prime minister.

In England, in the meantime, the reconstruction of an army was pushed to the utmost. For the protection of the work to be done, the coastal defense line was strengthened, and a civil defense was established, especially in the southern counties of England. At the same time, the building up of the resistance movement in German occupied territory was ordered by higher up and sustained in the western areas during the whole war under the control of the "War Office Intelligence Corps." Persons who had fled to England from occupied territory were taken back to their countries in nightly flights and landed there equipped with large sums of money and radio equipment and formed the first resistance movements.

Within a year, we confiscated, aside from the numerous weapons transports, 62 transmitters. Some of the male agents even wore women's clothing. Areas favored for such activities were the Netherlands, France, and the occupied territories of Poland and Yugoslavia. In Poland, the resistance fighters called themselves "A.K." After Russia entered the war, a communist organization called, "A.L." was formed in Lublin and worked together with the Russian partisan organization. The work in Yugoslavia was also handled by Russians after Stalin had declared the Balkan his sphere of interest and the English contacts had disappeared. The murderous anti-international actions of these resistance fighters made it necessary for the German authorities responsible for the safety of German personnel and materials to take actions which while still within the realm of international law nonetheless sowed a hatred which seems to go on forever but which seems to some of the creators of the "Franctireru," [sic] [Franc Tireurs - irregular military formations deployed by France during the early stages of the Franco-Prussian War (1870–71)] a condition which they don't mind at all.

After the surrender of France in June 1940, Hitler again allowed himself to hope that his threats of an invasion of England would soften the leading statesmen to agree to his wishes of a separate peace treaty. Under the code name "Sea Lion," directions were sent to the armed forces components to prepare for an invasion of England. They were, however, never forced with the kind of push one was accustomed to from him. In view of the insufficient defense capabilities England had until at least late fall of 1940, it seemed quite possible that a crossing would be successful; it perhaps would have meant less victims than the war which lasted five more years.

Obstacles were seen mainly in the English fleet which was still rather intact up to then, and in that area Germany had nothing equal to throw in as a defense for the crossing. A protection of the air space was possible since the German Air Force was far superior to that of the English. The plan could be prepared through clear and precise instructions to the air force leadership, and that it was feasible was proven by the attacks in the latter half of August 1940 on the many bases in the London area. Bases at Dover, Deal, Hawkinge, Lympne, Middle Wallop, Kenley, Biggin Hill, Croydon, Manston, West Malling, and Tangmere were lastingly destroyed. The 11th Fighter Group in that area received heavy losses. The English thought about bringing in the 12th Fighter Group stationed in middle England, but this idea was hastily rejected. The 12th Fighter Group had the duty of protecting England's industry. On the German side, there was also the possibility of landing troops to prepare for the crossing elements.

Due to the vacillating orders of the Reich's leadership, the German Air Force was fighting in these times against English shipping traffic on a line about from Harwich to Plymouth. Going by directives issued in 1939 to effect a disruption of the English life lines, it was of foremost interest to shut down England's most important harbor, namely London. From this resulted the aerial engagements which became known in England as "The Battle of Britain" which lasted from the beginning of August to about the end of October 1940. The official notification of a crossing to England (Operation Sea Lion) was given to the armed forces units only at the end of September 1940 but had been expected much sooner by the air force Ops Staff because of certain observations. I still participated in meetings together with the Chief of Staff of the Air Force as late as mid-September 1940 at which the technical details of action to be taken by the air force in case "Sea Lion" was executed were discussed. On the return trip, I allowed myself to remark that I found it strange to conduct such meetings since it was clear that these plans would never be realized. I received the answer it was done strictly for camouflage purposes.

London and its harbor were protected, as suggested before, by a great number of bases and fighter squadrons; their destruction had to precede any successful attack on the harbor of London. During September 1940, we succeeded in forcing the English Fighter Squadrons to bases further to the north. These attacks, as well as those flown against London harbor proper, gave us valuable insights into the use of strong squadrons. We had hoped in the beginning to give the bombers protection on the English side due to the short crossing time by using rendezvous tactics with our own fighter escorts somewhere shortly before the English coast. This would also have taken care of the speed difference and flight time discrepancies. These trials never fully succeeded. Add to this the fact that bomber crews in the heat of battle easily forgot Ops Staff directives to return the moment they came in contact with enemy fighters. The English were successful because of excellent detection methods, their high speed, and the interception of returning bombers even from bases further north. Thus, losses were incurred, but their actual number was far smaller than those published. From 10 July to October 1940 the German air force suffered the following losses:

Time Frame	Total Loss	Damaged/ Returned
10 July to 7 August (24 days)	192 planes	77 planes
8 August to 23 August (16 days) attacks on English coastal targets	403 planes	127 planes
24 August to 6 September (14 days) attacks on bases near London	378 planes	115 planes
7 September to 30 September (24 days) attacks mainly by heavy bombers against London harbor	435 planes	161 planes
1 October to 31 October (31 days) attacks by fighter bombers against London harbor	325 planes	163 planes
In 114 days	1733 planes	643 planes

This was a daily average of 15 total losses and 6 damaged returns.

English reports gave for the individual days of these missions higher losses for the German Air Force than actually incurred. For 15 August, they reported 183 German aircraft downed against an actual count of 76 losses and 9 damaged, and for 15 September, 185 downed German aircraft versus 56 actually lost and 21 damaged.

As a result of these air battles, which lasted almost four months, we were able to sink not only several English destroyers and numerous trade vessels, but also disrupt shipping lanes in the Channel and effect a far-reaching paralysis of the London harbor. Its capacity had sunk to about 35% according to reliable sources. Removal of cargo from ships could not be effected on the quays anymore and had to take place in the middle of the river. Actual attacks on the civilian sectors were not planned. But if you are familiar with flying bombers at night without escort and against fighter and anti-aircraft fire, then you know that misses are inevitable. Added to this was the fact that in London the harbor installations were far up the Thames in the area of the Tower Bridge.

The end of the "Battle of Britain" is looked upon by many as a great victory for the English Air Force; some even believe that its end influenced the outcome of the war for Germany in a negative way. That these allegations are not true can be seen from the missions of the air force after the harbor of London had been significantly disrupted. It is further said that we gave up the crossing to England of German army elements in August/September 1940 because the protection of these elements could not be ensured during or after the landings. The danger to these elements had been greatly reduced, in fact, by the heavy losses of the English Air Force and their move to more remote bases towards the end of August 1940. They could have been further protected as soon as the coastal bases had been repaired for use by the German Air Force. A limited protection could have been given against the English sea elements; this was proven by our destruction of English destroyers in the Channel as well as the successes of the German Air Force against the harbor of Plymouth in August 1940.

Other critics of the air war against England from August to October 1940 reached the conclusion that the German Air Force would have been incapable of gaining "air supremacy over England." The question of how this would have been feasible, without occupying all of the English/Scottish Isle cannot even be answered by the critics. The English Air Force always had the possibility to move to more remote bases from which to operate. Such bases had been continually expanded since 1939 along with the move of the industry to the north. How far the German Air Force was master of the sky over England is proven by the rather successful missions against harbor targets from November 1940 to April 1941.

Only after several months of disorganized missions with heavy losses did the Ops Staff receive, in November 1940, the possibilities of fulfilling all objectives worked out in the spring of 1939, namely the attack from the air as well as the mining of the English harbors. Earlier requests had been turned down continuously. The time that passed had not been idle, however, since it had given us important experience in missions, strategy, and materials used on the virgin field of air warfare. Especially important were the facts about missions of large, closed units operating by night against distant targets. We were successful in flying missions of 900 km in units of 700 or more aircraft against harbors like Glasgow and Belfast, all under cover of night and with rather few losses. The German units assembled for this purpose over the Irish Sea.

In October 1954, a German writer expressed his opinion in a renowned military newspaper that Britain's strategic situation had not been studied in time and sufficiently by the responsible German authorities. It is likely that the utilization of this man during the years 1939 to 1940, when he was most likely just a lieutenant, did not allow him to judge the work and the intentions of the offices of the General Staff, nor did he know the command structure of that time. Other opinions expressed in the article lead to the same conclusions.

In the time from November 1940 to the end of April 1941, we succeeded, through systematic actions, in paralyzing the harbors of Firth of Forth and on the Humber, the many harbor installations on the Bristol-Channel as well as on the Messey, [sic] [Mersey] on the Firth of Clyde, and in Northern Ireland. The English shipping traffic on the east coast of England as well as in the Channel had to be stopped already earlier. The overseas ships destined for England were forced to transfer their cargo at the north exit of the Irish Channel to coastal vessels, who then tried under the cover of fog or low clouds to reach the west shore of the coast of England. The reports going from London to Washington through the Ops Staff of the Air Force convinced the Ops Staff in April 1941 that England's war against Germany could only be fought until about the end of October or the beginning of November 1941. During my interrogation in London in 1945, I was asked what decisions of the English government we were expecting. I answered that if we had even discussed this unimportant question, then the overall consensus would have been that the English government and members important to its survival, as well as institutions, would have boarded the English fleet and sailed to Canada. I received the reply, "You may be right." We knew too well the English motto "never give up" to believe that the war against England and its vast resources would have been over.

The course of the war could have been totally different, however, if somebody had listened to the request of the Ops Staff already in October 1940 to either give up the attack against Russia or to postpone it at least until spring 1942. At least the British Isles would not have become the jumping board of the English and American aircraft units which influenced the operations in the west so drastically and destroyed Germany almost completely. Adolf Hitler, however, created, against the advice of his military advisors, a dangerous second front before the fighting on one had been brought to a successful completion. The English prime minister confirmed the above situation when he stated in his address on the occasion of "V.E. Day" before the House of Parliament: "In the beginning of May 1941, when the German attacks on our harbors failed to materialize, the great saving wonder happened."

Already in October 1940, the Ops Staff of the Air Force received directives which made it clear that the attack pattern would soon be shifted from the Western to the Eastern Front. Facts which materialized later made it clear that Adolf Hitler had already decided on a switch shortly after the capitulation of France. This might explain the listlessness in preparing for an invasion of England. Hermann Göring argued the point of the Ops Staff with Hitler energetically. However, it was very clear what kind of an influence other people had gained, mainly those in the Security HQs and Rosenberg's office who spoke of Bolshevik Russia as a giant with earthen legs who could be toppled in short order by a mighty push. Even negative reports arriving from the German Embassy in Moscow, especially those reports from the military attachés, were thrown to the wind. Herman Göring's useless interventions showed again the power he had lost over Hitler, a power which had received a big dent when he tried to intervene for peace before the war had even started. Göring's position became almost untenable around 1941-42, largely because of his animosity with Ribbentrop, Göbbels, and Himmler.

In October 1940, the Ops Staff received the order to move the first reconnaissance squadrons to the east for the purpose of aerial photography over Russia. In March 1941, the first bomber squadrons left for the Eastern Front. One group from each squadron was first returned for R&R to Germany. In intervals, the other groups followed. The patriotic and death-defying German pilots were, thus, robbed of their victory some short months before its attainment. The remaining inventory of airplanes in the Western Theatre around May 1941 amounted to a grand total of 35 planes. The enemy, however, got the opportunity to rebuild his destroyed harbor facilities, to replenish the low supply of all kinds of products through unrestricted imports from overseas and to arm himself again. A strong English air fleet, reinforced by the end of 1941 with American units, found on the English Isle the spring board for their devastating attacks against the German domain. The protection of that domain had been made impossible because of Hitler's negative position on the modernization of the air force which had been suggested already in 1940.

The Ops Staff left its position on 31 March 1941 near Beauvais, about 60 km north of Paris, and travelled in its special train in the area of Vienna and then to the Semmering [Semmering Pass in east Austria] to direct the operations of the air force during its Balkan offensive, the highlight of which was the capture of the Isle of Crete. The request to take Malta was refused by Hitler even after it had been softened up for assaults by air attacks.

After the Ops Staff returned in May 1941 to the HQs Air Force in Wildpark near Potsdam, the preparations for the Russian offensive began. I did not participate directly since my field was the Western Front. I was told to submit a detailed report of the present air situation in the west as well as figures detailing the strengths and armament capabilities of the western allies in light of a possible reopening of the air offensive there. To my question as to deadline on this report, I was told beginning August 1941 that Hermann Göring had to report to Hitler on August 15, 1941, and it was thought that the air offensive could be picked up again on September 1, 1941. Due to what seemed to me a rather short interval, I then questioned the liaison officer of the army at HQs Air Force and was told by him that according to his information under ideal conditions the planned eastern offensive was to be over in four weeks and under less than ideal conditions it would come to an end in about six weeks.

The German air activities in the west, as indicated before, were rather limited. My work was not as concerned with the Front as it was with the reconstruction of the English harbors, the resupplying of the Isle, the continued armament in the Commonwealth and the U.S., and especially the situation on the African Front. In this work, the air information troops under General Martini did an excellent job. Their listening posts on the west coast of Africa, as well as deep inside Central Africa, reported not only great troop transports, which were on the way to Europe from India and Australia, but also the movement of British air force units to the African Theatre. The airplane parts were transported to Lagos (Nigeria) to be reassembled. They then flew with stops in Kamo (middle Nigeria), Fort Lamy (Ischad-Lake), [Chad Lake] and El Fasher (Sudan) to Khartoum. Here their routes divided, depending on whether they were destined for North Africa, Kenya, or India, but the great mass went to the North African Theatre. The reports were so exact that we knew when one of the aircraft had to stop at one of the refueling points and on what day it would continue its journey. We knew exactly the strength of the units operating in Africa and were able to predict the English offensive of 18 November 1941 almost to the day. Other offices had believed the offensive would start much later mainly because of poor weather during that time of the year. The number of aircraft available had been estimated at 1600 by our intelligence. Contrary to all military rules, this figure was declared as too excessive and reduced to 900. The reinforcement of the German Air Force, therefore, was considered unnecessary and influenced the outcome of the engagements in a rather undesirable way.

The observation of the expansion of harbors on the Red Sea continued, and the construction of railroads, military roads, and new airfields was noted in the Near East. The observations made here reinforced the belief that the western powers were planning their big offensive through the Balkans, in which case the position of Turkey was to play a big role. This big plan was dropped, however, when Stalin declared that the Balkans were his sole area of interest.

After the conclusion of the offensive against France, I had taken over, in addition to the Group Foreign AF West, the leadership of the Group Roman Countries (France, Italy, Spain, Portugal, and South America). The presence of a strong contingent of the Italian Air Force in the HQs of the German Air Force brought out special problems. After Japan's entry into the war, the Chief of Staff gave me the additional duty of Liaison Officer to the Japanese mission in Berlin, consisting of Captain Toyoda for the naval air force and Colonel Izima of the Chief of Staff's Office for the army air force. My duties now were expanded to include all events on the Asian war front.

The cooperation with the Japanese colleagues became quite interesting since Japan was not at war with Russia, and therefore had a full diplomatic mission at the seat of Russian power. The members of the Japanese delegations in the Axis countries travelled to and from Japan through Turkey and Russia, and there were meetings in Helsinki and Istanbul of Japanese attachés stationed with enemy and friend. This required especially tactful conduct during our weekly meetings in Berlin. For my own benefit, I had all the question and answers recorded in shorthand rather inconspicuously by an escort. I soon found out that the questions which I had evaded were being asked again after three or four weeks. I had to answer in the same way as I had before if I did not want to arouse suspicions. It also was observed that our Japanese friends were sometimes very well informed about the location and strength of German units, especially those on the Eastern Front. I want to stress, though, that our mutual relations were always friendly and trusting; yes, even hearty from day one to the last day. But it also has to be said that we were made aware of the fact that the Reich's leadership was not liked at all.

I was always interested in all official and social functions as a means of gaining a deeper insight into the interesting mentality of the Japanese people. Having studied the thinking of Asian and African people for more than six years, I understood that six months was not enough for such a task. I gained a high respect for the principles on which the youth of Japan were educated in what once had been called "the Prussia of the East." As in the state of Prussia, which has been erased from the map because of alleged misdeeds, the Japanese had the concepts of patriotism, sense of duty, a willingness to die for one's country, and a simplicity of life. It is hoped in the interest of Japan that these ideals are not replaced by those of materialism and egoism as they have been in the rest of Germany.

The factual style of my reporting, which sometimes did not coincide with the wishful thinking of my superiors, led to the impression that I saw life too much through British or American glasses, and there were officers who called me an "Anglophile" and a "Roosevelt dependent." I was filled with deep regret that the reports we submitted, based on rather accurate information from overseas, were not given the full recognition they deserved. I later saw a report in which we had projected the strength of the British Air Force at the end of 1941. On the first page of these reports had been marked in red the words "too fantastic." Later observations confirmed that the figures given accurately reflected the real situation and could in no way be called bloated. A report demanded near the end of 1941 asked for the projected delivery of aircraft to the front by the U.S. in 1942. Again, based on information received from experts, we projected 38,200. Unfortunately, I later heard that this figure had been reduced by higher authorities to 24,000. If a certain feeling of pity about this spreading self-deception had not pervaded me, I could have laughed a little when I became witness to a heated argument between two very high officials later about who was to be blamed for all those rosy prognostications.

Opposing views clashed, especially at meetings with representatives of other Reich offices. They concerned the situation in the enemy territories, German foreign propaganda, and the setting up of British and American POWs in units fighting for Germany. I always had to accept either a complete misjudgment of the situation or describe the situation in self-pleasing, rosy colors.

During February 1942, I was advised by the Chief of Staff of my selection, with Admiral Canaris' concurrence, to the post of air attaché at the German Embassy in Lisbon. These posts were considered rather important and such nominations had to be approved by the highest authority. As this would take several weeks, I was asked to inform myself about the special situation in Lisbon by going to the Foreign Office. After three weeks, I was told that my selection had been turned down; the reason, as often was the case in these matters, was not given. They were mainly to be found in the untrustworthiness of my political convictions.

As a soldier, I had been educated to look at a situation in a clear and cool manner without regard to personal or official desires from above in order to analyze the matter objectively. The renewed disregard for such facts was again made clear to me. The armed forces attachés were briefed at certain intervals about the total picture with regards to the military situation. These briefings were the same for everybody and were in writing; this was called "speech regulation." Additionally, the gentlemen were called to Berlin for personal interviews.

In January 1942, the air attachés heard in my presence a report from the Director, Division of Foreign Armies East at the O.K.H. [Oberkommando des Heeres was the Supreme High Command of the German Army] about the initial position at the start of the eastern offensive. The surprise, yes, even terror, of the listeners was immense. The actual figures presented had no relation to those given to them in the official letters. These numerous self-deceiving practices and the resulting mistakes from these decisions made me realize that I wanted no part of this heavy burden. I asked for my retirement in March 1942 based on my age and shaky health, or at least for a different job.

On 24 April 1942, I was named "Commander of the POW Camps AF" with HQs in Sagan and also Commandant of the POW camp AF Nr. 3 (Stalag Luft 3) situated there. The duties and responsibilities of a Commander of the Air Force POW camps were totally unclear and soon led to differences. In September 1942, an officer was named without my consultation to the post of commandant of a camp under my jurisdiction. Because I thought him totally incompetent for that post, I fired off a letter of protest. The position of Commander, POW Camp AF, was terminated, and the "Inspection of POW Affairs" in the Air Ministry was created. From 21 October 1942 on, I was only the Commandant of the POW camp AF Nr. 3.

A discussion of my duties with the Chief of Staff of the Air Force, and in particular with the Ops Staff, cannot be complete without remembering the type of persons it took to fill these positions. The personal integrity of each individual, his character, education, and devotion to duty was exemplary from the Chief of Staff down to the draftsmen and telephone operators. I cannot fail but to mention certain individuals and want to start with the Chief of Staff, AF, "General der Flieger" Jeschonnek. He was mainly responsible for the excellent working relationships of the departments.

I will always be thankful that I was privileged to be so close to this humble and chivalrous gentleman. He possessed a high intellect and a strong idealism. When we talked of the ugly sides of the Nazi rule, he compared the German people, who had been shaken up pretty badly by the Versailles Accords, with a cauldron of boiling water in which the dirty elements first came to the surface to be taken off. This point of view cost him his life. In 1942, Adolf Hitler asked Hermann Göring whether it was feasible to supply by air the 220,000 troops fighting in the east. General Jeschonnek, having been requested to do the study, reported to Adolf Hitler that such an undertaking was not possible since the transport units were already serving the army in Africa and their capabilities already were being stressed to the maximum. From my work on Ops Staff, I know of the losses incurred, up to 126 aircraft in one day, with a delivery quota from German factories being only a fraction of those delivered to the allies. The discrepancies in the transport system had been spelled out repeatedly. Adolf Hitler's repeated refusal to occupy Malta was now taking its toll. General Jeschonnek asked Adolf Hitler for an immediate reassessment of the situation if the loss of one of the fighting theatres was to be avoided. Hitler refused to even listen. The same question was put to a higher officer in Hitler's entourage.

General Jeschonnek brought his personal doubts one more time to Adolf Hitler. He was rebuked rather sharply and had lost any sympathy the Führer might still have had. The final act came when Hitler appointed for certain high officials a kind of political watchdog in the guise of staff officers on the staff of these officials. General Jeschonnek protested very sharply. This led again to a tumultuous interview with Hitler, after which, so it is alleged, the general was sent a revolver. He took his life on 9 August 1943 but wrote a letter to Adolf Hitler which made it into his hands and had about the following text: "The path on which you, my Führer, are taking the German people and its armed forces must lead to their downfall. I have tried in vain to explain to you my point of view. I do not want to see the downfall of all that I hold precious and, therefore, depart voluntarily from this life. May my death be a sign to you to make you think and leave the path of destruction and save Germany from the worst." It was announced that General Jeschonnek had died of an ulcer.

Aside from General Jeschonnek, I would like to mention the excellent Chief of the Operations Section, General Hoffmann von Waldan, [sic] [Waldau] who perished in an aircraft over the Balkans, the Chief IC, Colonel Schmid, [Joseph "Beppo" Schmid], whose willingness to work, rapid grasp of ideas, and precise situation/reports, were the envy of everybody.

Structure of the POW System of the Air Force in Germany during WWII

The mobilization of the German armed forces delegated all matters pertaining to the POW system to the High Command of the Armed Forces where they were handled by a special section (Abt. Kgf., POW section). From this section were recruited the commanders, officers in the rank of general for the POW camps in the various Armed Forces Districts. The POW camps under their command were divided into transit camps (Dulags), officers camps (Oflags), and main camps (Stalags), the latter for NCOs and lower ranks. The transit camps were mainly located in the front lines. The fighting corps delivered their prisoners to them, and they, in turn, moved the POWs to the Oflags and Stalags located primarily in the homeland. At the beginning of the war, the POW system was run entirely by army personnel, and POWs of the enemy army, navy, and air force were housed in the same camps.

Later in the war, the position of General Inspector of POWs was created, last held by Infantry General Roettig. His chief of Staff was Colonel Müller, a man with a great sense for duty, yet very judicious, perceptive, and deeply human. It was his doing that avoided unnecessary confrontations between the military and political departments of the Reich, particularly in questions pertaining to the administration of the POW system. The seat of the General Inspector was first in Berlin and later moved to Ziethen near Torgan, due to the heavy bombing of Berlin. The protection of the POWs in enemy territory was guaranteed by the diplomatic representatives of a neutral country, "the protective power." [Protecting Power] During WWII, this role was held first by the United States, and after it entered the war, Switzerland took over. Their representatives, after clearance from the High Command, had the right to visit each and every POW camp and talk to the POWs about their grievances. The rights and duties of the detaining powers on one side, and the rights and duties of the POWs on the other, were regulated by the Geneva Convention of 1929. The spiritual and physical well-being of the POWs was delegated to two international institutions, namely the IRC [International Red Cross] and the YMCA [Young Men's Christian Association]. After proper clearance, they, too, could visit all camps and record the wishes of the POWs. NCO and lower ranked POWs could be assigned to work details by the Detaining Power, officers only if they so requested. Officers were authorized pay and had orderlies of their own country to attend to their wishes. Orderlies were assigned to either one officer alone or several, based on the officer's rank. Accommodations were also based on rank. Doctors and clergymen of various denominations from the homeland of the POWs attended to their physical and spiritual needs. They were afforded special privileges and were able to fulfill their duties unhindered.

POWs who were totally disabled and could not fight in the war any more were, according to international treaties, repatriated already during the war. To authenticate the cases reported to the German High Command, a commission consisting of a doctor from the Protecting Power, the Detaining Power, and the Enemy Power convened. The POWs selected for repatriation by the commission were sent to a neutral port for their return home.

During the war operations of the German army in Poland in 1939, hardly any Germans were taken prisoner. During the first nine months of the war in the west, only a limited number of army personnel were taken prisoner, the greatest number of personnel falling into enemy hands belonging to the air force. Their lot in captivity had to be influenced mainly by the treatment afforded the enemy air force personnel in German hands. It was, therefore, understandable that Hermann Göring, as Commander in Chief of the German Air Force, was interested in bringing the department detaining the downed enemy flyers under his command.

The air war in the west began on September 4, 1939, with an attack of ten English Blenheim fighters against the battleship, Scheer, docked at Wilhelmshafen. [sic] [Wilhelmshaven] Five of the Blenheims were shot down, and the two surviving sergeants were taken prisoner. The first RAF officer taken prisoner was Pilot Officer T. Edwards, shot down on

September 6, 1939, in his Anson near Helgoland, picked up by a German seaplane, and admitted to the army hospital in Wesermünde. During his 5½ years in captivity, he stayed remarkably healthy and in good spirits, was well known as one of the best rugby players, and returned in May 1945 in good health to his loved ones. On September 8, 1939, a Whitley, which had started for a leaflet drop, developed engine trouble over Thüringen, and its crew bailed out. Squadron Leader W. Murray and Pilot Officer T. Thomson [sic] [Alfred Burke Thompson] of the RAF were taken prisoner. Hermann Göring ordered their transfer by POV [privately owned vehicle] to his headquarters in Wildpark near Potsdam. He explained to them that the German Air Force would do everything possible to ease the lot of the flyers taken prisoner and ordered first that their belongings be returned which had been taken the day before. Both officers, after going through camps Itzehoe and Spangenberg, ended up in the newly-built POW camp of the Air Force Nr. 3 at Sagan and returned home at the war's end. Squadron Leader Murray was held in high esteem by his comrades and Germans alike. Pilot Officer Thomson [sic] was a member of the 76 officers who escaped in March 1944; luckily he escaped the lot of the 50 dead.

Hermann Göring's efforts to have downed flyers incarcerated in camps under the control of the German Air Force were successful in that the German Air Force was authorized to take over control of the interrogation camp of the army at Oberursel in the Taunus Mountains. It had been, up to then, under the command of Reserve Major Alvieni, in peacetime the director of the metal works at Frankfurt A.M. Thus, was created the "Transit Camp of the AF at Oberursel" which became well known to all Allied powers as "Dulag Luft." It was under the command of the Military Council of the AF; its administration, like that of later erected POW camps of the AF, fell under the control of the German Air Corps District HQs in whose districts the various camps were located. The first German Commander of Dulag Luft was Lt. Colonel von Donat. He was replaced after a few months by Major (later Colonel) Rumpel, and in December 1941, Lt. Colonel Killinger took charge. Once the air force took over, the members of the enemy armies detained in Oberursel up to then were transferred to other POW camps of the army, and from those were pulled the British, French, and Belgian flyers and transferred to Dulag Luft. After the capitulation of the French and Belgian armed forces, AF personnel of these enemy countries were transferred, with a few exceptions, to officer and enlisted camps of the army so that the camps of the AF from July 1940 until the entrance of the U.S. into the war housed only members of the AF of the Commonwealth – later also of the U.S.A.F.

Based on directives from Reichsmarshall Hermann Göring, the POWs were to be treated not only honorably and commensurate with their rank, but also given all available benefits. They received, early in the war, from the goods the Germans captured, rations of cigarettes, wine, and whiskey. A small, well-stocked PX made it possible to purchase items to make their dull lives more pleasant. Even sports equipment was organized. After giving their word of honor not to escape, the POWs were authorized long walks into the Taunus, escorted by only two German officers. Visits to cafes, public baths, Catholic mass in Oberursel, and skiing on the Feldberg were also allowed. During a meeting at the military council HQs in France in early1941, the German camp commander reported to Hermann Göring about the general situation of the POWs and their wishes. He stated that the greatest wish of the POWs would be to listen to the BBC. They were positive that the German POWs in Britain were authorized to listen to the German news. Hermann Göring granted their wish, provided the German POWs were afforded the same right. Thus, it was that the English flyers were enjoying a right which was denied the German population under severe penalties. However, one wish could not be granted to these young and enthusiastic flyers, and that was to sit in an airplane again. They were of the opinion that if we gave them only a few liters of fuel, they would be forced to return to the airfield after a couple of rounds. Indicative of the mood of the POWs after a few months of captivity was the following incident: On one of my earlier trips through Oberursel, an older officer stated his wish to make a phone call, or rather to talk on the phone again. A granting of this wish could not have any serious consequences, so the designated phone was disconnected temporarily at the switchboard and the officer made his call to an imaginary partner. Judging from his reaction, he seemed rather happy after his phone call.

The ties with the outside world were understandably weakened tremendously with the beginning of the hostilities, which impaired the collection of information, especially from enemy territories. A substitute source could be found in the statements provided by POWs. Therefore, their objective and expert interrogation was given over as an important task to Dulag Luft. Among the most sought after information was the identity of the POW's unit, as was equipment, strength, and location of this unit. Through these interrogations, it was possible to maintain the accurate picture of the war organization of the air arm of the enemy which had been formed at the beginning of the war. Until my transfer in May 1942, we had, despite ongoing new formations, reorganizations, and shifting of the enemy air forces, an accurate picture of the enemy's strengths, formation, and posting. The interrogation of enemy flyers, versus army personnel, also yielded more important insights into the enemy's operational and tactical actions, since the former were more familiar with the overall picture due to their need to know. Added to this was the need to determine the type of aircraft flown, including weapons and instruments on the plane.

The experience of the first war years had shown that the interrogation of downed flyers right after their capture by inept personnel gained little intelligence information and that the downed aircraft often had parts removed by souvenir hunters. The AF military council succeeded, finally, towards the end of 1939, in implementing strict orders by the High Command demanding the immediate transfer of downed flyers to Dulag Luft, without first going through local interrogation, and safeguarding downed aircraft until the arrival of competent personnel. The immediate notification of the nearest AF installation was required, which, in turn, was responsible for the immediate transportation of the POW to Dulag Luft and the notification of competent AF engineers to start the inspection and evaluation of the downed aircraft. This latter measure repeatedly had excellent results, among other things, the German AF was able to copy the English radar unit and named it the "Rotterdam instrument."

It had been proven prudent to give the new POW arriving in Dulag Luft at least two days rest, since a certain state of shock after being shot down was noticed. Only then was the interrogation by a specially-trained officer started, and only after its completion was the flyer turned over to a POW camp. There they met up with friends, some who had been thought dead.

The personal belongings taken from the POWs were immediately registered and turned over to the escort. Military property, with the exception of clothing and watch, was confiscated. Among the items which were confiscated were often bags with foreign currencies which had been given the flyer to be used in the event of a forced landing or bail out. After a while, considerable amounts of German, Dutch, Belgian, French, Swiss, Danish, Norwegian, and Swedish currencies amassed. An item of controversy remained the watches of the flyers, which had RAF stamped on them. It was thought that officers had to buy them, and "other ranks" were issued these watches. The latter were, therefore, considered government property and confiscated. Other than that, the private possessions of the POWs were considered untouchable. If they were not allowed to keep them due to security reasons, they were given a receipt for them upon processing through Dulag Luft. When the prisoner was transferred to another camp, the confiscated possessions were transported by the escorts to the POW's new destination. If a POW reported that an item from his personal belongings had disappeared after his apprehension, intensive investigations were conducted in all the places the POW had gone through during and after his capture. Documents pertaining to these complaints traveled sometimes for years through the German territories. In the spring of 1944, Stalag Luft 3 had, based on a population of 6,500 POWs, 34 of these cases. The endless search for sometimes rather cheap items was the terror of every German unit. The search documents grew to fat bundles traveling back and forth between military units, mayors, police and constabularies, and numerous other units. How differently, however, were the German soldiers treated when, after the unconditional surrender of May 1945 the victorious powers seemingly regarded the Geneva Convention as nonexistent. During repeated rigorous searches of German soldiers, things like watches, rings, fountain pens, and other valuable items disappeared. The Germans tried to hide their wedding bands on their toes or other places, without much luck however. Many hundred thousands of watches and other valuable items, even engraved pocket watches, were not recognized as personal property.

In February 1941, we received complaints from German POWs in Canada (Fort Williams) by way of the Protecting Power demanding that we take immediate action to alleviate their lot. Two hundred enemy POWs were brought to Thorn on the Weichsel where they were kept in a fort of that garrison much like the one in Canada. They were then transferred to the barracks of the Polish military school. This action had the desired results, for the Protecting Power could report after a short while that the living conditions of the Germans in Fort Williams had greatly improved. The stay of the 200 AF officers at Thorn could, therefore, be cancelled after only one month, and they were transferred to Spangenberg. One other incident, which required regrettable actions against POWs, was the tying up of German soldiers captured in 1941 at Dieppe. The order was given to tie up the British AF sergeants incarcerated at Lumsdorf [Lamsdorf] in retaliation. This action not only was very humiliating for the victims, but to take care of even the most basic human needs the assistance of a comrade was required. Our repeated pleas for humane treatment of our soldiers were finally heard, and the POWs were untied. It is a fact that reprisals are condemnable and are easily the beginning of an endless chain.

Within a few months, the number of POWs grew so much that the facilities at Dulag Luft were deemed inadequate, yet the transfer of AF POWs to army POW camps like Spangenberg, Lubeck, Warburg, Kirchhain, Dössel, Bad Sulza, and Lamsdorf was seen as rather undesirable. It, therefore, was decided to open up a new POW camp of the AF Nr. 1 at Barth in Pomerania. When the British flyers in Dulag Luft heard that 50 of them were to be transferred to Barth, a long-planned escape plan was executed. Eighteen of them escaped in July 1941 through a tunnel, but all were apprehended again. Two of the escapees laid the foundation for their growing fame as escape experts during this attempt. They were Wing Commander (later Group Captain) H. M. A. Day, a pilot since WWI, and

Squadron Leader Roger Bushell, a London lawyer of South African birth. Further worth mentioning, as a member of the above elite group, was Johnny Dodge, a major in the British army. He had started as a lieutenant and made it all the way to colonel in WWI. Recalled in 1939 as major in the British army, he was captured at Dunkirk (as Lt. Colonel "temporary") and was transferred to Dulag Luft, Oberursel, by mistake. Despite repeated separations of English army and AF personnel, he remained somehow throughout the whole war in air force POW camps. Lt. Colonel Dodge's behavior, coupled with an extremely high intellect, made him well liked and respected not only among his friends but also among the Germans. This was not diminished, even though he participated in various escape schemes and attempts, and at his age he even jumped out of a moving train. He also was involved in the Great Escape of the 76 on 24-25 March 1944, but was spared the fate of the unfortunate 50 who were killed. The political circles thought maybe of using him as a hostage or negotiator at the appropriate moment. In early 1945, he was to be brought to the Italian Front by the S.D. [Intelligence Agency of the SS] but was liberated by American troops in Upper Bavaria.

The escape from Dulag Luft in July 1940 gave Heinrich Himmler the opportunity he sought to protest in a report to Adolf Hitler the humane treatment afforded the enemy flyers by the German Air Force, which in his view was stirring up the German population. This report went to Hermann Göring, who passed it on for comments to the Chief of Staff of the Air Force, General Jeschonnek. He, in turn, ordered me to investigate the allegations against Dulag Luft. I stayed for three weeks in Oberursel, Frankfurt A.M., Darmstacht, and Kassel and had my first immediate contacts with members of the security main offices, which were followed by so many less pleasant contacts in later years.

Due to the continuous increase of POW flyers, the following POW camps of the Luftwaffe were established in succession:

1. Dulag Luft, Oberursel, December 1939
2. POW camp of the AF Nr. 1 at Barth in Pomerania (on the Baltic), June 1940, commanded at first by Lt. Colonel Oertel, then Colonel

Scherer. After opening of Stalag 3, Sagan, it was temporarily closed but was reopened again in October 1942.

3. POW camp of the AF Nr. 2 at Litzmannstadt - Set up in August 1941 to serve as a transit camp for the flyers downed on the Eastern Front in the style of Dulag Luft in Oberursel on the Western Front. When representatives of the S.D. arrived to pull out the Russian commissars and Jews and bring them to a swift "justice," the commandant refused them entry. Extensive differences between the political and military units followed, but access to the camp never was granted. The camp was able to fulfill its role as an interrogation camp only in limited form, since the continuous shifting of the Eastern Front resulted in the transfer of only a few Russian flyers. Its last commander was Colonel Stephani.
4. POW camp Nr. 3, Sagan, March 1942
5. POW camp Nr. 4, Gross-Tychow, spring 1943 - Commanded by Lt. Colonel Bombach
6. POW camp Nr. 5, Heydekrug in East Prussia, May 1943 - Commanded by Colonel Kirstein
7. POW camp Nr. 6, Königsberd [sic] [Königsberg] I.D. Neumark, fall 1943 - Commanded at first by Colonel Braune then after April 1944 by Colonel von Hormann
8. Colditz, reserved for repeat escapees and those known as notorious escapees

POW Camp of the AF Nr. 3 (Stalag Luft 3)

Refer to attached map of the City of Sagan and plan of the camp. The order for the construction of Stalag Luft 3 was given in October 1941. It was supposed to become, according to the wishes of Hermann Göring, a model camp in which all POW officers of the enemy air forces would eventually be housed. It was purely an officers' camp, but the name "Stalag" Luft 3 had been given to it originally and remained. The total number of members of the enemy forces incarcerated in Stalag Luft 3 for the whole war was about 31,000, 13,115 of which were members of the RAF.

When I moved to Sagan in May 1942 to take over my new position, the town had a population of about 24,000 inhabitants who made their living primarily in weaving mills, dye works, beer breweries, and sawmills. Sagan lies in the upper northeast corner of Silesia on the rail line Berlin-Breslau (Wroclaw) situated 193 kilometers from Berlin and 139 kilometers from Breslau. It lies at the junction of 6 rail lines, the aforementioned Berlin-Breslau line, the Soran [sic] [Sorau]-Cottbus-Halle, Hausdorf-Görlitz-Dresden, Sprottan- [sic] [Sprottau] Glogan-Lissa-Posen, Freystadt-Nuesalz, [sic] [Neusalz] Neuhammer-Löwenberg. The location of Sagan as such an important and lively railway junction facilitated the numerous escape attempts by the POWs.

Silesia was, at the beginning of the era, a Germanic domain. From the east to the area we call Poland today, and down to the Black Sea, lived the Goths, Vandals, and Burgundians. In Silesia lived a branch of the latter tribe, the Silingians. The name Silesia is derived from them. After the Goths had given the impetus to the great migration, Slavic elements began occupying the deserted areas around 560 A.D. Around 700 A.D., Sagana, the daughter of a Slavic prince, settled near the present day location of Sagan. The town derived its name from her. Around the year 1000, Silesia came under Polish rule, and from about 1100 on the dukes from the House of Piasts [sic] [Piast] ruled the area. Under their rule and encouragement, a gradual reverse migration of German settlers took place. In 1163, the Duchy of Silesia gained independence under Polish supremacy. Sagan became a city in 1230 under German law, and Breslau became a city eleven years later in 1241. In 1335, the kings of Poland gave up all claims to Silesia in favor of the House of Luxembourg ruling in the Kingdom of Bohemia. The reformation of 1522 encompassed almost all of Silesia until the counter-reformation took place from 1580-1740. Due to the continuous practice of inheritance division in the House of Piast, Silesia was finally divided into about 30 small principalities, whose rulers called themselves dukes. In 1628, the Duchy of Sagan was given in fief by the German Emperor and King of Bohemia to Sagan's most prominent citizen, Albrecht von Wallenstein, Duke of Friedland and Mecklenburg and now also Duke of Sagan, born 24 September 1583, assassinated on 25 February 1634. He began the construction of the remarkable castle at Sagan, for which 65 freemen houses had to be torn down. In this town, which is still 80% Protestant, he settled the Jesuits and directed the transfer of 60 of the town's most prominent freemen's sons to his Jesuit school in Gitschin in Bohemia. He worked hard for the growth of the city, ordered the River Bober be made navigable, and called the famous astronomer and mathematician Johannes Kepler to Sagan. After the death of Wallenstein, the Duchy returned to the German Emperor who sold it to Prince Wensel Eusebius Popel von Lobkowitz. In 1742, Silesia became part of the Kingdom of Prussia, and Sagan became a Prussian principality held in fee. In 1786, Duke Peter Biron von Kurland bought, among other things, the principality of Sagan, for one million Danzig guilders, money he had received for the renunciation of the Duchy of Kurland to Russia. He was succeeded by his daughter, Wilhelmine, who became known to the world as "The Sagan," the confidante of Prince Meternich [sic] Metternich. Her successor was her youngest sister, Countess Dorothea de Tulleyrand-Perigord [sic], [Talleyrand-Perigord] nicknamed, "the beautiful Dorothea," Duchess of Valencay and Dino. She settled completely in Sagan and brought all her important art treasures from her French possessions to Sagan. With the help of Count Puckler-Muskan, [sic] [Pückler-Muskau] she built the famous park of Sagan, had a brilliant court, and was a friend of the Prussian royal family. After the death of her son, Ludwig, in 1898, who had also been living in Sagan, the property which had been renamed "Forest Dominion Sagan" after the fall of the Prussian monarchy went to members of the Talleyrand family living in France. The present owner is Juan de Valencay. The castle in Sagan was cleared of its art treasures by the Russian and Poles in 1945, the city 75% destroyed. Of the 6½ million inhabitants of Silesia, the 5¾ million Germans, and with them the surviving citizens of Sagan, lost, due to the agreements of Yalta and Potsdam, the right to their homeland which had not been in doubt for more than 700 years.

It was soon discovered that to house the intrepid young POWs of the Allied powers a more unsuitable location could hardly have been found. The camp was located about 1200 meters south of the Sagan train station, which saw hundreds of trains daily going to all directions of the compass. The station itself was located about 2000 meters south of Sagan. The camp was bordered on the east, south, and southwest by the extensive forest of the Duchy of Sagan under the administration of the Board of Woods of Karlswalde. About 2500 meters to the west of the new AF camp was a POW camp of the army, Stalag VIII, occupied by about 26,000 French and Russian POWs who were working for the Germans outside the camp. The ground was excellently suited for underground tunneling and afforded the captives many chances at escape attempts. In the course of time, the POWs reached a mastery of tunneling which was unexcelled. The flyers were all between 21 and 30 years old. Only a few staff officers were a little bit older. As flyers, they had been trained well, physically, as well as technically. Their escape attempts were aided by materials cleverly hidden in packages from home, as well as items smuggled into camp. During the time of my command, from 10 May 1942 to 25 March 1944, (21 months and 24 days) a total of 262 attempts were made. Of those, 100 were tunnel constructions. Many hundreds of POWs participated, but only five reached their homeland by escaping in such a manner. The increased perfection of the escape preparation resulted in an increase of the countermeasures of the German personnel. At least in this area, Stalag Luft 3 became a model POW camp. New personnel to be used in the POW system came here for training. The escape material, which had been either found or confiscated, filled two huge barracks after only two years and was known as the "escape museum" and served as training aid for personnel tasked to duty in other camps as well as for the local criminal police.

The biggest problem during the initial layout and construction of the camp was the procurement of personnel and material. This problem increased until the end of the war and with the expansion of the camp could never be solved satisfactorily. If we succeeded in getting people and material, they sooner or later were withdrawn from [sic] [by] higher authorities for projects deemed more important. It wasn't until 21 March 1942 after an initial construction start of October 1941 that the first RAF officers and sergeants could be transferred from the POW camp Nr. 1 at Barth in Pomerania to Sagan.

When I took command on 10 May 1942, Stalag Luft 3 consisted, aside from the "troop compound" for the German administration and guard personnel, of an East Compound with 401 officers and a Center Compound with 873 NCOs and sergeants, all members of the RAF. Their number climbed within three months due to new arrivals from Dulag Luft, the POW camp Nr. 1 at Barth, and from army POW camps at Spangenberg, Bad Sulza, Kirchhain, Dössel, and Lamsdorf, to 751 officers and 1,823 other ranks. The humane housing of all these people proved rather impossible. The situation was eased somewhat by the occupation of an abandoned army POW camp at Schubin (New-Brugund) [sic] [Burgund] in West Prussia and the reopening of Barth. The continued expansion of the camp made possible the completion of the North Compound in March 1943. The return of the POWs redirected to Schubin was possible, but their number had also grown due to receiving direct transfers. The first U.S. officers of the U.S.A.F arrived in June 1942. A new POW camp of the AF Nr. 5 at Heydekrug in East Prussia was opened, to which were transferred all NCOs and sergeants of the RAF formerly housed in Stalag Luft 3. The "other ranks" of the U.S.A.F were sent to an army POW camp at Gueisendorf [sic] [Geisendorf] near Krems on the Danube. A special section for about 2,500 AF POWs had been opened there under the command of German AF Major Eigl. The increased transfer of POW officers to Stalag Luft 3 can be seen from the fact that from 17 September to 1 November 1942, a period of 6½ weeks, we received exactly 1,000 officers. In September 1943, the South Compound was ready for occupancy, and in January 1944 the repairs on the old Russian camp, Belaria, about 2½ kilometers north of Sagan, were finished and the camp ready for occupancy by officers. It was fully under the command of Stalag Luft 3. It housed only officers and should have been named Oflag, but the name Stalag Luft 3 had become known to friend and foe alike so it remained. The orderlies assigned to the officers were drawn from the enemy army POWs, since the RAF and U.S.A.F sergeants, with a few exceptions, refused to do orderly duties. When I was put under court martial at the end of March 1944, there were in Stalag Luft 3 a total of 6,169 flyers, of which 2,581 were officers and 408 orderlies of the RAF and 2,643 officers and 537 orderlies of the U.S.A.F. Their number climbed until January 1945 to about 12,600 POWs of the enemy air forces.

After the completion of the aforementioned constructions, Stalag Luft 3 consisted of six sections. In the main camp south of the city were:

The German troop camp in the middle and to the east of it:

>East Compound. Occupied since 21 March 1942 with Britains [sic] [Britons]; senior officer Group Captain Kellett, later Group Captain Willets

>Center Compound. Occupied since 11 April 1942 first with British sergeants and after July 1942 with Americans, senior officer, Colonel Delmar T. Spivey

Immediately in front of these two compounds was the Front Compound East (Vorlager Ost). In it were located the sick quarters and arrest cells as well as the food stores and the living quarters of the Russian POWs drawn for work.

To the west of the German troop camp were:

<u>North Compound</u>. Occupied since 29 March 1943 with Britains [sic] [Britons]; senior officer, Group Captain H.M. Massey; after his repatriation on 2 July 1944, Group Captain Wilson

<u>South Compound</u>. Occupied since 8 September 1943 with Americans; senior officer, Colonel Goodrich

<u>West Compound</u>. Occupied since July 1944 with Americans; senior officer, Colonel Alkire

Positioned in front of these three compounds was also a Front Compound (Vorlager). In it were side quarters, food stores, and the coal shed. Added to these compounds was the partial camp Belaria, north of the city, occupied January 1944 with the senior officer being Group Captain . . . [no name given].

The main camp south of the city occupied an area of about 145 ha (58.7 acres) with a circumference of about 6¼ kilometers. Each compound was strictly separated from the others and could only be entered with a special pass. The compounds were all surrounded by two parallel-running 3 meter high fences about two meters apart and tightly strung with barbed wire. The space between the fences was filled up with coiled and tangled barbed wire about one meter high. This was called the "Löwengang" (Lions walk). In the actual compounds, and about 10 meters from the inside barbed wire fence, were affixed small stakes with wire circling the compound. This marked the so-called "warning line." The crossing of this line was expressly forbidden; it was comparable to the first "halt" shout of the guard who was authorized to shoot after giving two more warnings. This practice was protested at first by the POWs, but because of the state of affairs at that time their protests were ignored. Outside of the prison camp, watchtowers were located every 75 meters.

They were manned night and day with guards who had been issued binoculars. Also positioned on these towers were one machine gun and a searchlight to sweep the fence and interior of the compound at night. The towers were connected to the watch room by telephone. At night, two guards patrolled the outside of the fence between two towers. Access to the actual compound of the POWs was controlled in such a way that a visitor had to go first through the front camp, consisting of two gates with armed guards. An escape over or through the fences of the compound, by day or by night, was, thus, greatly hampered.

German dog tag found at Stalag Luft III over 65 years after von Lindeiner's time there
Courtesy Marek Lazarz

Attempts at escape, therefore, concentrated mainly on passing the gates in clever disguise and [with] forged papers. The POWs soon showed a remarkable talent and expertise in this area due mainly to their technical know-how and available time.

After the POWs realized that an escape above ground would not be very successful because of the German countermeasures, they moved their operations underground. The construction of "tunnels" increased rapidly. In general, the tunnels led from one of the barracks under the fence into the surrounding woods. As a countermeasure, the Germans buried microphones about two meters down and 100 meters apart along the outer fence. The mikes [sic][mics] were hooked up to a central listening post in the German camp and were supposed to register earth movements in their vicinity.

The main body of the POWs was made up of flyers from the U.S. Air Force, RAF, Royal Canadian, South African, Royal Australian, and Royal New Zealand Air Forces. Captured while serving in the RAF were also members of the former Dutch, Belgian, Polish, and Czech Air Forces and

From Commandant to Captive

volunteers from many neutral countries. A budding diplomat could have received excellent schooling here studying the mentality of almost all the peoples of the globe.

As varied as their nationalities, were the professions of these POWs in civilian life. Aside from the career soldier, were represented such jobs as: tramway conductors, sons of millionaires, waiters, lords, Hindu princes, horse trainers, race car drivers, professional dancers, pro-hockey and football players, school teachers, bus and horse buggy drivers, cowboys, photographers, actors, policemen, traveling salesmen, movie house operators, ski instructors, artists, miners, veterinarians, reporters, missionaries, private detectives, singers, diamond miners, lawyers, organists, jockeys, bacteriologists, plantation owners, hotel managers, porters, cardsharps, chauffeurs, band leaders, firemen, pianists, and high school teachers.

In the individual compounds, the POWs had established a form of self-rule under an American or British senior officer. He was assisted by a deputy, an adjutant, and a translator. He had also at his disposal a vast staff of functional experts for any imaginable situation. In first place should be mentioned the kitchen staff, then the staffs for sleeping accommodations, clothing, dispensary, mail and newspaper office, parcel distribution, academic programs, sports, theater, music, gardening, artistic endeavors, workshops, and expositions. Many of these groups were subdivided into smaller groups. A lack of qualified personnel to fill all these positions was never apparent, mainly because of the great number of highly intelligent men available. An organization which was kept secret from the Germans and "supposedly" also from the senior officer was "Organization X." It supervised all work relating to the preparation and execution of escapes, including the shielding of said activities against discovery by the Germans. The leader of this secret organization was called "Big X."

Strangely enough, the general organization mania was more apparent with the Britains [sic] than the Americans, or at least the latter handled everything more calmly. A diversified occupation of so many young officers could only be to our advantage, since it kept them from thinking the undesirable thoughts we knew the members of "Organization X" were contemplating. The objective observer could also note in many other things differences in the behavior of the Allied Anglo-Saxons, if one can call the Americans, with their heavy German and Irish heritage, Anglo-Saxons in the British sense. This became most apparent in work which could be accomplished by the POWs in their own interest. It was noted repeatedly that materials for the expansion or beautification of the quarters were available, however, German personnel for the work to be done was not. The British did nothing. It was their point of view that the completion of such work was the duty of the Germans; a takeover by the British would unburden the German work force and free German workers for the purpose of warfare. This point of view was rather nonsensical since not a single German worker was pulled from the war work force to undertake a beautification project in a POW camp. How different were the Americans. They helped themselves and made their quarters more livable. The British were also much less careful with German property. They thought it possible that they were harming the German economy by destroying these items, especially since we were required to replace them in accordance with international laws. It is rather obvious that replacements were released only after a thorough investigation. The behavior of the members of the various Commonwealth air forces also brought out interesting differences. The New Zealanders made the best impression on us. Their high intellect, their life styles directed towards peaceful and beautiful things, was probably the result of life on an island without green borders and without neighbors who envy you your wealth. The South Africans and the Canadians were also rather pleasant fellows. The Australians, along with the Britains [sic], were the most defensive against the Germans. Of the other nationalities serving in the RAF, the Dutch tried to be more British than the British, whereas, the Poles were preoccupied with a deep worry about the future of their homeland, regardless of the outcome of the war. I was asked repeatedly by Germans whether the arrogance of the British was not a disturbing factor. My standard reply to that was that nobody could be as arrogant as I, if I deemed it necessary.

The attitude of the senior officers was a great influence on the other POWs in the compounds. With the British, the most outstanding personality was Group Captain H.M. Massey, B.S.O., [sic] [S.B.O - Senior British Officer] D.S.O., M.C. Apparently, he wished to be regarded as the representative of all POWs in Stalag Luft 3. He objected that, upon the arrival of more and more members of the U.S. Air Force, they were understandably segregated in their own special compound.

Group Captain Massey had been shot down in July 1942 over Essen. A leg wound which he had received in 1933 in Palestine got worse again, and he could hardly walk. His obstinate vigor had not suffered, however. He was the typical conservative and correct Englishman who stood up for the rights of his comrades in a most emphatical manner. I believe I can say that he and I had a respectful trust in each other. When my apartment in Berlin was destroyed in March 1943 by English bombs, Group Captain Massey and several of his officers reported to me and expressed their regret over my loss. He added that I should never suffer harm at the hands of the RAF. I thanked him for his conviction and replied that I was a German, and, as such, wished to share the fate of my fellow Germans in every way including the consequences of the bombing war. From time to time, Group Captain Massey asked me for support in strengthening his authority towards the POWs of the RAF, thus, he asked me, among other things, to solicit the POWs to partake more often in the Sunday church services. Furthermore, he asked me to punish those POWs not following his orders. He would then not have to report these officers for punishment upon their return home. I was, naturally, in no position to comply with his wishes.

When in the summer of 1943, a well-known English surgeon arrived in a POW camp in Central Germany to perform rather complicated operations on wounded Englishmen, I succeeded, with great difficulty, in transferring Massey to the hospital of that camp. He was escorted by one of our doctors and a medic. About two months later, I was contacted by phone by the commandant of that camp, and he told me that Massey was under suspicion of inciting his fellow prisoners to mutiny. The commandant asked me whether I thought him capable of doing that, since he would then start proceedings against Massey. I vouched for his conduct. Several days later, the commandant called me back and asked if I were willing to take Massey back into my camp. After some serious considerations, I agreed and even had him picked up. The impetus to this discussion had been received days earlier in the form of a letter from Mrs. Massey, who was living in Devonshire at the time, thanking me for supporting her husband. I regretted my decision later since I had a very serious discussion with Group Captain Massey shortly before the Great Escape of 24-25 March 1944, and he chose to disregard my serious warning, therefore, breaking the mutual trust which I thought we had for each other.

In addition to the British POWs named so far, two more deserve special mention, namely Sq. Leader Jennens and Sergeant Deans. Jennens was the adjutant of S.B.O. Group Captain Massey and had been a civilian pilot on the London-Kohl [sic] [Köln (Cologne)] route before the war. At Sagan, he became a "Jack of all Trades." If somebody needed advice, whether Englishman or German, you went to see him. His many services to his friends shall not be forgotten. Sergeant Deans was the camp leader for the British NCOs and sergeants housed in Center Compound until June 1943. He then led the transfer to the air force POW camp at Heydekrug in East Prussia which had been constructed in the meantime. According to rank and age, one of the younger sergeants of the more than 1,800 NCOs, he nonetheless knew how to treat his men with tact and a firm hand. I was sorry to hear his health deteriorated after his return home. The leading personalities among the American POWs during the time of my command in Sagan were Colonel Delmar Spivey and Colonel Goodrich. They and their fellow staff officers gained the respect of everybody through their honorable, just, and yet understanding ways. It was their task to strengthen the spiritual and physical lot of their younger POWs in any way possible.

Colonel Goodrich had been shot down in Tunis and admitted to a German military hospital with serious injuries. After his arrival in Sagan, he handed me a letter addressed to the German High Command in which he expressed his thanks for the care which he had received, care which saved his life and gave him back his health. Colonel Goodrich was a quiet and reserved gentleman who liked the company of books. He fulfilled his duties as senior officer of South Compound with the tact and understanding so characteristic of an American colonel.

Colonel Delmar T. Spivey was the born leader of the American POWs in Stalag Luft 3. He knew how to unite the young flyers from various economic and social backgrounds, making the heavy lot of being a POW much more bearable. His correct manners secured him the support of the German administration to the greatest extent possible. I am convinced that every German, who ever came in contact with Colonel Spivey will always hold him in high esteem. I personally valued him as a model officer and knew his younger comrades were in the best of hands.

The numerous tasks demanded of the German personnel and the insufficient manpower available to us necessitated the use of foreign personnel. Thus, French and Belgian POWs were used as hospital orderlies, barbers, tailors, and cobblers. They proved themselves very well and were living in a barrack situated in the German troop compound which they had decorated nicely and surrounded with flower beds. In the big communal room of their barracks hung a picture of Marshall Petain which was always decorated with flowers. They did not want to return to France during the war since they firmly believed that they would have to join the fighting again in one way or another.

For the various other duties, which are necessary in such a big and complex installation as Stalag Luft 3, I had requested already in 1942 the assignment of Russian POW officers. Their number climbed to 300, and they also proved themselves very well. Since Russia had not signed the Geneva Accords, officers could be drawn to manual labor. They willingly took over the transportation unit, including the care of the cars, horses, and carts, maintained and operated the electrical plant, took care of the pigs and chickens, and worked in the big vegetable garden. The Russian officers were in miserable condition when they arrived, undernourished, in rags, and desperate. After consulting with the doctors, I contracted with nearby slaughter houses for the healthy blood of animals which had to be slaughtered. Blood soups cooked with stinging nettles and the tips of Scotch pine needles performed miracles. The Russians regained their strength and will to live. Only two deaths occurred mainly because of advanced TB. The Russians performed miracles in restoring clothing, furniture, cooking utensils, and other items which their fellow prisoners had thrown away. Also worth mentioning was their striving for cleanliness; a piece of soap was a most treasured possession and their living quarters were always immaculate. One certain incident might illustrate their way of thinking. The POWs of all other nations had their permanent senior officers who held these positions on a permanent basis. The Russians, however, changed their senior officer on a regular basis. Such frequent personnel change could lead to unwanted problems and friction. Questioned as to their motives, the Russians strangely requested that they be allowed to keep their system. Each and every one of them wanted to avoid taking sides, even unknowingly, and transgressing against the laws of camaraderie, a definite possibility with the prolonged rule of one individual. The Russian POWs were also subject to especially severe penalties ordered from high German places in case of escape attempts. They signed a declaration desisting from such attempts and vouched one for all to abide. Experience, however, had shown that with the advent of spring and rising fervid activity, the escape attempts increased. Thus, one spring morning in 1943 two Russian officers had disappeared. After barely 48 hours, they reported back and asked for their punishment. When asked for the reasons for their behavior, they replied that after such a long incarceration they had felt the need to taste freedom and hear the birds sing in the morning. It is unnecessary to mention that the treatment of the Russian officers in Stalag Luft 3 as "also human" brought sharp protests from certain high places. My extensive involvement over the years with Russians of varying age, background, and education gave me the opportunity to gain some insight into the mentality of these people. Among the many hundreds I met in the course of the war, I did not find one who was not a devout communist. Opportunist [sic] reasons toward me could not have been a motive, since a critical view of the communist doctrines would have been more in character. They were also ardent nationalists. "Mother Russia," the holy soil of Russia, represented more than their own beings. How different from other parts of the free world where the concepts Fatherland and tradition are seen as outdated today. They had been raised with high moral standards, the family was considered holy and the unmarried woman was untouchable. Their military training seemed rather good to me; it had been obtained in plants of the aircraft industry and in their own air force. They were filled with a sense of military honor. One of them was shunned by his comrades because he had failed to destroy his aircraft after a forced landing. Most interesting was their inner attitude towards their allies. The great enemy in the fight for the final aim of all aspirations, to wit, the propagation of communism throughout the world, was the Americans. They were the representatives of the despised capitalism, but their power was respected and feared. The British considered on their way down in the order of the world were less respected, the other peoples of Europe did not count at all, though the traditional sympathy of the Russians for the Germans was apparent. They regarded national socialism as remotely kin to communism but were of the opinion that Hitler and his cohorts were not drawing the correct conclusions from their teachings, neither in the social nor in the economic areas. The centuries old, deep-rooted hatred between Poles and Russians is too well known to require elaboration.

After the landing of American and British troops in Morocco and Algeria on 8 November 1942, the "Führer order" came down dictating that all French POWs be removed from the camp. This meant that we, regretfully, had to say goodbye to those quiet and trusty helpers. They were replaced in their duties by Russian personnel who handled the situation quite well. British POWs, however, protested the use of Russian male nurses and attendants in the sick bays. When the protest was positively supported by the Protecting Power, a new change had to be made, not between the Russians and British, but between the Russians and Americans. The changeover could only be achieved gradually, and the limited room in the barracks made it necessary that Americans and Russians were housed in the same rooms for several days. The doctor in charge conferred with the Americans, and they did not mind this situation. Our surprise the next morning was rather great, though, when we found that after having assigned two Americans and two Russians per room, the latter chose to sleep not in, but right outside, the room in the corridor. Asked for the reason of their behavior, they replied that if at all possible they did not wish to live with capitalists in the same room. Another incident portraying their attitude is worth mentioning. Several months after the arrival of the Russians, I received an invitation to one of their concerts which I accepted. I not only found an excellent choir but also a rather large orchestra with many different instruments. Since the Russians were only making ten pfennig each a day, I inquired where they had gotten all that money to pay for the instruments. After some hesitation came the reply, "Capitalists dumb, Russians smart!" They finally admitted that during their time as hospital attendants they had played cards with the Americans and British and had won the money to purchase the instruments. Occasional cheating when playing with capitalists must have been considered meritorious rather than sinful.

Shortly after taking command, I called together the staff officers of the POWs to detail to them the general guidelines along which I wanted our mutual conduct shaped. I said something like:

> "The basis of our future relations are the Geneva Accords of 1929 which are very clear on our mutual rights and duties. It is my wish to behave towards you as I would expect our present enemies to behave towards me, were I ever so unfortunate as to become a POW myself. The basis of our aspiration to make life for the POWs as pleasant as possible is that they resign themselves honorably and quietly to their unfortunate position and behave accordingly."

At this point one of the English staff officers replied:

> "We respect your views and will try to live up to your expectations. However, we would like to point out one thing right away. It is not only our right, but also our duty

to try, through a successful escape, to rejoin our troops at all costs."

I recognized this point of view, but interjected that, as it was their duty to escape, it was my duty to try everything to keep them from a successful escape. The flyers should not again come into a position in the war where they could harm Germany or ever drop bombs on German territory. We, therefore, came to a "Gentleman's Agreement." In it, we stated, "The armed war is over for the POWs in this camp. They recognize the international laws and camp rules, however, they maintain the right to rejoin their units through escape. In the place of a war of weapons, they are now in a 'war of brains.' Absolute fairness is to be observed in all actions."

Two examples may illustrate how much we tried to live by this code of fairness. Two British officers approached the first "ferret" in the East Compound and asked for a map of the area of Sagan, for good pay naturally. Sergeant Pilz, whom the POWs nicknamed "Charley," reported the incident to me and received orders to agree to the deal. It must be said at this point that it was strictly forbidden for the POWs to have German money in their possession and that it was our duty to confiscate it and find out how it came into the camp. So Charley agreed to the deal, and after three weeks of haggling a price of 50 RM was agreed upon. The exchange of the map for the money was to take place one morning during roll call when the two officers would stay in bed playing sick and Charley could bring them the map. Well, Charley appeared, pulled out the map, the Britains [sic] gave him a 50 RM bill, and Charley pocketed money and map and delivered everything to me. The English were rather indignant about the incident and called the behavior of the German soldier "unfair." They reported the incident to me and insisted the "Gentleman's Agreement" had been broken. In rather lengthy debates, we finally convinced the participants that the German had not been unfair, rather that he had shown more "brains" than his adversaries.

The other incident happened while a friend of mine, a high-ranking German officer, paid me a visit. We drove in his car to the North

Compound to view the almost completed theater which had been built by the English. A rather large crowd of English officers gathered around the car, a model unknown to them until then. It was a Tatra 8-cylinder with rear mounted engine. My visitor wanted his chauffeur to explain the construction of the car to the ever-growing number of spectators who were arguing noisily among themselves. Since I was well aware of the uncanny ability of my protégés to appropriate objects which they deemed desirable I had my doubts. I finally gave in after the doors and windows had been carefully locked. After looking over the construction of the theater, we returned to my quarters. Shortly thereafter, a rather distraught chauffeur appeared and reported that a book had been stolen from the locked vehicle. I requested the acting senior officer of North Compound to report to me and explained to him that my friend had his car explained to them at their request and, in complete trust on their fairness, I would have to regard the disappearance of a book from the car as a violation of the "Gentleman's Agreement." I demanded the return of the book within two hours. It was returned within the specified time; however, two stamped entries had been made: "Passed by the British censor" and "Seen by Winston Churchill." The POWs were masters in producing in a short time any desired stamp made out of rubber soles. Fortunately, the book contained no classified information.

At the meeting with the staff officers of the POWs where we discussed the principles of our mutual conduct, we also touched upon the question of the word of honor. It could play a role in POWs taking walks and in the temporary issuance of tools, typewriters, and such, all of which could be used for escape purposes. We came to an agreement whereby the word of honor had to be given in writing on a case by case basis, signed not only by the parolee, but by his senior officer as well. The written agreement of the latter was a necessary requirement. During long projects like the construction of the theater barracks, sports fields, garden, etc., the word of honor of the senior officer was given to ensure that the supplied materials were not used for unauthorized purposes. I know of no instance which would have given me reason to doubt that the word of honor had been kept.

The German Camp Organization at Stalag Luft 3

The German camp administration was divided into the following groups:

a. Group 1 - Commandant and Court Officer
b. Group 2 - Administration of the various compounds
c. Group 3 - Counterintelligence
d. Group 4 - Administration
e. Group 5 - Medical Branch
f. Group 6 - Mail and Censorship
g. Group 7 - Guards
h. Group 8 - Military Officer of the Barrack

Such a big and diverse organization as Stalag Luft 3 required an extensive number of personnel tasked with innumerable duties. These duties went above and beyond the primitive concept of guarding and reached into the areas of foreign affairs and internal politics. Incidents touching upon the latter areas could have far-reaching implications. The special situation of Stalag Luft 3 had been recognized by the German Foreign Office. I briefed the German officers, doctors, and administrative personnel on my expectations as to their behavior in much the same way as I had briefed the POW staff. In essence, I said the following:

> "The Geneva Convention is the basis for our behavior. It is against the tradition of the German soldier to violate the precept of law, humaneness, and chivalry even against an enemy. In the last war, there persisted even until the last days, especially between the German AF and its enemies, a spirit of chivalry and fellowship. Our commander in

chief has expressed his wish that in this war also this spirit should guide the actions of the organization under him.

As the representatives of the Detaining Power, we have to look upon the POWs as persons, who had and still have the duty to fight for their country, as we are doing. The imprisoned enemy is defenseless. To violate his human dignity is contrary to the spirit of chivalry as mentioned before. Vexing insults are a part of this. Provoking violent behavior towards defenseless people is proof of cowardice.

It is absolutely essential that all German personnel employed here are aware of their rights and duties as representatives of the detaining power and also of the rights and duties of the POWs. I ask the individual section commanders to make sure their subordinates are informed accordingly.

The basis of our behavior is the correct conduct of the POWs. Violations of individual POWs are to be reported; they will be punished. However, the actions of a few should not prejudice you towards the others. I have personally warned the POWs about the consequences of repeat incidents. It is the right of a POW to rejoin his unit by trying to escape. It is our duty to prevent a successful escape. We shall try our utmost to do our duty with the resources at hand.

I shall ask you not to forget one important fact: any war has an end sooner or later, and after a war the nations have to live together again. We cannot ask for the sympathy of the POW we will release when this is over, but what we want to instill is a feeling of respect. They can say, 'I hate the Germans,' but they must think, 'I respect them.'"

The assignment of personnel destined to serve at Stalag Luft 3 was marred by problems which were not easily recognized higher up. This was not only in reference to the intellectual and physical abilities of the newly assigned. One could easily get the impression that certain circles thought that officers and enlisted personnel, who could not be used anywhere else, were just good enough to guard a POW camp. They overlooked the fact that especially these officers were representing the German armed forces to the foreign officers who could easily get the wrong impression about the German Officers Corps in general. Since Stalag Luft 3 was especially blessed with young and well-educated POWs, the German officers, doctors, and civil service employees were required, aside from tact, culture, and self-discipline, to adhere to a certain standard of grooming. The retired officers serving in the beginning in Stalag Luft 3 did an excellent job; however, it is incomprehensible how some of the later assignments were handled by the responsible units at Luftgau III. To mention just a few examples, we received once an officer who was so shortsighted that he could not distinguish a German from an American or English soldier at 12 paces; another officer was so handicapped that even with a walking stick he could not go 300 paces without stopping for a rest; and a third officer, a mental vegetable due to alcoholism, had been let go by another unit some nine months earlier. These officers could hardly be accepted as superiors by the well-trained and rather critical young officers of the enemy AFs.

Strength of character to resist temptation was a main requirement demanded of the NCOs and sergeants. The POWs, who had plenty of food, cigarettes, and other items, tried to win over the confidence of the German personnel who were subsisting on minimum rations. Once the order not to accept presents was broken, the German was in the hands of the POW. The demands for material used in escape attempts increased. The POW called his German delivery man his "contact." In April and May 1944, it was discovered that of the 2,000 German soldiers pulling duty in Stalag Luft 3, seven soldiers and one civil servant had given in to the first harmless, then escalating demands of some POWs. One could understand the civil servant, since he had provided a sick wife and four little children with cocoa, condensed milk, margarine, and egg powder; however, the corruptible behavior of the soldiers was highly reprehensible and disgraceful. In one of his books published after the war, Mr. Paul Brickhill writes in his usual style: "One could bribe 90% of the Germans, including officers, with a little coffee and chocolate." Apparently, it is his style to disregard the most basic precepts of truth and chivalry toward a conquered enemy. Possibly he thought that by insulting the German people he could increase the sale of his books and consequently increase his earnings. The people who were familiar with the situation at hand were rather surprised to find that after 1945 two of the guilty seven soldiers were employed in positions of confidence in the service of the English occupation force. We had believed up to then in the English proverb: "We use the traitor, but we despise him."

Within a time span of 16 months, I made eight requests in regard to strength and composition of the German personnel. The Luftgau III Headquarters in Berlin-Dahlem, however, chose to ignore them. During my entire assignment at Stalag Luft 3, not one representative of the Luftgau ever showed up. On the contrary, well-qualified personnel under my command were continually reassigned elsewhere. In addition, I received urgent requests to reassign NCOs and soldiers for training as officers. Since the educational level of the personnel assigned to Stalag Luft 3 was well above average, Luftgau III thought it had found an ample reservoir of officer candidates. We once received 30 non-German volunteers more or less as compensation. Within a short time, however, they were actively involved in black marketing with binoculars and other important items. Another time, we received for 138 departing soldiers, 62 men who had been retired during the demobilization of 1919 and had held civilian jobs since then.

We did not see any results from our constant efforts to alleviate the personnel shortage until the summer of 1943 when the Inspection of the Air Force XIII entered the picture. They recognized the existing troubles right away and pressed for a solution. The personnel responsible for the daily routine were somewhat relieved, however, since Stalag Luft 3 had become a kind of school for the personnel employed in POW administration, and a constant rotation of officers took place. They came for their training, graduated, and then were transferred to other camps. Other officers came on temporary detachment to us for their training; their number climbed to 14 at one time. Even training schools for the army and the home front came on field trips to look around and gather information. This all took up a lot of time of the assigned personnel.

During the investigations by the "Reich's Kriminalant" (Bureau of Criminal Investigation) and the "Reich's Militargericht" (Military Court) in 1944, and the actual court martial in October 1944, I was charged with systematically removing all officers and civil servants who showed too much interest in National Socialism. This was definitely not true. Only achievements and personal conduct were a deciding factor. I did request the removal of personnel in sensitive positions, such as those who made the issuance of leave papers, dependent on how much food the person brought back for them, or people, whose life styles were not in concordance with moral standards, or who committed irregularities in the issuance of food rations.

The commander had the punitive authority of a regiment commander towards the assigned personnel and the POWs, which in the case of Stalag Luft 3, did not suffice. Proposals for the broadening of these powers, endorsed by the Luftwaffen Inspection, were without success. The duties of the court officer, a Lt. of the Reserve, Roske, were expanded rather extensively. Due to the increasingly-harsh decrees of the High Command, a summary of evidence had to be submitted on the smallest act of vandalism, a summary which was reviewed by the representatives having military jurisdiction. Added to this were the requests of the Gestapo which we had to handle also.

From the beginning, it was clear that Heinrich Himmler wanted to control not only the key positions of the German governing apparatus but also the POW administration. The High Command gave the order to the armed forces units to coordinate all activities having to do with POW camps with the criminal police and the Gestapo. To prevent further expansion of controls, I immediately contacted the individuals responsible for the Sagan area. This resulted in a rather smooth co-existence, for some time at least. Control visits by uniformed Gestapo troops did not take place. Visits of individual Gestapo agents were done in civilian clothes at my request. Nevertheless, a few months after taking charge of Stalag Luft 3, I was warned by good friends in the High Command that my friendly behavior towards the POWs had aroused indignation in political circles and especially in the Reich's Security Headquarters. I was also aware that my behavior was heavily criticized in the circles around the party district director of Sagan. These actions did not change my behavior; I continued fulfilling my duties as I had been taught as a soldier of the old army. I also knew that two members of the camp personnel had volunteered to report my activities on a weekly basis, one to the district director, and the other to the Gestapo. Acting according to the motto, "An alerted man is twice as valuable," I let these two "gentlemen" do their pitiful duty.

Repeated differences with the Gestapo arose out of the fact that they did not deliver captured flyers immediately to the armed forces but tried to keep them in their own custody. I was informed by POWs that several of their friends were held in the cellars of the Gestapo prison in Fresnes near Paris and subjected to unauthorized and rather distressing interrogations. Prompt steps led to their delivery to the proper authorities of the Wehrmacht. Rather lengthy negotiations were required to effect the release of Sq. Leader Roger Bushell who had been located in a Gestapo prison in Prague. After his release to Stalag Luft 3 was obtained, he was again claimed by the Security Headquarters in Berlin after having spent only a couple of weeks in Sagan. When he was not returned after what seemed a rather excessive length of time, I personally intervened repeatedly to effect his return to Stalag Luft 3. He became a victim of the Great Escape of 24-25 March 1944.

A case which attracted a lot of attention was the case of Flight Lieutenant Bob van der Stock. He had been an officer in the Dutch AF at the beginning of the war and was included in the capitulation of 14 March 1940. He escaped to England, joined the RAF, was shot down, was taken prisoner, and taken to Stalag Luft 3. The Gestapo in Holland demanded his extradition for court martial. Two similar cases had resulted in the death penalty for the accused. His extradition was refused and the dispatch of his dossier requested for court martial by the Wehrmacht. This led to rather intense and exceptionally harsh correspondences over a period of at least a year which ended without his extradition. Had I known then how Bushell and van der Stock would behave later on, I might not have compromised myself so much on their behalf.

The requested delivery of two British POWs held by the Gestapo in Warsaw could not be pushed through, since I was placed under court martial in March 1944. A rather lengthy matter was the request by the Gestapo in Prague for the return of ten officers and seven enlisted. These seventeen had been members of the Czech AF. They had fled to England in March 1939, joined the RAF and became British subjects, all this clearly before the beginning of the war. An edict of Adolf Hitler's made them into traitors anyway. During a whole year, I was able to delay their extradition. Only after my removal from office in March 1944 were they transported to Prague. These controversies came also to light during my court martial.

The accomplishment of our duties was increasingly hampered by rigorous orders of the High Command. These orders were sometimes unbelievably contradictory. One order from 23 March 1943 declared that chivalry belonged in the time of the cabinet wars and that in today's war it was unnecessary, that any contacts with the POWs should be kept to a minimum, and that violators would be prosecuted. Only a few days later, a new order arrived which directed all personnel involved in POW administration to actively seek the company of POWs, to distribute propaganda slogans, and win the POWs over to the German ideals. Yet, proposals by several hundred POWs to take German lessons were bluntly refused. The granting of this request would have been easily feasible, since we had no less than twelve modern language teachers among the German personnel. The POWs asked, furthermore, to be instructed in German history with special emphasis on the eastern problems. Again, we had at our disposition highly-educated gentlemen who possessed an excellent knowledge of English, but this request also was denied. The POWs held regular discussions in the evenings and asked for the participation of the German personnel. All these requests were refused and in no uncertain terms. One order of the High Command declared imprisoned

POWs unworthy of treatment as officers, because they all were not only "Mordbrenner" ([murderous] incendiaries), but also always broke their word of honor. As a result of this order, we were also prohibited from performing burials with military honors. The execution of especially this order required a lot of tact, since depressing and provoking actions were to be avoided. The list of these examples goes on and on.

As mentioned earlier, there were two international organizations which had the interest of the POW at heart, the IRC and the Young Men's Christian Association, the most honored and blessed YMCA. The representatives of the IRC appeared only sporadically at Stalag Luft 3. Their area of concern, as best we could determine, was mainly the confirmation of the state of health of the POWs and the checking of the sanitary conditions they lived in.

To honor the work of the YMCA to the fullest is impossible to do in words; it was an expression of deepest human concern. In a very short time, we had a rather pleasant working relationship with the YMCA. When their main office in Berlin, Wilhelmstrasse, was destroyed by English bombs, we succeeded in relocating them to Sagan. The recreation of the POWs in Stalag Luft 3 could not have taken on the extent it did had it not been for the YMCA. Far-reaching plans were contemplated. The church [unnamed and not described in memoirs] was to be surrounded with a small grove of trees. Unfortunately, the plan failed. In consideration of the incessant escape attempts by the POWs, no trees could be kept within the confines of their living areas.

I can only recall the names of a few of the representatives of the YMCA who devoted themselves in such a noble-minded and unselfish way to the commandment of Christian charity and who reaped high praise in caring for the lot of their incarcerated fellow man. The gentlemen's names were: Hugo Cedergren, Eric Christensen, C.G.R. Christiansen, Eric Berg, and Henry Soderberg. May they never be forgotten and may their accomplishments motivate others to true deeds of humaneness.

The efficacy of the YMCA truly came to light when the allies, after the unconditional surrender of Germany on 8 May 1945 more or less revoked the Geneva Accords of 1929 for the members of the German armed forces in their custody. Then, as before, the YMCA was there to ease the lot of so many unfortunate people. I neither heard, nor saw, anything from the IRC. As mentioned earlier, from the end of 1941 the affairs of the enemy powers in the German domain and consequently also the interests of the POWs in Stalag Luft 3, were handled by Switzerland. Gentlemen of the Swiss delegation in Berlin visited Stalag Luft 3 in intervals of two to three months unless special circumstances made more frequent visits necessary. The overall control of the affairs of the POWs at the delegation in Berlin was in the hands of Mr. von Steiger. Councilors of Legation Nayville [Narville] and Büchmuller were the gentlemen who came to Sagan as his representatives. Their visits were appreciated by POWs and Germans alike.

Upon their arrival, we had a short meeting in which we inquired about the state of their work and then they were free to move among the POWs as they pleased. The end of their visit was preceded by a conference which was attended by the representatives of the Protecting Power, the leading personalities of the German camp administration, the senior officers of the different compounds with their deputies, adjutants, and interpreters, and also the foreign clergymen and doctors. All questions were discussed in ruthless candor. The representatives of the Protecting Power absolved their duties with great diplomatic skill and absolute objectivity. I believe that they recognized our efforts to ease the lot of the POWs, in accordance with what conditions allowed. The POWs, however, could not or would not--at least the English behaved that way--understand the special conditions in a Germany ruled by dictatorial National Socialism. Repeatedly, I requested of Legation Councilor Nayville [sic] to explain the situation, which he did, but apparently without success. When we were in English captivity later on, there, unfortunately, was no Protecting Power for us.

At the request of his duty section, Privy Legation Councilor Reinhart from the German Foreign Office visited Stalag Luft 3 toward the end of 1943 to inquire into the state of affairs of the British POWs. Before WWII, he had been German Consul General in Seattle and Liverpool, successively, a fact which made him well-suited for the task at hand. After he had moved freely among the POWS for three days, he bid me farewell with the following words, "I have discussed the conditions in this camp with the British and American officers for the last three days. All, without exception, have expressed their highest esteem and thanks for the treatment afforded them. This conduct is extremely valuable in molding the attitude of the Anglo-Americans towards Germany after the war."

In the fall of 1943, the newly-appointed General Inspector of the POW system and Special Deputy to the Führer, General of the Infantry Roettig, visited Stalag Luft 3 which had been described to him as a model POW camp. He was accompanied by his Chief of Staff Colonel Müeller. The captive officers staged a really remarkable military review. The following day, I was asked by the British senior officer how the general and I had liked the parade. When I complimented him, he replied, "Sir, when you visit the RAF in England after the war, we hope to show you a parade not hampered by lack of uniforms and the like." I did not visit the RAF, but my conduct was very much distorted in the publications of one of its members. After the lifting of the state of war, I protested against this kind of defamation without much success however.

The discussion of the basic duties of the Commandant of Stalag Luft 3 cannot be complete without paying tribute to those who were my immediate helpers and patrons in the daily camp routine. To be mentioned are: my adjutants, first Captain Dr. W. Huenemoerder and from November 1942 on, Lt. W. Awe; the first secretary, Miss L. Knüppel, now Mrs. Hatfield of the U.S., and the imperturbable first clerk, Ofw Schulz. Their devotion to their work was exemplary. Even after it became very dangerous to be associated with me after 25 March 1944, they remained loyal to me. My deepest thanks for their standing by me shall always be theirs.

On the following pages I shall describe the working of the individual groups of the Stalag Luft 3.

Group 2 - Administration of the Various Compounds

The camp administration regulated the life of the POWs within the various compounds. This responsibility was on the shoulders of Major of the Reserve, Prof. Dr. Simoleit. He was responsible for the smooth interaction of almost all aspects of camp life, and he absolved his duties in a most exemplary manner. His actions were dictated by a strict sense of duty, untiring devotion, and deep human sensitivity. All these attributes were coupled with an extremely high intellect. (It is regrettable that he and his family during the first years after the collapse of 1945 had to endure so much suffering.)

Major Simoleit had at his disposition a vast staff of equally qualified people. Aside from the office staff, each compound was manned by two compound officers, one camp NCO, and five sergeants of lower ranks. They all spoke English, had a higher education, and even academic titles. Among them were many former members of the Austrian Armed Forces. The assignment of the POWs in the different compounds to individual barracks and rooms was under the supervision of the senior officer in charge. Liberal allowances were made for personal preferences as to room assignment. The room assignments were normally handled in such a way that the senior officer had a room for himself. Staff officers were assigned two or, if necessary, three to a room, while the remaining officers were bunked four-to-six to a room. Experience had shown that it was necessary to maintain a bed card for each barracks. On it were the names of the occupants of each room broken down into who slept in an upper and who slept in a lower berth. To aid in escape attempts prisoners tried to change places at times. An exchange between an officer and a sergeant or an orderly was very popular, since they could be assigned to work outside the camp and, thus, find a way to escape.

The Russians lived strictly segregated from the Anglo-Saxons in the front camp of East Compound. They were under the command of Ofw Wichmann, a peacetime hotel owner in Königsberg in East Prussia. He had several soldiers under his command, two of whom spoke fluent Russian. Aside from this, the Russians were eagerly learning the German language.

In the last stages of the war, the influx of POWs was so great that occupation strength of the rooms, as mentioned earlier, unfortunately, had to be exceeded in a lot of cases. This was not done due to a lack of care or even chicanery, but simply resulted from the fact that construction could not keep up with the influx of POWs.

Each morning, all camp compounds simultaneously held roll call to determine the presence of all registered POWs. Due to special circumstances, roll calls could be increased temporarily. At these roll calls, the POWs had the opportunity to present wishes or grievances to the camp officer on duty, who, in turn, passed them on to the group leader. Requests for appointments with the group leaders or the commandant were always granted. Frequent meetings between the group leader and the senior officer of the individual compounds in the presence of their staff officers were also held.

The camp administration kept a card file on all POWs in several copies. Right after roll call they submitted their daily written report to the commandant, broken down by compounds, nationalities, and rank, including details of sick bed reports and special events. Tuesday of each week saw a conference in the commandant's office including the group leaders, all senior officers with their immediate staff, and the clergy and doctors, including those of foreign nationalities.

The descriptions of camp life in some of the previously mentioned English books leave the impression that the behavior of the German personnel towards the POWs was often marred by rudeness or even brutality. The Germans allegedly only yelled around; it has even been alleged that NCOs and soldiers were threatening the captive officers with arrest. I have to protest against these allegations very strongly. Punishment was only handed out by the Commandant and only after consultation with the appropriate senior officer. The international rules, whereby NCOs and lower ranks could only do their duties, like roll call, searches, and the like, under the supervision of the officer of the Detaining Powers, were strictly adhered to. An agreement with the senior officers named two Ofws [Oberfeldwebel - Staff Sergeants] who could, if the circumstances warranted it, act as officer representatives. Especially in dealing with older POW officers, the German personnel showed the same exceptional courtesy as they did in dealing with German officers. If a staff officer of the POWs entered a German office, it was natural for the German soldiers, even the officer working there, to rise for a salute. I mention this, in particular, because later on the German officers were treated entirely differently when they were POWs.

Due to the lengthy confinement, the nerves of the POWs were taxed to the utmost leading sometimes to depression and even suicide. The compound administration was trying with whatever means possible to combat these symptoms. They tried to provide mental and physical diversion. Symptoms of depression in fellow POWs were to be reported to the compound leader, so that he could take appropriate action.

The spiritual care was primarily a function of the clergymen of their own nationality, practiced during personal interviews or during church services. The program ran into trouble in the beginning because a sufficient number of the clergymen of different nationalities were not available. During that time, the clergy of both confessions of the city of Sagan placed themselves at the disposal of the POWs. Much later, we had one or two clergymen of their own nationality in each of the compounds. While the Catholic care was rather uncomplicated, the Protestants had their problems because of their various denominations. This was especially true with the Americans, but these problems were solved in time to everybody's satisfaction.

Experience had shown that of the total POW population, a certain percentage was more or less involved in the activities of "Organization X," which, as mentioned, dealt with escape attempts. About 15% of the Englishmen and 5% of the Americans were involved in some form or another. The difference in participation may be explained by the fact that England lay closer than America, and the English had had more time than the Americans to expand and even perfect their organization. They hoped to reach ports like Danzig, Stettin, and Bremen, find refuge on Scandinavian freighters docking there, and eventually reach their homeland.

For educational meetings of the POWs, special barracks were put at their disposal, and if those did not suffice then the numerous theater barracks and dining halls could be used. At least the intention for mental exercises was highly developed at Stalag Luft 3, and a neutral visitor one day compared the camp to a university. If somebody spent his days underground to dig instead of learning something for his later life, then that was his free decision. Each compound had a large library with valuable scientific literature and novels. Many POWs had amassed a sizeable library of their own during their extremely long captivity. Among the many books were extensive works on history, geography, natural sciences, technology, languages, philosophy, and the like. There were many study groups and classes, among them courses in German, Spanish, French, Italian, and Russian. Even for Asian languages like Malayan and Sanskrit, there were teachers and students among the POWs. By way of the Protecting Power, the POWs corresponded with their home universities. Academic centers sent tests upon request which were administered under seclusion in the camp and returned via the Protecting Power for grading. The teaching staff was drawn from the many academicians among the POWs, and the British also had many personalities among them who had served in the colonies or as diplomatic representatives in foreign countries.

Worth mentioning are the highly-interesting discussion evenings of the POWs. Somebody "moved a motion" which the person detailed in front of everybody. Then a first speaker spoke for, and a first speaker spoke against the motion. There was a second speaker for and against, and at the end the whole assembly, made up of several hundred spectators, voted for or against the motion. When we still had 1800 NCOs and sergeants of the RAF at Stalag Luft 3, the older English officers suggested that they, too, should have similar discussion evenings. This points out the desire of the English to train everybody for the unprepared usage of oration, a trend visible in the English school system.

Excellent results were obtained in the theater productions. Each compound had a theater, and in some there were two. The theater erected in the North Compound turned out quite nice based on the experiences gained in previous ventures. The POWs gave their word of honor not to use any of the issued materials or tools for the preparation of escapes. The foundation production room and fire wall were built from solid bricks, and a wooden barracks was erected on the foundation. The interior was decorated rather artistically, and construction of the side scenes and other theatrical properties showed great perfection. The greatest problem here, as in other theater barracks, was the lighting system, but even this question was solved with the help of the many technically-educated POW officers and the assistance of the German personnel. The auditorium in the North Compound differed in no way from other theaters. There were 350 seats, mostly folding chairs constructed from the wood of the crates in which the Red Cross packages arrived. The man responsible for the theater organization was Wing Commander Lackin. [sic] [Larkin] The texts came in via the Protective Power or the YMCA and then were reproduced on typewriters and handed out on word of honor. Superintendent of the theaters in the East Compound, and later North Compound, was Flight Lt. Kenneth Macintosh. His assistant was Flight Lt. T.N.E. [sic] [T.N.C.] Rothwell. Responsible for the lighting was Lt. McKay. They had dressing rooms where even wigs were manufactured and workshops where simple costumes were made from pyjamas, [sic] towels, handkerchiefs, etc. Costumes too hard to reproduce were rented from theaters and rental places in Berlin, Dresden, Liegnitz, or Görlitz. The rental of the historical costumes, armor, and weapons of the 11th century for Macbeth cost the POWs more than 2000 RM. Since the shelves of the PXs were rather bare due to the hard times, the substantial salaries paid to the officers were freed for other things.

In the course of the years, a great number of theatrical productions, revues, and other things were played. Let me just mention those that I remember:

1. Classical productions – Macbeth, Hamlet, Mary Stuart, Joan of Arc, Summernight's Dream [A Midsummer Night's Dream], As You Like It, The Importance of Being Earnest
2. Variety productions – George and Margaret, The Dover Road, [Dover Road] Design for Living, Rockery [Rookery] Nook, Twinkle Twinkle Little Star [Twinkle, Twinkle Mr. Starr], Escape, Tony Draws a Horse, Arsenic and Old Lace, Blithe Spirit, The Man Who Came to Dinner, I Have Been There Before, Thark, The Flashing Stream

3. Revues – Aladdin's Lamp (with ballet), Between Ourselves (with ballet), Music Hall with Krakowiak, [Polish dance] Palina Panic, Messalina.

The acquisition of theater properties and their transport posed additional problems for the German troops which they were able to solve by giving up their already sparse free time.

Each piece ran in each compound for several days. The POWs of all compounds were to have the opportunity to see theater productions which had been produced in other compounds. It was, therefore, necessary every evening to lead a certain number of POWs from one compound to another. This also tasked the few free evenings of the German personnel, and as a thank you they received a rather unfair treatment in English books.

Aside from the above mentioned actors, the following gentlemen deserve mention:

Dominic Page, Peter Butterworth, Peter Gates, John Dowler, Peter Allan, Anthony Hudson, John Madge, David Porter, John Casson, and Malcolm Freegard.

This list, as is the one on the repertoire, is rather incomplete, but more than 14 years have passed, and I rescued from Sagan only what I wore on my body.

Music found as much interest as theatrical plays. Already in early 1943, Stalag Luft 3 had five orchestras, among them symphony, dance, and jazz bands. One of the symphony orchestras, under the direction of Arthur B. Creighton, [Crighton] consisted of 42 members in classical arrangement. The best known dance and jazz bands were, The Swing Club and The Ron Birch Band. The many musical instruments had to be procured from all over the Reich, but even this work was done without grumbling by the supposedly brutal and yelling German soldiers.

Another major part of the POW's life was taken up by sports. Each compound had a particularly large sports field which first had to be converted into such by the POWs on a reserved area within the barbed wire enclosure. It was necessary to remove tree stumps, flatten out the area, etc. The tools for this job were loaned out under word of honor not to use them for illegal purposes. The actual sports equipment was procured for the most part by the YMCA. Athletics, high jump, broad jump, discus throwing, and the one hundred, two hundred, and five hundred meter dash were practiced feverishly. In team sports, the English preferred football and rugby, the Americans softball, but the Canadians also like to play softball. During rugby matches, the presence of the first aid personnel was desirable, since broken bones, bruised ribs, and other injuries were no rarity. For the older gentlemen, there was the possibility of playing golf. In winter, ice skating and hockey were possible since some of the sports fields became flooded and froze. The presence of the Canadians ensured a high game standard. Sunday afternoons saw competitions and a band playing. Even a tote board was used. There were enough racing experts among the POWs to ensure a correct operation. Every once in a while, there were elimination matches between different compounds, which, naturally, became the highlight of camp life.

Despite immense problems in the procurement of materials, we succeeded in installing a PA system in the different compounds. The POWs could choose the radio programs, but were restricted to German stations. That they succeeded in building secret receivers even with the most primitive means shall be discussed later. The camp administration had a section for photos and movie presentations under the expert guidance of Offzs Eichacker and Ettlich and Corporal Friedrich. We amassed a rather large stock of photographs, which, if they concerned POWs, were given to them upon request to be sent home. Unfortunately, even those pictures were used in rather expert ways to send uncensored news back home. They were being checked at a German central office, and several times secret news was found between the gelatine layers and the paper of the pictures. After movie presentations were made possible in the German troop camp, the POWs were given the possibility, according to the available space, to attend the showings.

Walks outside the camp perimeter were planned, but they were restricted due to the large numbers of POWs and the non-availability of German personnel for escort duty. Added to these difficulties was the fact that the increasing destruction of German cities brought out an ever-increasing hostility in the German populace which came especially to light in the many people who had been evacuated from western Germany to Sagan and its surroundings. To preclude any incidents it was soon necessary to avoid towns entirely. Walks finally had to be restricted to persons of the clergy, doctors, and camp administrators, and to those POWs who showed signs of depression and who, therefore, needed a maximum of diversified distractions.

The German camp administration tried very hard to supply the POWs with German newspapers of which the ones with technical information were preferred for obvious reasons. These papers were screened and retained if they contained articles too offensive to the Enemy Powers. The "Organization X" derived from these newspapers, as we found out later on, material for their escape attempts in the form of ads from German industrial companies to which the escapees had their forged papers made out.

The daily routine was more or less left to the discretion of the POWs. After roll call in the morning came the walk to the bulletin board, on which was posted important news for all or for single individuals. Included was the news whether mail or packages had come in and for whom.

Courses were generally also held in the morning. A great amount of time was dedicated to the washing of the laundry which the POWs undertook themselves. Linen and other things went to a German laundry. The afternoons were mainly spent with sports. A solemn ritual for the British was tea time at 1600 hours. Sports matches could actually be interrupted because of tea time. In the evenings, there were theater visits, concerts, discussions, and demonstrations of newly-received records from home. Many POWs spent their time with handicrafts of many sorts and some beautiful accomplishments were made in that field. At various intervals, there were shows of these works.

The English officers had the habit of preparing their noon and evening meals for small table groups of six-to-eight persons in the barracks kitchen provided for that purpose. Since several cooking groups were trying to use the same kitchen during any eating period, the individual groups had to make do with a 25-minute kitchen time. The big camp kitchens in the English compounds limited their activities generally to the preparation of the potatoes as well as the hot water for the wash and for the preparation of tea.

Mr. Brickhill talks in his book, *Escape to Danger,* on page 47, about the way the food was distributed to the POWs in Germany and says, "The Germans interpreted the Geneva Convention in their own way. The POWs received rations which delivered them to starvation." The Geneva Conventions prescribe that the POWs receive the same rations as the garrison troops of the Detaining Power. These rules were strictly enforced. If the British POWs who could lead a perfectly calm life thought they were not able to subsist on the same rations as the German soldiers who were pulling rather harsh duty then that is a sign that the British population was rather spoiled, even in war. The alleged starvation rations of the POWs were augmented since June 1941 with packages from the Red Cross with the contents of which the recipients could live a life of excess in comparison to the war-time rations allocated to the German personnel. It went so far that the English threw a part of the food rations provided by the Germans, like tea and cheese, onto the garbage pile. When the responsible POWs were denied their allocation of these rations, the expected indignant protests took place.

The English, Canadian, and American Red Cross provided each POW with a weekly ration package of ten pounds (German). These packages contained high grade foods and assured the recipient better and more nutritious nourishment than any German had. In Stalag Luft 3, about 25,000 of these packages were distributed monthly. In case of delivery delays due to war activities a reserve of three months was kept on hand. To these deliveries were added the great number of packages which the POWs received from their families at home. In some cases, there were so many that the recipients had no use for their contents and had them stored in the German depot. This went so far that one of the English officers kept a supply of 72 packages on hand. The storage and administration of finally more than 100,000 packages brought the responsible German offices to the breaking point and led to the directive that the number of private packages an individual might store in the German depot be limited to ten. The happy owners of extensive supplies found less fortunate comrades with whom they could share their wealth.

In similar excess to the arrival of food, clothing, and the like, was the arrival of tobacco and cigarettes which came in big heavy sacks on a regular basis. Matches, however, were extremely scarce, since they could not be shipped due to the fire hazard. Like the German personnel, the POWs received one box of matches per month. This led to the value of a match being equal to a cigarette in the daily trends of the POWs. Many helped themselves by constructing small lamps made from tin cans filled with margarine and a wick made from a pyjama [sic] or pullover thread. Each barracks had a lamp of this kind in a fireproof place and under the supervision of a POW.

The various contents of the packages led to the temporary excess or shortage of many foods or luxury items. This led to the establishment of a regular food exchange with variable exchange prices fixed by a commission.

The consumption of alcoholic beverages was prohibited. This, however, did not exclude the delivery of beer to the POWs for big holidays like Christmas even though its procurement for such a large crowd was rather difficult. It is well known that the highlight of the Christmas season for the English is the second Christmas day, the so-called "Boxing Day." Already in Dulag Luft at the beginning of the war when the delivery of alcohol from captured stock was still possible we could observe that the English did not consume their weekly rations in daily portions but saved them up for one time usage with the corresponding consequences. In Stalag Luft 3, they soon began producing their own alcohol. The numerous packages contained great quantities of raisins and prunes. These were fermented in large containers in secret places and distilled in artfully-constructed stills made from old tin cans. The procedure did not remain hidden from us. If a certain POW community had shown itself a rather unpleasant side, we conveniently, by accident, found one or several of their stills and threw away the contents. Some of the more artistic and technically-superb stills were the pride of the escape museum.

The heating of the living quarters and assembly rooms was left to the discretion of the POWs, each compound receiving firewood based on the occupation strength. The English converted some of the iron stoves by means of an addition to a kind of fireplace around which they spent their tea time and evenings. We were less interested in the excessive consumption of firewood in such fireplaces, since the wood allocation of the compounds was fixed, than in preventing fires. The barracks were closed at 2100 hours, and nobody was authorized outside after that time. In the event of emergencies within a barracks, a red light was mounted on each roof which the barracks senior could activate from his room. Its glow called German personnel without fail.

I cannot end this chapter dealing with the group camp administration without mentioning the persons in leading positions, who were responsible for the smooth operation of the business at hand, even though sometimes it had to be done under the most difficult circumstances. They were, aside from the previously mentioned director Major of the Reserves Prof. Dr. Simoleit, Major Wiedemann, Captain Pieber, Dr. Gralka, Schultz, Hallwachs and Gallatowicz, [sic] [Galothovics] and the Offzs Dr. Eidmann, Hohendahl and Schmutzler.

Group 3 – Counterintelligence

If the POWs thought of the group "camp administration" as the unit most concerned with their welfare, they all were rather apprehensive towards the counterintelligence group. The duties of counterintelligence in general were to protect the German domain against acts of espionage and sabotage. Since one could expect, based on experiences from WWI, such acts not only from escaped forced laborers but also from escaped POWs, there had been established at Supreme Headquarters a counterintelligence department called, "Abwehr III Kriegsgefangene, O.K.W. ABW III Kgf" (counterintelligence III/POWs) which dealt in affairs connected with POWs. It was under the command of Colonel Witte, and after his death in October 1942 came under Captain, later Major, Salewski.

Under him, came the chiefs of counterintelligence in the various armed forces districts. Stalag Luft 3 came under the Armed Forces District VIII in Breslau. Its Intelligence Chief 123 gave his orders pertaining to countermeasures directly to the intelligence officers in the various units stationed in the district, consequently, also the intelligence officer in Stalag Luft 3. This intelligence officer had to report in all matters directly to the chief of intelligence of the armed forces district which led to the fact that the responsible commandant of the camp could only find out about the orders his subordinate had received, and his report, in turn, to District VIII, by reading it when the report was disseminated. Such subordinations were contrary to any military chain of command and had to lead to complications if administered to the letter. My personal relations with Colonel Witte and Major Salewski made possible the prevention, i.e., removal of any disturbing events.

The position of First Intelligence Officer in Stalag Luft 3 was held by Major Peschel. When the POW camp Nr. 5 in Heydekrug opened up in May 1943, this excellent intelligence officer was transferred there. His successor was the Second Intelligence Officer, Captain Broili. He was court martialed with me in June 1944. These officers usually had two assistant officers and a greater number of military personnel for administrative and outside duty at their disposal.

The outside duty of intelligence was delegated in Stalag Luft 3 to the so-called "Spurers" (trackers). Each compound had one FW [feldwebel], or officer in charge, and four or five soldiers of various grades as helpers. It was their duty to observe the POWs in whatever manner they chose and determine whether their behavior betrayed any escape preparation. They were the German fighters in the so-called "war or brains" in which the POWs with their escape intentions were the aggressors. Attack and defense were refined over the years and developed to a fine art with the most well-known trackers gaining international fame. Standing out from all and in first place, I have to mention Ofw Glemnitz, an energetic personality with exemplary dedication to duty, and an untiring worker of determined reliability against sometimes quite enticing attempts at bribes. He also knew how to garnish his behavior, if and when necessary, with the right degree of joviality. Almost equal in their accomplishments were Uffz Pilz and Griese, as well as the younger, but talented, Uffz Seifert. The shadowing was divided as follows: East Compound Uffz Pilz, Center Compound Ofw Glemnitz, North Compound Uffz Griese, and South Compound Uffz Seifert. Glemnitz was the recognized master and prime expert. The British had nicknamed Uffz Pilz "Charley," and Griese was called "Rubberneck" because of his long neck. Like their assistants, these main trackers wore dark blue coveralls which made it possible to check out inaccessible places. They were also equipped with big flashlights and a kind of thin rod about three feet long which was used to poke into piles of any kind and also to check for underground tunnels. In the accomplishment of their duties, they also had to check the ground under the barracks for tunnel entrances or evidence of fresh sand. Since they were forced to crawl around under the barracks, they had been nicknamed, "Ferrets" or "Fretties" by the POWs.

To secure against unwelcome visitors, the POWs had created their own watch network within the confines of their compound. It was supposed to keep them continuously informed as to when and which Germans were entering the compound, what they were doing there, with whom they talked, and when they left. This security system was used mainly to secure "Organization X" in its work on escape attempts against the unwelcome surprise visits by Germans. The system required the posting of one or two POWs rather innocently reading or talking in front of a barracks, but well in sight of the inner gate. Those were the "duty pilots" who kept a log on every German entering or leaving the compound. Close by was a box or a chair with a shovel or something like that on it. A change of position of this object indicated what category of German had entered the compound. This change was recorded by a second guard inside the compound who relayed the information either directly or via a third person. The most vulnerable members of "Organization X" were in this way continuously and most expeditiously kept informed on whether the commandant, ferrets, or members of the regular camp personnel (the latter being considered harmless) were within the compound. The presence of "ferrets" meant general alert. The POWs pulling this duty were called "Stooges," while the German guards on the towers and outside the camp were called "Goons." A tower with its guards was a "Goonbox" in the POW language. The security system described above, naturally, did not remain hidden from us since we confiscated enough logbooks which showed the warning system used. Countermeasures on our part were hard to implement since the warning system was flexible enough to adjust to our measures. The warning signals were changed, and it was hardly possible to forbid the POWs the closing of a door, the opening of a window, or the blowing of one's nose. These and other signals changed constantly.

It was in the trackers' interest to get into the living quarters of the POWs without being seen. They let themselves be locked in the communal rooms, hid in the attic of the living quarters, etc., while the POWs were at the assembly areas being counted. The POWs, in turn, ensured themselves against undesirable visits by stringing thread at strategic places in the attic or elsewhere, which was checked at intervals to ensure it had not been disturbed. The trackers crawled at night through the concertina wire or climbed over the fence on especially dark nights. They hid in cars bringing materials into the camp, or observed camp life from hiding places outside the camp erected in treetops during the dark of the night.

The most logical escape attempts were those in broad daylight. The leaving of the camp by day required special preparations, like the copying of German uniforms or mannerisms of known persons, or the sewing and creation of civilian clothing. In all cases, the preparation of forged papers was necessary. In all these endeavors, the POWs became in time real masters. It happened one day to the well-known tracker Uffz Pilz, that he met himself in the German compound. He stopped short, thought he saw his mirror image walking towards him, arrested the individual and had captured a POW in disguise. The color of Pilz' hair and face as well as his clothing had been copied exceptionally well. One help, naturally, was the color similarity between the uniforms of the German and Royal Air Force. The color tone of the latter had been darkened slightly with a combination of soot and graphite from pencils which was applied in liquid form to the uniform. The insignia were cleverly copied from leftover pieces of material.

One other time, Uffz Hohendahl arrived at the main gate in the German compound after having passed the gates of East Compound to leave the camp area. When he presented his ID card, the guard on duty was rather perplexed since Uffz Hohendahl had already left the camp ten minutes earlier. The only difference was that the first Hohendahl had worn dark pants while the one at the gate was wearing white pants. His suspicion having been aroused, he examined the latter Hohendahl closer and discovered a POW. He looked quite like the real Hohendahl except that he had had darker hair. To alleviate this problem, he had received over a period of several weeks, small amounts of hydrogen peroxide from friends being discharged from the dispensary. He then colored his hair until it matched the real Hohendahl's. The possibility of forging IDs, or as was once the case, the forging of a service and pay book, could always be traced to the inattention of the German soldiers who had not been trained in those things. It was possible that one of the soldiers took off his uniform jacket to do some physical task of some kind or another. Immediately, his attention was distracted by other POWs, and his ID card had disappeared out of his coat. In painstaking work, his ID was copied, and after some time the ID was returned with the most honest of faces as having been found somewhere. These were IDs for escapers who wanted to disappear in German uniforms; later there was a well-organized production of IDs of forced laborers who were being transferred from one work location to another.

These escape attempts in broad daylight culminated in one attempt which was admired by all. In early 1943, there was only one bath facility for POWs situated in the front camp of East Compound. At certain intervals, POWs of the different compounds, were escorted by German personnel to this facility. One day, at 1400 hours, a troop of 24 POWs escorted by two German Offzs arrived at the gate of North Compound. The papers of the German soldiers stated their duty to escort these POWs to the bathhouse in the front camp of East Compound. To reach the front camp, after having exited North Compound, the group had to use the public road for about 600 meters before it entered again the fenced-in area at the main gate. So, the two "Uffzs" arrived with their bathing group at the gates of North Compound, the IDs of the "Uffzs" who spoke fluent German were checked, and the whole thing was a routine matter; no suspicions were aroused. Unfortunately, the guard failed to check the bathing bundles the POWs were carrying with them. Out of sight of the guard in North Compound, the whole group disappeared. After about 300 meters in the adjoining woods, the bundles which contained the escape clothes were opened, everybody changed, and all 26 men took off. Fifteen minutes later, a second group of bathers appeared at the same gate of North Compound, this time led by one "Uffz." The guard found something amiss here. He stopped the detail for closer inspection, and the intelligence officer was called on the phone to come over right away. By chance, the guard mentioned that he had already let pass a detail of 24 men led by two NCOs. The intelligence officer felt like lightning had just struck next to him since he knew with certainty that bathing was not planned for that afternoon. A quick check confirmed the successful escape of 26 POWs. An escape of more than four men was considered a mass escape and resulted in a country-wide alarm of all police stations and other units involved in camp security. At least 42 telegrams, aside from the telephone notifications, had to be sent to all departments involved in security within Germany and corresponding units involved in border guarding. Security headquarters had photos of all POWs. After an escape notification, an exact description with pictures of all escapees, was published in the Reich's criminal Most Wanted list. In this case, however, we succeeded in recapturing 24 of the escapees within a short time, and only two of the officers remained missing and seemed to have vanished. Twelve days after the escape, two corporals of the German AF appeared at the huge Kupper airfield located about 8 kilometers from Stalag Luft 3. They approached a parked airplane, searched around, but discovered that the starter handle was missing, so they then turned their attention to a second plane which was also parked outside. One of them climbed aboard while the other tried to kick over the propeller. A sergeant passed by and asked, "Where do you guys want to go?" The two corporals were, naturally, the other two English escapees. They felt they had been discovered and replied, "We just wanted to fly to Sweden." Supplied with the so-called escape food, they had hid out in the forest near the airfield for the last eleven days, studied the duty cycle and the general goings on at the airfield, and had waited for a quiet noon hour to try their take-off.

In the chapter of the daylight escapes needed to be mentioned are those during big train transports. To jump from slow moving trains brought no success since guards were posted at the doors and in the corridors. Some tried to saw through the compartment floor with a small saw smuggled in their sacks. Two POWs dropped through this opening. This was discovered by the guard, and the escapees were recaptured rather quickly. During larger transports, we finally took away the POWs' shoes, suspenders, and belts, since running through the countryside without shoes and with dropping pants is rather cumbersome. Some POWs hid in boxes being loaded in the same transport. This was rather primitive since we discovered them missing already when the POWs climbed aboard the train. As a precaution, however, we started putting a guard on the wagons carrying boxes and the like.

A favorite method was to infiltrate a troop of Russian POWs, who had come over from Stalag VIII to do work in Stalag Luft 3, and, naturally, had to be taken back. Other POWs tried to hide in horse carts or trucks carrying trash or in felled trees taken out of the camp. To make their escape, they would jump from a road onto the moving car. All vehicles were, therefore, stopped at the gates. The guard on duty would yell, "I am poking into the load." If a POW had hidden out in there, it was in his interest to come out if he did not want to be skewered alive. One other attempt at a daytime escape deserves mention. The POWs had calculated the field of vision of the guards on the towers and had enlisted the obscured areas of the camp on a map. This resulted in the discovery that a short section of fence could not be seen by the guards on two of the towers. This became the basis for their plans. The guards on three consecutive towers were distracted by incidents within the camps. Close to one tower, two POWs seemed to get into a fight. A crowd gathered, and the guard was also watching the fight. Close to the second tower, a match took place. Here, also, a crowd gathered, and the guard looked on. At the third tower two POWs appeared and begged to call to sick bay so that a doctor might come. These diversionary tactics were used by two officers to bridge the 80 steps to the next fence to the exact spot which could not be controlled by the towers. They cut the wires with lightning speed, crept through, and made it to the woods. They actually succeeded in reaching the Baltic where they took a boat to reach Denmark, a safe haven for them. They did not reach their goal, but perished on the high seas.

All escapes were doomed to fail if the escapee could not properly identify himself at the numerous control points. Extensive preparations were, therefore, needed. Anybody who has ever been in captivity knows how material is collected. A POW leans to pick up any object, however useless to a free citizen, and delivers it to the proper people, be it rusty nails, bits of iron, leather, thread or the like. Added to this in Sagan was the collection of parts of the camp proper. Nails were pulled out in inconspicuous places. If workers were in the camp, one tried to appropriate some of their materials, like cement, cable, trowels, etc. Wire cutters were fabricated from knives and oven doors. A very important chapter in the acquisition of materials was the question of bed boards. The 1200 beds of one compound contained seven 12-inch wide boards on which the mattress rested. If three boards disappeared from each bed, that totaled up to 3600 boards. This was enough to shore up a tunnel of about 400 meters (1200 feet) on the sides and on the top. It is self-explanatory that after we discovered the first tunnel shored up with the help of the bed boards that they were taken away and a net of rope was substituted for the mattress to rest on.

The escapees had to prepare themselves to live, for the first few days anyway, on a food concentrate which could be hidden on the body. This concentrate was a mixture of sugar, cocoa, condensed milk, margarine glucose, oats, Bemax, chocolate, and crushed crackers; all those were foods which arrived in plentiful supply in Red Cross packages. This mixture was cooked in the kitchen in flat cocoa pans which could be attached to the belt. Calculations had shown that one can contained enough nutrition for three days.

The escapees needed maps and ID cards. Soon after the arrival of the first flyers, we discovered that they had sewn into their clothing silk maps of Germany with special emphasis on border crossing points. On them were indicated what guards were present at the crossings and especially whether they had dogs. Even though the major part of these maps were found, some made it through and formed the basis for mass reproductions. As noted earlier, the POWs were able to acquire some guard IDs, mainly because of the clumsiness of a few German soldiers. They were also able to get transfer documents which the many foreign workers had to carry with them on their way from one work place to another. The idea was that the escapee would pass himself off as a foreign laborer, who was, for example, on his way from a work place in lower Silesia to a work place near the Swiss, Czech, Dutch, Belgian, or French border, or to a coastal city. As mentioned earlier, the German newspapers, with their ads of industrial companies, gave them the necessary information. The copying of the maps and the IDs was handled by expert draftsmen or cartographers. The necessary drawing instruments and ink, unfortunately, were supplied by so-called "contacts."

The work did not stop when the maps and IDs were drawn. They had to be duplicated in great numbers. According to British descriptions, gelatine was used which had been procured in the dispensary. This gelatine was soaked in hot water and then wrung out in a towel until all the sugar had been removed. The remaining mass was melted down again, and poured between flat metal sheets constructed from tin cans. The draftsmen drew the map or ID to be copied on a piece of paper by means of ground lead from copy pencils and then pressed the paper onto the gelatine plate. It was then possible to make hundreds of copies through this process.

Compasses were also made entirely by artificial means. Broken records were heated until pliable and then formed to make the housing for the compass. A kind of compass card was drawn and glued to the bottom of the housing. A record needle was mounted on the bottom as the pivot point for the actual magnetic needle. It was made from a sewing needle, whose point had been made magnetic. They even succeeded in making this needle glow in the dark. The top was closed with glass from broken windows cut under water. The solder came from old tin cans and the resin from trees.

If the escapee wanted to pass as a German soldier, i.e., escort for a group of POWs, it was necessary to carry a holster with visible pistol butt on the sergeant's uniform; or if he pretended to be a member of the regular guards, he had to carry a carbine. The copying of individual carbines proved quite difficult. During conversations with German soldiers, a second POW close by was drawing the picture of the carbine. A detailed and accurate sketch, naturally, required several sessions for corrections. The discovery had been made in the camp that one in 3000 bed boards was beech wood rather than pine and, therefore, particularly well-suited for carving rifles. Since a single board did not suffice to make a carbine, two boards were glued together and secured with clamps from ping-pong nets. Slowly, the copy took on the form of the original. The holsters of the sergeant's uniform were made by expert leather craftsmen from old leather shoes.

For the work in the tunnels, which became longer and longer, they used air pumps to provide fresh air to those working underground in tight quarters. To do this they used old kit bags, whose open ends were stretched over a wooden frame. Inside the kit bag was a round wooden disc on a long stick which stuck out of one end of the bag and had a handle. The movement pressed air out of an opening on the other side of the bag. The necessary rubber bands were made from suspenders. From the air pump, a pipeline led into the tunnel. The pipeline was made from tin cans, whose ends fit perfectly together. The joints were additionally protected with resin and paper. This pipeline was embedded into the floor of the tunnel. The removal of stale air was accomplished through an identical pipeline which ended in the masonry of the barracks floor. The air coming out of the tunnel proper was guided into the chimney. When the escaping air could be seen, a smoke-producing fire was started in the oven.

The biggest problem in the tunnel construction was the disposal of the accumulating sand. Considering the length and depth of some of these tunnels, many cubic yards had to be disposed of. The trackers were naturally always looking for signs of fresh sand. If sand could be found, then a tunnel was under construction. Even in the camouflage of sand, a certain expertise was attained. First, the sand was distributed under the barracks. This soon became impossible since the ground was being watched. Then sand was packed in the attic of the barracks. But that was also discovered after some time. It was dangerous to amass great amounts of sand in a limited area since the sand could easily be distinguished from the dry ground. The POWs finally tried to distribute such great amounts of sand away from the tunnel entrance by dispersing it over wide areas of the camp with the aid of old pant legs. The pant legs were sewn together and the sand packed in these "hoses." The hoses were carried in the coat arms [sic] [pant legs] on strings, and the POW then went for a walk, releasing the sand slowly through a small opening. When even that did not help any more, the sand was hidden in small shafts distributed throughout the camp. The discussion of the great tunnel construction in North Compound in a later chapter in this manuscript will permit us to look at these techniques more closely. Work on the great tunnel had taken eleven months. Ninety-nine tunnel constructions had been discovered over a span of two years by the trackers. The coincidence of various unfortunate events prevented the discovery of the 100th tunnel. Its discovery was supposed to be celebrated in grand style; the intelligence people had even taken up a collection for this purpose. But this 100th tunnel proved fatal for Germans and POWs alike.

A constant source of our worry was the construction of secret radios on the part of the POWs. Old cracker boxes cut to the right form and insulated with melted Victrola records were used. Paper rolls held the wires for condensers while a piece of paper with a graphite line became a resistor. The tube was the only part which was not manufactured in the camp to complete a radio. The "contacts" mentioned earlier were used for that. It was sad to discover later on that a German had been found who used his position of trust to do such traitorous duties for the POWs. It goes without saying that we were constantly on the lookout for those radios which we knew were somewhere, and our searching was sometimes successful. One of the radios had been built into an accordion. One side was removable and in it the radio had been built. The whole contraption had been put together in such a way that the accordion was still playable. Later on, the POWs started the practice of hiding the individual parts of a radio in their belongings and only on certain nights, when they thought themselves safe, did they put the radio together to listen to English broadcasts. One instance happened where during a surprise search of the barracks, a radio tube fell out of the hair of an American first lieutenant. The Germans believed that with special equipment it was possible to detect the location of an unauthorized radio. Postal inspectors were called in with their equipment, and the POW barracks were observed at night through closed shutters. Unfortunately, we never discovered a set that way.

A great help in the fulfillment of the work of the intelligence division was the dog detail attached to them. We had 32 excellent dogs and 24 dog handlers who did a superb job. A watch dog could cover at least a 350 meter wide area of the woods surrounding the camp, whereas a guard could only control about ten meters.

When the time had come to expect another tunnel breakthrough at any moment, a cordon of watch dogs 350 meters apart was posted at least 150 meters deep into the woods, between the last fence and its towers and the patrols in between them. It was impossible that an escapee climbing out of a tunnel could escape the attention of a dog. The only problem was to determine in which compound a tunnel was nearing completion. This is why we were undecided in the days before the Great Escape of 24-25 March 1944 whether the dogs should be outside the East or the North Compound. Unfortunately, we decided to bet on the East Compound. The coverage of both compounds was impossible even with 32 dogs. The dog handlers had the additional duty of patrolling the inside of the compounds at night to discourage POWs from leaving their barracks. In the rare instances where this was tried the dog stopped the perpetrator immediately. The dogs were continuously exercised in a special fenced off area within the German camp. Jumping and seizing of a person was exercised with the man portraying a POW walking around in a heavy-tufted armor. The dogs were also excellent for tracking. Nobody but the handlers could even get near them. If I met a dog handler and his animal at night during one of my rounds, I usually kept at least three paces away from the man. If I had come any closer, the dog would have attacked me.

Intelligence was also in charge of package control. It was rather obvious that the home offices of the POWs were trying by any means possible to smuggle in unauthorized items in the packages, especially items that could be of help in escape attempts. The packages were, therefore, thoroughly searched. We soon realized that the packages sent by the Red Cross did not contain contraband. Spot searches conducted on the hundreds of thousands of packages never came up with anything. The private packages, however, necessitated a thorough search. The number of items found is legion; they were hidden in the cleverest ways possible. Apparently, certain large companies had even given themselves to hiding contraband in original company packages. For example, compasses were hidden in original tooth powder boxes. Several of these companies were on our black list. To own German money was strictly forbidden for the POWs, and yet our searches continuously uncovered considerable sums of money, in one month alone 4,000 RM. The supply of money dropped considerably after we discovered that it had been hidden in Victrola records. The center part of the record had been hollowed out, the labels put back on, and in between the money had been hidden.

The more POWs turned towards the construction of tunnels, the more the German sections were on the lookout. The first tunnel had already been dug in 1940 in Dulag Luft. In the POW camp Nr.1 at Barth, digging was rather impossible since the water table was at 50 cm, and a tunnel at that depth was impossible.

To discourage any digging activity completely heavy trucks were driven through the compound, causing the tunnels to collapse. At Stalag Luft 3, the ground composition was much more favorable for the POWs. The sandy soil had a rather peculiar composition. The surface was covered with loose sand which hung in a cloud over the camp whenever the wind blew. At a certain depth, however, the soil was rather consistent. Of the 99 tunneling attempts made during my command, only one succeeded, the so-called lightning tunnel of Squadron Leader Eric Williams,whose book, *The*

Wooden Horse, was translated into many languages and made into a movie. Williams thought of the daring plan of digging a small tunnel close to the surface under the fence and into the woods. A wooden vaulting horse was constructed for this purpose. Inside, there were handles where one or two men could hang on and also attach bags of sand. This jump horse was positioned after roll call between a barracks and the fence, and the POWs did their exercises for everybody to see. Every day, the people hidden in the horse dug a little deeper and then tunneled towards and under the fence. This was a very sporty, but also rather dangerous undertaking, since the whole thing could cave in rather easily so close to the surface and consequently suffocate everybody. This idea and accomplishment of this feat elicited admiration from anybody with any sense of objectivity.

POWs, who had succeeded in getting outside of the camp, had to be informed about the direction in which to travel. If their goal was a seaport on the North or Baltic Seas, and if they succeeded in reaching it, they looked for a Swedish freighter. The captain would hide them until departure time from the German controls and would receive a handsome reward from the British Government upon delivering the POWs to a neutral port. If POWs tried to get to the German border, and if they crossed it, they found assistance from the underground in those occupied areas. They were then taken from place to place to reach their destination. This kind of escape route was written about by Charles Morgan in his book and play, *The Riverline.* Both were translated into German. The German version was called, *The Way Back.* The German intelligence was trying to smuggle their own personnel into this escape route who, naturally, revealed the escapee's identity at the appropriate time. This succeeded several times, and we received prisoners in Sagan who had been captured deep in occupied territory. Volunteers for this kind of work were rather scarce, however, since they were killed by loyal members of the underground upon discovery.

Escapees recaptured on German territory were picked up by guards from Sagan in those towns where they had been found and detained unless repeated escapes made it necessary to have them incarcerated at the POW camp, Colditz. Escapees returned to Sagan received the obligatory two weeks arrest. The escapee was put in solitary unless occupancy made it necessary to bunk two in a cell. Newspapers, books, and cigarettes were authorized. Such a segregation from the rather crowded mass quarters was sometimes looked upon as a relief.

A POW returning to his compound had to report to his senior officer and give a detailed description of his escape and the experiences gained. These reports were kept secret from the Germans, however, during the numerous searches we did find a large number of these reports. They contained interesting and sometimes humorous details, some of which are listed below:

1. Warning about entering the city proper of Bresau, [Breslau] especially the harbor, controls exceedingly severe
2. Notes on the control of travelers using the ferry at Gedser. Tips on how, if at all, these controls can be circumvented
3. Notes on how controls are made at train stations and in trains
4. When buying ticket for train, go to counter that is rather busy and ask a German soldier, possibly NCO or officer, to buy your ticket, since train is leaving shortly.
5. Advise to use night trains which are normally darkened and almost always overcrowded, which makes it possible to elude control
6. Go to German hotels only if absolutely necessary, and then only late at night. It is better to sleep in movie theaters. It's dark there too. Don't spend the whole afternoon and evening in the same theater.
7. Advise finding temporary refuge in camps with French POWs. Beware in approaching same, since German undercover agent may be present.
8. Tips on successful usage of hitchhiking with German motorists. An English officer at one time escaping through the Black Forest had been taken along for more than 30 kilometers on the rear seat of the motorcycle of a gendarme.
9. Escapees who feel they are being watched while going through a town are advised to go to the police. The watcher will drop his suspicions if he sees the man go to the police.

Group 4 – Administration

Already as a Staff Officer during the first World War, I thought it my duty to ensure that all deliveries of food and supplies reach the troops for whom they were intended and not be used for selfish purposes by a few. Such violations are hardly tolerated by the masses and the fight against them, through stringent security, is a special duty of those persons entrusted with leadership positions.

With deep regrets, I found out shortly after taking command at Stalag Luft 3, that the director of the camp administration had weekly packages sent to his family living nearby. Even excellent tortes baked by the local baker were among the items. A preliminary investigation revealed that the POWs had been shortchanged 1800 kg sugar, 84 kg margarine, and 540 loaves of bread over a period of three months. But that was not all. The German officers, doctors, and civil servants all had their meals at the officers club, their menu being the same as all the other German personnel. The authorized 50 portions were cooked in the main kitchen, delivered to the club, and reheated. I noted after some time that some of the younger civil servants were often absent at these meals and without any justifiable reasons. Rumors had it that they were eating a lot better meals in their quarters. This was the last straw, and I had the meat rations weighed several hours after their arrival. I found a constant weight loss of ten per cent to fifteen per cent which could not have resulted from the meat drying out, especially in such a short time. The civil servants in question had stolen the missing meat and eaten it at meals with their friends.

The facts were reported to the Luftgau-Command III at Berlin-Dahlem with the request for immediate relief and prosecution of the perpetrators. The relief took place, but the prosecution was never started, and persons in question were employed elsewhere. The Luftgau-Command sent a fact-finding commission after some time and after three days they left again, declaring everything was alright. The successor of the administrative branch soon discovered that more irregularities had been committed in the past. One hundred seventy-eight kg of soap had actually been recorded as 178 pieces of soap. We also discovered that three months after the occupation of this camp and of the partial camp Belaria, no inventory had ever been taken in either camp. Hundreds of furniture items were missing and had been missing before I took command. I mention this fact because the court martial against me in October 1944 used this as one of the accusation against me. It was alleged that my lack of control had caused the loss of valuable goods of the Reich, especially in this time of war, even though I had been the one to uncover and stop the embezzlers. Staff paymaster Schmidt, who had accused me in front of the Gestapo in April 1944, had to retract his statement during the actual court martial as not true.

Problems were also encountered in supplying the POWs with needed clothing to which they had a right under the Geneva Convention. In the beginning, we supplied them with captured stock of the Czech and Polish army, but when these supplies were exhausted, we could not deliver any more. The POWs demanded what was due them, and we had to negotiate for a long time and under rather shameful circumstances to stall them for a couple of months. They, naturally, were not supposed to find out that clothing and other items, being in short supply, were not being delivered to them as required by the Geneva Convention. After long negotiations and the intervention of the Protecting Power, a solution was found. A kind of transit camp was erected in Frankfurt A.M. where the British, Canadian, and American Red Cross set up a stockpile of uniforms and other items of the various air forces. The POWs being transferred from Dulag Luft to other camps of the air force received from it a complete new change of clothes from uniform, underwear, and other things up to the toothbrush.

The third director of the camp administration installed since late 1943, the previously mentioned paymaster, Schmidt, seemed to follow in the footsteps of the director relieved in the summer of 1942. Soon after his officiation, I was notified by the city of Sagan that he had requisitioned an apartment there with his family still living in Berlin, under less than truthful declarations and that it was being renovated by craftsmen employed by the camp. Schmidt had to admit to the truth of these allegations when questioned. I demanded a report about the number of workers and the length of their work for private purposes as well as restitution of the pay due them to the public fund. Schmidt apparently hated me since this incident, because after the arrival of the fact-finding commission of the political police in the last days of the month of March 1944 he became rather chummy with the leader of this commission, the ill-renowned criminal commissar, Dr. Absalon. One of the allegations which he passed on to Absalon, should be mentioned here, since it was proven untrue already before the court martial of October 1944. He alleged that I had misappropriated 4000 m^3 of carpentry wood which had been created through afforesting by the continuous expansion of the POW camp, sold it privately, and embezzled the 30,000 RM profit. An immediate investigation by the investigating judge of the armed forces revealed that the afforesting was conducted by the Reich's Forestry Department, the felled wood taxed by them and sold by the appropriate duty sections of the department.

My fight against all irregularities in the provisioning, especially of the POWs, should be apparent from the previous detailed notes. Mr. Brickhill, however, rather strangely takes exception to this in his book, *The Great Escape*. Describing the events in Stalag Luft 3 of March 1944, he reports about the investigation by the Gestapo in the following manner: "And look there, they (the Gestapo) were successful. They discovered a black market organization in which were involved, unbelievably, von Lindeiner and V.M. [von Massow].They produced wines and foods from Denmark and kept a supply of it under the kitchen of the commandant's quarters. Von Lindeiner was relieved of command and court martialed." A more brutal defamation of character is not thinkable. The truth is that I already fought to the utmost any kind of hoarding, even within my own command, and even dismissed a staff officer because of such an incident. Travel permits to the occupied zones were issued by me, only rarely, and mostly upon the request of other offices. Mr. Brickhill must have known, only too well, that my relief from command as commandant and the start of court martial proceedings were a direct result of my continuous strict compliance with the Articles of the Geneva Convention and that I intervened on behalf of his own comrades, regardless of the consequences to me or my family. His descriptions must be in line with his own thinking and also increased the attraction of his publications even if it meant distorting the truth and hurting the chivalry which according to my thinking exists among officers. A motion to desist, filed by me at a later time, was without success.

Group 5 – Medical Branch

The routine of medical treatment ran to everybody's satisfaction and that cannot be contested by anyone. In charge of the medical branch at Stalag Luft 3 was the rather young, yet industrious and prudent staff physician, Dr. Lechtken. He was assisted by a German physician and a German dentist. Added to them, were a number of American and English doctors. Their team work went rather well and in colleague-like fashion to the advantage of all POWs. Among the foreign doctors were also two dentists. The supply of dentures and false teeth, which could not be handled through German stock, was finally augmented through deliveries from Switzerland.

The sanitary facilities at Stalag Luft 3 were in no way adequate upon its opening; however, ameliorations were constantly strived for. With time, we were housing on a limited area about 9,500 persons and the army Stalag VIII closely housed about 24,000 persons.

There was no sewer system, and the cans from the latrines were hauled about three kilometers into the woods and dumped there. With a total population of 35,500 persons in the area, the consequences can well be imagined; it can lead to sicknesses, even epidemics. In the creation of solutions to this untenable situation, the experience of the American officers was an enormous help. Since camp life in the U.S. had educated them to some healthy sanitary practices, we were able to make use of their know-how. One man in particular stands out in this endeavor, Lt. Colonel Clark of the U.S. Air Force. But here again the shortage of materials played a significant role. It was almost impossible to procure window screens for the windows of the latrines. It took almost a year until we had an adequate sewer system for Stalag Luft 3. This in turn did not sit well with the town of Sagan which had no sewer system of their own either. We could only appease their tempers by pointing out that the system built for Stalag Luft 3 reduced their risk of getting sick.

Sick POWs reported in the morning during roll call. They were then sent to the sick bays situated in the front camps and found themselves in good hands. The existing facilities were not adequate enough to care for gravely ill persons, so they were transferred to the hospital at Stalag VIII run by the army. After some time though, the duty sections at Stalag Luft [sic] VIII [Stalag VIII] refused to admit British officers from our camp since they were inciting the Russian and French POWs there to riot. After some great difficulties, it was possible to readmit the British patients in a specially secured area of the hospital.

Special attention was given to those young people who had been denied their freedom for so long and were prone to mental disorders, the so-called "mental cases." Experience had shown that many POWs, after an incarceration of nine-to-fourteen months, showed more or less signs of mental stress depending on the will power of the individual. Similar symptoms were later on observed in Germans in camps in England. To catch these disorders in the early stages the POWs as a group were asked to observe their comrades for any signs of changes. As a distraction, the affected man was either transferred to another compound or he was given a different occupation. If this did not help or if his condition worsened, he was sent to a mental hospital for further observation and to determine if he should be sent home or whatever other steps could be taken to help him. Anybody who has had any dealings with POWs knows how far their talent goes, especially in playing a mental case; therefore, in many cases medical authorities were sometimes the last resort to determine the accuracy of the case. Despite all precautions, two instances led to a terrible end. One time a POW had been in the mental hospital for six weeks for observation, and the specialists had determined that he could be returned to the camp. He was picked up by a medical orderly for the return to Sagan. When the train entered the station, the POW jumped in front of it, and the orderly jumped after him to rescue him. The POW, unfortunately, was killed, and the orderly seriously injured. Another time, a POW admitted to the sick bay for observation jumped out of bed, ran outside, and hurled himself on the barbed wire fence apparently to climb over it. The German personnel on watch ran after him to prevent the guards from shooting him, since this seemed to be the POW's objective. He had, however, inflicted such grave wounds on himself that he died. For these two, and fortunately only three other officers, who died in captivity, a small grave yard had been created in the heath which the POWs kept in nice shape. The funeral was held, as was the custom with German soldiers, in a dignified way with full military honors and with German dignitaries present. As mentioned earlier, we had received orders in the fall of 1943 from O.K.W. to drop all military honors at funerals. Where possible, we still afforded the dead this last honor; however, the three salvos over the grave had to be dispensed with. The reason for this rule we told the POWs was that because of numerous bombing raids the German population had become gun shy.

A successful remedy to liven up the spirits of the POWs seemed to have been the occasional change of compound which was done with the blessings of the English and American senior officers. The members of the air forces are more or less a big family. It, therefore, was rather thrilling to greet new arrivals to the camp. These were distributed to the individual compounds where a lively exchange of experiences and news from home took place, and old friends were reunited. The logistics of these moves created an additional heavy workload for the German personnel, since with each move new lists had to be established and the bedding arrangements changed.

The previously-mentioned plans of distracting the POWs through walks could not be implemented as desired. We had to restrict it because of the increasing number of POWs in the camp. We already had more than 6,000 POWs in March 1944. It had been feasible at first to let out 50 POWs and two German escorts, one familiar with the surroundings, the other as legitimation towards the German populace. However, already with an occupation strength of 3,000, this became impossible. If each POW was supposed to get out of the camp once a week, this would have led to about 200 walks in a six day week or 36 walks a day. This would have necessitated 72 escorts daily for 540 POWs dispersed over a five kilometer radius around the camp. Aside from the logistics of getting 72 escorts, the civilian population would have protested rather loudly. In addition, we had problems with the depositions of the word of honor by the POWs. We, therefore, came to an agreement with the American and British senior officers and the camp doctors to have a list made up of those persons needing a walk outside. Special consideration was given to the mental condition of the individual with despondent POWs getting preferential treatment.

Group 6 - Mail Service and Censorship

Stalag Luft 3 was, since May 1942, the central office for the whole postal service to the POWs in the hands of the air force and the accompanying censorship division. It was under the command of First Lieutenant of the Reserves von Massow. The total of all air force POWs was already at 13,400 in the early days of 1944, the mail for one month at times amounted to 280,000 pieces. For the censoring of mail, we had at Stalag Luft 3 about 30 male and 180 female translators. Each person employed in the censorship division had among the foreign letter writers and/or recipients their "permanent mouths." On their incoming and outgoing letters, they kept a detailed log. They learned a lot about the individual POWs and their relationship with their homeland. The expeditious handling of the mail was demanded, and the translators even worked Sundays on a voluntary basis, if the load became too heavy. Their working hours were held at seven hours daily since the reading of sometimes almost illegible handwriting put a lot of strain on the eyes. When the work week was increased to 68 hours in 1943 within Germany and the air force, the translators' work week was kept at seven hours per day at the insistence of medical personnel.

Comparisons of transit times from sender to receiver for POW mail were made between Germany and its enemy counterparts. The German

POWs in England and its Dominions complained in the beginning that their mail to Germany took an unusually long time, letters from England about seven weeks, those from New Zealand and Australia 11-13 weeks. Through the Protecting Power the enemy countries were advised that the German side saw itself forced, much to their regret, to slow down the mail destined for POWs in Germany from the countries indicated by an equal length of time. This action had the desired quick result, and letters from England could be delivered within ten days, those from Australia and New Zealand within 9-14 weeks.

The hiring of translators was rather difficult in the early stages since their pay, food, and housing had been better in the navy and also in the occupied countries. Due to the large number of translators needed here the deciding factor had to be their special treatment at our installation. We ensured that they were treated like we would have liked to see our daughters and sisters treated, and we had total success with this plan. Despite their living in large segregated barracks within a huge rather isolated camp with about 1800 young men, and despite the rather charged moral ethics of the national socialists, not a single shameful incident was ever reported.

The reading of letters arriving from enemy countries gave a rather interesting glimpse into their life styles. It is perplexing how much can be read out of such a letter, even if the letter writer is making an effort to talk only of harmless things. Rather unwillingly we can derive from the great mass of letters important news about the general sentiments, work conditions, housing situations, food procurement, and the like in the countries of the letter writers. Such information was extracted by the translators and compiled in monthly reports. This made possible a rather precise, reliable, and extensive determination of the conditions in countries like the U.S., Great Britain, Canada, Australia, New Zealand, South Africa, etc. These reports were reproduced in 22 copies only and sent to strictly identified offices with a commitment to absolute secrecy.

Group 7 - Guard Unit

The number of German personnel detailed to strictly guard duty within the German POW system had been relatively low in relation to the number of POWs to be guarded. It was realized rather quickly, however, that to guard young flyers a much greater number of German personnel was needed. Their strength in Stalag Luft 3 was increased until the end of 1943 to about seven companies of 150 men each, with two of those companies detailed to the Belaria compound north of Sagan. It was their duty to provide guards and patrols within the camp as well as escorts during transports. The men employed were part of the territorial army, older men, sometimes only partially fit for duty as well as only or sole surviving sons of families. In general, they showed themselves as trustworthy, dedicated, and very duty conscious.

The many diverse duties of the Commandant of Stalag Luft 3 made it impossible for him to dedicate much of his time to the training and education of an ever-increasing guard contingent. Already in the summer of 1943, incidents on the Eastern Front and many other observations made it desirable to look at military contingency plans. The possibility of parachute drops of unauthorized, even armed resistance, yes, even air rescue operations, had to be considered very carefully. Including the occupants of Stalag VIII, a contingent of more than 32,000 POWs was concentrated within an area rather bare of defensive units, and the POWs' numbers increased steadily. We, therefore, requested and were authorized the position of a staff officer at Stalag Luft 3 who was entrusted with the military aspect of such possibilities and who could take over the commandant's duties if necessary. Among several of the recommended officers, the commandant chose Lt. Colonel Cordes. He violated the trust put in him rather shamefully in April 1944.

Group 8 - Military Officer of the Barracks

The rather deplorable condition of Stalag Luft 3 upon its opening in March 1942 had been mentioned earlier. Difficulties in the procurement of materials and the ever-increasing flow of new POWs forced us to help ourselves since the Luftgau Command III as Berlin-Dahlem, responsible for the expenditure of such funds, denied us their assistance outright. The construction of shelters, as required by international law, confronted the command structure of Stalag Luft 3 with tasks comparable to settlers in a new land. Among the officers of Stalag Luft 3, we found one who distinguished himself as a master of self-help, Major of the Reserve Jakob, during peace time one of the most important and honored craftsmen of the town of Sagan. The town of Sagan did have a garrison construction office (C.E.), however, despite good intentions their possibilities at helping us were rather restricted. They did help, though, in the supervision of static calculations and other technical security precautions.

Major Jakob soon created his own construction staff. He had the good fortune of finding among the camp personnel many technically-schooled craftsmen. First there was Uffz [Unteroffizier]of the Reserves Weiss, during peace time an architect in Düsseldorf, and the two OGefrs [obergefreiters] from the construction business, Berger and Kuhnemund. The personnel detailed for the actual construction had been sent from higher up, in this case two battalions (detachments?) of Jewish slave laborers. The way they were guarded and treated by the special personnel with whom they had arrive, elicited the highest indignation from the German soldiers at Stalag Luft 3. To avoid having to look at such humanly-degrading conditions on a daily basis, the immediate transfer to other duties of the most unfortunate Jewish slave laborers was requested and actually complied with. Their place was taken up by Yugoslav and Russian POWs who were, however, in no condition to work after their long ordeal. There again we saw the good heartedness of the German soldier. They happily agreed to share one meal with all the workers detailed from outside the camp after the work had been done. This actually shortened their own meager rations.

To the permanent work force of Major Jakob belonged also the numerous Russian POWs detained at Stalag Luft 3. Not only did they work hard and successfully in the workshops maintaining cars and caring for the horses, pigs, and chickens but also they served as a regular fire control unit. Major Jakob rented several parcels of farms and grazing land situated near the camp. He made possible the installation of vegetable gardens to augment the diet and the collection of hay for the horses. Within the compound, he helped the POWs establish their own gardens around their barracks and provided other small amenities. The POWs immediately interwove the necessary garden work with their escape plans. To the dismay of the trackers they inconspicuously mixed the sand extracted from the tunnels in with the soil while doing their garden work. Similar incidents also made it necessary to remove the trees which had been left within the compound with the best of intentions. Major Jakob also found a rich and deserving field of endeavor in the construction of special baths within the individual compounds as well as the huge sewer system. The continuing growth of the whole camp necessitated the afforesting of considerable areas all around the compound. There again Major Jakob was in charge. After the start of the court martial proceedings against me, as mentioned earlier, it was alleged that the proceeds of 30,000 RM from the sale of the wood had been embezzled by Major Jakob and myself. Investigations proved beyond the shadow of a doubt that all afforesting was done in accordance with Forestry Department directives and sale of the wood handled exclusively, without any intervention on our part, by the military administration.

During the occupation of Sagan by the Russians, Major Jakob refused to leave his industrial and agricultural interests in and around Sagan. He was arrested and while being taken away by the Russians succumbed to the wounds inflicted on him.

The Great Escape of 24/25 March 1944

It was on 25 March 1944 around 4:10 a.m. when the patrol on the north side of North Compound between towers 14 and 15, upon making his turn, saw a silhouette near the woods. He went towards that location and saw an English POW with hands raised in the air. At the same time, two more silhouettes stepped from behind a nearby bush and also raised their hands while in the same instance a fourth man climbed out of a previously unnoticed hole in the ground and joined his comrades in raising his hands. The guard gave off a warning shot and kept the four POWs at bay.

After only a few minutes, a patrol arrived from the guard compound of North Compound which was only about 170 meters away. The Officer of the Day, the First Intelligence Officer, and the commandant were notified by phone. The preliminary investigation revealed that the tunnel breakthrough expected for months had become a reality. The following shall help shed light on its construction.

Construction of the Tunnel

Towards the end of March 1943 the construction of North Compound was nearing completion. First occupation occurred 23 March 1943 with 224 officers and 38 orderlies, almost exclusively from the RAF with only a few members of the U.S Air Force. The latter moved to South Compound after its completion in September 1943. Strength within North Compound rose to about 1248 by March 1944. Senior officer was Group Captain H. M. Massey, accompanied by his adjutant, Squadron Leader Jennens.

Even on the part of the Germans it seemed wise to allow a select few POWs access to the new complex several days before its actual opening so that they could plan in advance for the distribution of officers and their orderlies to the individual barracks and also get an idea of the location and equipment in the kitchens and other facilities. Already during the formation of this advanced reconnoitering there came together the most fanatical and expert escape specialists under the leadership of Squadron Leader Roger Bushell who thought of getting a head start and possible advantage for their future escape attempts.

Based on the information collected, Mr. Bushell discussed his plans with his comrades at arms, among them Mr. Floody, Fanshawe and Kerr-Ramsay. It was decided to start the construction of not one but three tunnels in the belief that the Germans would be extremely happy if their search would uncover one of the tunnels, thereby letting up on their vigilance. The work in the other two tunnels could be considered less prone to discovery and could be forced more. It was also decided to drop the tunnels to at least a depth of 7½ meters and then lead, if possible, close to the watch towers under the barbed wire and fence. The reason for these precautions was the knowledge about the microphones buried two meters deep midway between each set of towers. The POWs believed that this would prevent the German intelligence division from discovering their underground tunneling activities via the mikes [sic]. It was clear that German measures like the burial of mikes [sic] could not stay hidden from the more or less idle POWs. Mr. Bushell, with his closest associates, finally decided on the construction of underground workshops in conjunction with the actual tunnel construction. It was envisioned that the materials needed by the POWs for their escape be created during daylight hours and between roll calls in these underground workshops away from the scrutiny of the ever-present Germans. The conclusions drawn from the discovery of the last tunnel in East Compound, also inhabited by Englishmen, had been that at least 200 POWs were to break out. It was confirmed later on that "Big X," Squadron Leader R. Bushell, having moved to North Compound was basing his new tunneling activities on the same figures. He ordered Mr. Walenn to start working on 200 passports or IDs for foreign workers, Mr. Guest was to change 200 uniforms into civilian clothing, Mr. Hake had to fabricate 200 compasses, and Mr. Plunkett had the task of running off 400 maps of the area around Sagan by using the gelatine technique described earlier. Finally, Mr. Travis was tasked with the construction of air pumps and the like for the tunnels as well as the construction of the underground workshops. All aforementioned officers had to select the necessary techniques, lithographers, tailors, etc., from among the available personnel of North Compound.

Extremely important for the guaranteed success of an escape attempt was the creation of an absolutely foolproof and reliable security system which had to protect the personnel working on the escape from surprises by the German personnel. One had to bear in mind that we continued with daily unannounced thorough searches of individual barracks in a rather random fashion either by day or night, that during the day there were at least four or five Germans, among them one or two trackers continuously within the confines of the compounds, and that the POWs were continuously watched at night by the guards in the towers with the help of huge searchlights. Finally, as previously mentioned, we had a dog patrol in each compound. The leader of compound security in North Compound was at first Lt. Colonel Clark from the U.S. Air Force, our specialist in getting the hygiene problem solved. He carried the name "Big S" (security), and working for him were Mr. Kirby-Green (British) and Mr. Harsh (American). "Big S" was also in charge of all stooges. Mr. Clark divided the compound into two security zones, namely a more and a less vulnerable zone. The most vulnerable zone carried the designation "D-zone" (danger), the less vulnerable zone, "S-zone" (security). If a German entered the D-zone, then a stooge would shadow him, and if he came too close to an area where forbidden activities took place the stooge sounded the alarm. All work ceased, and the tools were hidden. After Mr. Clark and Mr. Harsh were transferred on 8 September 1943, to the new South Compound [sic] [Mr. Harsh was transferred to Belaria] occupied by the Americans, Mr. Kirby-Green took Mr. Harsh's place.

After the preliminary decisions and personnel selections mentioned earlier, Mr. Bushell went to the senior officer of North Compound, Group Capt. Massey, and filled him in on his plans. Mr. Massey reminded Mr. Bushell of the risks he was taking in his self-appointed role. He reminded him also that he had been twice in the hands of the Gestapo and that there would be no doubt about the outcome if he fell in their hands a third time.

Mr. Bushell replied that he had learned a great deal in the last four years of his captivity, and because his present undertaking had been planned so well and all eventualities had been taken into consideration, he thought nothing humanly possible could stop it. Group Capt. Massey repeated his warning but assured him of his own full support.

After everybody had moved to North Compound, Mr. Bushell could begin with the execution of his plans. He first selected a confidant in each barracks for "Big X" as well as a second one for Lt. Colonel Clark, "Big S." The number of people actually involved with the tunnel construction was only about 45, the number of stooges about 180. They were all sworn to secrecy in regards to their duties and organization even towards their friends. Confessions, if at all available, could, therefore, not be verified.

Mr. Bushell then set about with his staff and selected the entrances to the three tunnels. We had shown earlier that the barracks did not rest on soil but were built on foundation columns about 70 cm high and 40 cm wide. Solidly connected to the ground were only those areas that contained the washrooms and those where the heavy iron stoves were standing in the individual living quarters. Here alone, were deep-reaching connections between the barracks floor and the actual ground. The floor of the washroom was cemented and sloping towards the middle to a grate through which the overflowing water could escape. They had hoped in the beginning to use the drainage pipes running out of the compounds as a means of escape. Their hopes were soon shattered, however, for the pipes were so narrow that the thinnest of men could not slip through.

The continuing research finally culminated in the decision to use Barracks 122, 123, and 104 as the starting points of the tunnels. The tunnels starting from there were code named "Dick" (Barracks 122), "Tom" (Barracks 123), and "Harry" (Barracks 104). It was expressly forbidden from then on to use the word tunnel in any way. If one had to talk about them, one talked about Tom, Dick, and Harry as about a good friend. The actual location of the tunnel entrances was only known to the 45 men working on them.

Barracks 122 (Dick) was in the southwest corner of the compound as seen from the fence in the second row. They thought that because the position of the barracks deep inside the compound would require construction of a longer tunnel, it would be less conspicuous. The entrance was located in the washroom with its cemented floor and solid foundation. The drain for the washroom was in the middle of the room covered with a metal grate with overall dimensions of 50 × 50 cm. Underneath the grate was a shaft about one meter deep. The actual drainage pipe reached 25 cm into this shaft so that there was always water standing in there, mixed with sand and other debris. They took out the grate, removed the standing water, cut out a side wall and replaced it with a concrete slab made from cement collected when the workmen were building the compound. To get in and out of the tunnel one only had to remove the water and the side plate. If no one was in the tunnel, the plate was put back and water let into the reservoir. The actual opening and closing took about two minutes each. During work in the tunnel, the washroom could not be used.

Barracks 123 and tunnel "Tom" lay about 25 meters away from the fence in the furthest southwest corner of North Compound. Outside the fence, the woods started at a distance of 50 meters which would hide them coming out of the tunnel. Here also the washroom was elected for the tunnel entrance. A concrete slab was made, this time 65 × 65 cm. In the darkest corner of the washroom, next to the chimney, an equal area of concrete was removed from the floor and a frame inserted on which the slab would rest. Small wire loops had been attached to the sides, which could be hidden in the cracks once the slab was in place. If the plate was to be removed, you took a fork, reached into the crack, pulled up the loops, and then lifted off the slab. At rest, the cracks were covered with a flour and water mixture covered with sand. When you stepped on it, it sounded hollow. Since this could cause suspicions, a frame was added underneath the slab and sandbags put on it. After this preparatory work had been done, Group Capt. Massey was called and asked to look for an entrance in the washroom, a task which he could not fulfill. After it had been shown to him, he was asked to stomp on it. It proved solid, and no noise could be heard.

Barracks 104, the starting point for tunnel "Harry," lay in the northeast corner of North Compound close to the German guard office.

Camp traffic moved by rather close to the barracks, and the escape committee thought that the barracks would, therefore, be less suspicious. The direction of the tunnel was to be to the north. Not only did it have to go under the barbed wire fence but also under the whole front camp and under a much-travelled road outside until it would finally end in the woods. The tunnel length was more than 100 meters long at that point. It was hoped that this unlikely route would also make 104 less suspicious. In 104, the entrance was put in the foundation on which the oven in the most northerly living room, Nr. 23, rested. At first the stove was standing on a platform made from colored tiles which were connected to the foundation. It was, therefore, necessary to remove the stove, carefully lift the tiles from the foundation, and drive the entrance down through the cement to ground level. Some of the tiles were damaged in the lifting process which was rather worrisome since the trackers were after such details in their hunts. It was found, though, that the kitchen barracks had the same tiles and that they could be exchanged easily. The danger of discovery due to a hollow sound was also minimized by adding blankets underneath. After numerous tries, they succeeded in fastening the platform in such a way that it resisted attempts at being pushed off and still could be removed and replaced in short order. The moment it was feasible to start a fire in the stove this was done to increase its aspect of harmlessness.

Critical days were those when in the washrooms, part of the foundation and the side wall, and in 104, the breakthrough to solid ground, had to be accomplished. The noise generated would have to awaken the attention of the Germans. "Big X" looked for a way out and finally found one. Close by the work areas groups of POWs were posted busily and noisily working on tin cans and wood pieces. In yet another place, choir practice was held. Within the endangered barracks, straw mats and blankets lay ready near the work area as a last ditch measure to be thrown over the work area.

In all cases, a shaft, 7½ meters to 8 meters deep, and a width of 65 cm, was driven into the ground and shored up with bed boards. Despite these measures, and despite a remarkable solidity of the sand starting at one meter in depth there were occasional sand breakthroughs. They endangered the lives of the men working below, but it always ended well.

At the bottom of the shafts, the tunnel entrances and the three work rooms were installed. In one, the tools and boards were stored, and in a second especially large room the excavated sand was kept until it could be taken away for dispersal. In the third room was the air pump with room enough for the operator. The supply of fresh air was drawn in through the air bricks of which the barracks' foundations were made. Two pipelines made from milk cans were laid in the tunnels. One brought the fresh air in, and the other removed the stale air through the chimney. It was, thus, assured that the workers underground could work even with closed entrances without worrying about the stale air.

The most serious problem was the dispersal of the sand from the three long tunnels. Responsible for its smooth distribution was Mr. Fanshawe. The fresh yellow sand contrasted sharply with the grayish surface sand, and it showed the trackers that tunnel constructions were going on again. I described earlier how certain people distributed the sand by carrying it in tubular sacks under their overcoats while taking walks. These men, due to their appearance, received the name "penguins." They liked to mix with the football and rugby players during their games since the sand mixed well with all the dust flying around. Garden plots of the POWs also afforded the possibility to hide fresh sand, and they had to be curtailed rather sharply because of that. In those places, where the sand came out of the shafts, blankets had been spread to catch any particles falling down. Despite all precautions, it was this fresh sand which set the POWs back. One has to remember that according to calculations made at a later date during April 1943 to March 1944, at least 250 tons of sand were brought to the surface.

Despite all precautions, the problems for the men working underground grew as the tunnels became longer. They worked lying down in a space 65 × 65 cm. The front man removed sand and installed the shoring boards. He then pushed the sand under his body to the next man who was lying with his head to the entrance. He filled the sand into bags, crawled to the work room at the end of the shaft, and crawled backwards to his comrade, laden with new boards and empty bags. This procedure proved more and more time consuming and rather disturbing the longer the tunnel became.

Somebody had the idea to construct a small trolley car on rails. Thin baseboards were used as rails which had been removed in areas where beds stood etc. The construction of small carts posed no problems. The wheels were sawn from beech wood with a saw made from the spring of a record player. Each wheel was made of two discs glued together with the inner circle larger to prevent derailing of the trolley.

The illumination of the tunnel during work hours was electric as long as the lights were on in the compound. Over a period of time, the POWs had succeeded in swiping lengths of cable and light bulbs from electricians working in the compounds. From the regular electric lines, they spliced lines into the tunnels which could only be used after dark when the lights were on everywhere. Since no electricity was available during day time, little oil lamps were used similar to the ones made to replace the matches.

In June 1943, the construction of South Compound was begun in which all American POWs were to be lodged. To get the project started the woods south of North Compound had to be cleared for about 70 meters, something which, naturally, did not escape the attention of the POWs. They calculated that the new compound should be finished sometime in September 1943. To give the Americans who had participated in tunneling in North Compound a chance at escape, "Big X" decided to concentrate work on one tunnel and temporarily idle the other two. The choice fell on Tunnel Tom from Barracks 123 where work had progressed the most and which was also rather well situated. Tunnels Dick and Harry were used for storing illegal articles after the precious boards and other valuables had been removed from throughout the compound.

The German personnel were again put on alert by the discovery of traces of fresh sand. Further observation brought them to the conclusion that the tunnel under construction started from one of the most westerly Barracks 106, 107, or 123. The usual tracking methods were first employed. Heavily-loaded trucks drove around among those barracks, and a trench three meters deep was dug between the barracks and the fence and sounded with two meter long rods which would have led to any tunnel up to five meters deep. Aside from these measures, intensive searches of these barracks day and night were undertaken. When this did not reveal anything, a further strip of forest 20 meters deep was removed. Finally, hidden observers logged the movements of the POWs to and from these barracks to discover which barracks had an increase in activities.

All these measures brought no result until a search of Barracks 123 in early July 1943, during which the entrance to the tunnel was discovered in a corner of the washroom. During the sounding of the concrete floor, the iron rod had disappeared in a crack. The platform was removed, and we had found Tunnel Tom. At a depth of seven meters, it had already a length of 75 meters and was adorned with the latest POW technology. Its destruction could not be undertaken by us, and a demolition technician from Glogau garrison had to be called in.

This setback shortly before the completion of a masterpiece, which had taken four long and dedicated months to build, disappointed everybody. Even though they could assume that the controls by the Germans would be less intense now, and construction on the other tunnels could proceed rather unhampered, a certain rest period started especially since the bed boards were becoming rare. The work did continue in the manufacture of compasses, maps, false papers, and clothing; tunnel construction, however, was stopped. But after several months, "Big X" did decide to start tunneling again even though tunnel constructions were normally not undertaken during the winter months because of the frozen ground.

The dispersal of the sand during winter time was rather difficult. Tunnel Harry was the one selected for the renewed tunneling activities. It started in Room 23 of Barracks 104. The deciding factor to start tunneling again was the fact that a way had been found to dispose of the sand. It had been found that the theater barracks built on a continuous foundation had an air space between ground and actual floor. This was believed to be the solution.

The continuous watch of the POWs by German personnel again confirmed the fact that tunneling was in progress. The searches of the barracks by day and night, checking of the barracks' double walls, bodily searches of the POWs, sudden roll calls, meticulous inspection of the washrooms, trials to move the stoves on their pedestals, everything was in vain. Especially, the stoves seemed glued to their platforms because fires were burning in them due to the time of year. Construction of "Harry" progressed despite the repeated interruptions. Our estimates placed its length at 100 meters before an exit could be made in the forest. Because of its length, the POWs were forced to build two more chambers in it. Thus, they progressed under the fence through the front camp northward under the heavily-traveled road until they thought they were eight meters within the woods on the other side of the road. During the night of 21 March 1944, we had the last great search of Barracks 104 including roll call of its occupants. Nothing was found as the last workers had left the tunnel shortly before.

Construction on "Harry" had been completed that same day, and "Big X" could now name the day for the escape. A preliminary condition was a moonless night with high winds to cover up unavoidable noises. Dark nights were forecast for 23, 24, and 25 March. The number of personnel to escape had been set at 220. Sixty-five of those were the actual tunnelers during the last year; the other 155 were chosen by lot among the volunteers. They all received papers, compasses, maps, and escape food. The 65 who wanted to use the train also received as much civilian clothing as possible. Time of escape had now been set for the night from 24 to 25 March.

Before I continue with the events on and immediately after 24 March 1944, the following is inserted for clarification.

During 1943, Adolf Hitler had come to the conclusion that the national socialist ideology, as he understood it, did not sit too well with the German armed forces, especially among the ranks of the older officers. A comparison with the successes of the commissars in the ranks of the Russian armed forces came out to Germany's disadvantage. Hitler, therefore, decided to create an institution similar to the Russian commissars among the units of the German armed forces, namely, "The National Socialist Leadership Officer."

In February 1944, a special training course for higher officers had been created in Oranienburg-Luisenhof which I had been ordered to attend. The purpose of the course was to show the participants how to instill the desired education in their subordinates. Renowned representatives of the national socialist ideology gave us lectures on the appropriate subjects. At the end of the course, several of the participants, including myself, voiced the desire to visit the concentration camp of Oranienburg that everybody was talking about. Our request was denied.

After the completion of the course, a meeting of POW commandants of the air force took place at the HQs AF Inspection XIII which had been moved from Berlin to Fürstenwalde on the Spree because of heavy bombings. We were notified during these briefings that Adolf Hitler's increased irritability due to military setbacks had reached an almost unbelievable degree of rage directed towards POWs. In December 1943, about 140 Dutch POWs, [*] and in January 1944 about 120 French POWs, [**] had escaped from their camps which necessitated pulling tens of thousands of German workers from other duties to effect their recapture. This gave Heinrich Himmler the much desired chance to attack those officers of the armed forces responsible for POW affairs. Again, he tried to get the administration of the POW system transferred to the Reich's Security HQs which was under his command; those efforts finally succeeded in 1944.

The commandants of POW camps of the air force present at Fürstenwalde in February 1944 were verbally given the contents of order "Step III" of the O.K.W. which General Field Marshall Keitel had issued on Hitler's orders. It should be mentioned that at such times orders like

---

[*] [The massive escape of approximately 142 Dutch officers took place in Dec. 1943 as they were on their way by train from Stanislau to Neu Brandenburg due to the advance of Russian troops. They rode in a three-train convoy and during the journey from 10 to 15 January 1944 more than one hundred Dutch officers and NCOs managed to escape by cutting their chains. Some died after jumping off a train or were caught afterwards, the rest making a successful evasion.]

[**] [Oflag 17A, an Austrian camp that held 5,000 French officers defeated in the Battle of France close to the border with Czechoslovakia, was the location of the biggest POW breakout of World War II on Sept. 17, 1943. The men not only dug the tunnel, but they also filmed their efforts, calling their film, *Sous Le Manteau (Clandestinely)*. Their tunnel was shorter but deeper than Tunnel Harry. See - http://www.youtube.com/watch?v=YCSk9qZaSV8 http://www.youtube.com/watch?v=5pPkTNbBX1Y]

that were not given in writing. The order "Step III" said, "All recaptured POWs, with the exception of British and American POWs, shall not be released to the authorities of the armed forces anymore but rather delivered to the Gestapo. Furthermore, the authorities of the armed forces shall not be informed. Until further notice, British and American POWs shall not be returned to their camps; they will remain in the custody of the Gestapo, their names kept secret, and only the O.K.W. shall be notified. The O.K.W., in turn, will decide who shall be returned to their POW camps and who shall remain in the custody of the Gestapo."

Furthermore, we were told of orders that POWs were to be shackled during transports. The great number of shackles necessary was not readily available, but the army camp Stalag VIII received 300 shackles which could be requested as needed. To circumvent this order HQs AF Inspection XIII had already ordered the installation of special security locks on their transport wagons.

It should also be noted here that the much talked about, infamous "Bullet Decree" from the desk of Obergruppenführer Müller, whom I met during several meetings as early as 1939 at Reich's Security HQs in Berlin, Prinz Albrecht Street, was not then, nor later, given to us. It allegedly contained instructions that all recaptured POWs, with the exception of the British and Americans, were to be taken in shackles to the concentration camp of Mauthausen to be shot without legislation.

The above mentioned new measures filled me with deep worries. They were not only contrary to the Geneva Convention of 1929 but also against all traditions of an honorable German soldier. Immediately after my return to Stalag Luft 3, I called a meeting of my staff officers. I demanded absolute secrecy about the matter and recounted to them the news I had learned. I stressed explicitly my belief that more far-reaching unlawful and inhumane orders could follow given the jumpy and severe orders concerning the POW system which had just been released. I informed the gentlemen present that I, as a Christian and German soldier, would never carry out such orders. I was aware that the gallows would await me in this case and that I would die by my own hand, if necessary, to avert such a shameful end.

I then assembled the senior officers with their staffs, a number of staff officers, the clergy, and the doctors. In the presence of the German personnel responsible for the camp operation, I said the following: "During my travels through Germany within the last week, I have noted a certain feeling of disgust among the German population caused mainly by the inhumane air attacks of the enemy against the German territory and its inhabitants. People who are condemned to look on as their homes, which are without any military importance, are senselessly destroyed as ten, yes, even hundreds of thousands of defenseless women, children, elderly, and sick are killed, as people working in the field and children going to school are gunned down from the air, those people have to be gripped by a feeling of disgust, yes even hatred and revenge. As much as the attacking flyers are violators of the commandments of human decency, the tortured German civilian population might be pushed to acts of violence towards downed flyers and escaped POWs. I, therefore, beg of you, the rightful representatives of the men incarcerated here in Stalag Luft 3, to exert your influence in such a manner as to discourage escape attempts of any kind. I have pointed out to you at numerous occasions that it is our combined task to preserve the physical and mental health of the large numbers of sons of the U.S., Great Britain, and its allies, no matter how hard it may seem. They are all very young and hopeful individuals. Even this war, which already has lasted four-and-one-half years, will come to an end, and then we hope that the present POWs can return home, where they can accomplish many things for their country and their families, more than if they tried to escape now. I beg of you to think of the mothers, women, and children of your friends, whose happiness will be in jeopardy if some young hotheads try something foolish which has no bearing on the outcome of the war. Here, within the confines of this POW camp, I am responsible with my life for the lives of the POWs entrusted to me; here I will protect you within my means--outside of the barbed wire fence I am powerless. I beg of you to take my words very seriously and act accordingly."

At the time I made this speech, nobody even dreamed that Adolf Hitler would ever issue such orders as the shooting of fifty escaped and recaptured POWs. However, anybody observing the inner German developments for the last eleven years had to be very concerned about where the rage of an uncontrolled madman might lead. Nobody could influence Hitler's decisions in those times, except maybe his constant companion Bormann; it is said that even Göbbels approached him with shaky knees. That Göring's influence had disappeared completely has been mentioned before. The British officers incarcerated in POW camps could not comprehend the immensity of the terror role which had Germany in its grips even after they had been warned more than once by Germans.

Even after my speech, I detected the continuance of escape preparations for a massive escape, especially with the members of the RAF. We were aware that the escape should coincide with the impatiently awaited Allied landings on the Atlantic coast. The POWs assumed that the time of such a landing was influenced by the tides and had anticipated a landing in January 1944 but now thought that the end of March 1944 was the right time. Our observations caused me to transfer thirty of the most active officers in the retinue of "Big X" to compound Belaria situated north of Sagan. Among them was originally "Big X," himself, Squadron Leader Roger Bushell. His transfer was stopped, however, at the last moment due to the intervention of some of my co-workers on his behalf.

To explore all possible avenues of preventing a major disaster, I finally visited the most influential personality among the British POWs, Group Capt. Massey, and talked at length and rather seriously with him. I reminded him that after two years of working together he should know me well enough to give my warnings the attention they deserved, and I repeated with emphasis the warnings given earlier to the POWs.

I was rather deeply hurt when I found out later that Group Capt. Massey not only knew every detail of the plan of his subordinates but also approved their actions. I believed that he, being responsible for the well-being and future of so many young men, would stop them from going through with this senseless, if not childish, adventure. How bitterly I was deceived.

The Escape Proper and First German Countermeasures

On the evening of 24 March 1944 after roll call, the persons selected for the escape exchanged their beds with the other inhabitants of Barracks 104 so that after lockup of this barracks all escapees were assembled there. Around 8:00 p.m., Group Capt Massey showed up to bid them farewell and wish everybody good luck. At 8:45 p.m., the first escapee climbed down the shaft, lay on the small trolley, was pulled to the first transfer room, climbed on a second trolley, and thus reached the end of the tunnel. Three tunnel diggers had in the meantime opened the exit. To avoid spilling light towards the outside two sacks had been affixed in the tunnel as curtains. The first one getting out made a rather dismal discovery, the tunnel was three meters too short, and its exit, therefore, was three meters away from the edge of the woods. After a fast evaluation of the entire situation, it, nonetheless, was decided to go ahead with the escape as planned.

For one, it seemed too risky to cover up the tunnel entrance in such a way that the Germans wouldn't find it. Secondly, all IDs had been stamped for 24 March and would have become invalid if the date had been changed. Since German guards were patrolling about twenty meters away up and down the fence, the first escapee hid behind a bush. He had a rope in his hands which led into the tunnel entrance, and he would pull it the moment the guards turned their backs. Upon this signal, one or two men would jump out of the tunnel, creep into the woods, and hide in silence. This led to rather lengthy delays in the whole escape routine. Added to this was the fact that we had an air raid warning shortly after midnight, and all the lights were turned out, including those in the tunnel. It took forty minutes to get enough fat lamps into the tunnel and have them lit. Additionally, some minor technical problems crept up such as falling sand in the tunnel and the breaking of the rope used to pull the trolley, etc. Thus, the whole escape scheme went slower than anticipated, and Nr. 83 had just entered the shaft, when the shot resounded at about 4:10 a.m., which indicated that the whole operation had been discovered.

When I arrived at the tunnel entrance at about 4:35 a.m. on 25 March 1944, in the presence of the First Intelligence Officer Captain Broili, preliminary investigations convinced us that this was a large scale, cleverly executed operation. All necessary actions required in a case like this were immediately set in motion, to wit:

1. Alert of all officers and all other personnel of Group Intelligence and Camp Administration
2. Reinforcement of the guard detail in North Compound by about 125 men from the guard unit
3. Telephone notification of the train station officer as well as the train police
4. Telephone notification of the criminal police at Breslau for the preparation of an eventual mass search
5. Search of the woods between Stalag Luft 3 and the Sagan train station as well as the area around it by all available police dogs
6. Telephone or telex notification of the 42 duty sections involved in cases of mass escapes
7. Counting the POWs in North Compound to determine number of escapees and their names

The reinforcement of the compound guards seemed necessary after the experiences we had had when the former Wing Commander Douglas Bader was transferred to a special hospital camp in Lamsdorf. This officer tried to provoke the German personnel as he had done before in other camps where he had resided. He also had been able to influence his comrades more so because of an exaggerated egotism. He refused the order to depart the camp and was supported by his friends who amassed by the hundreds at the North Compound gate to prevent his departure. Such an active revolt, naturally, could not be tolerated, and I alerted the guards to have the order carried out by force if necessary and only after repeated instructions did Mr. Bader acquiesce. Since North Compound on this 25 March 1944 was exclusively inhabited by officers of the RAF, as had been East Compound in which Mr. Bader had lived, I believed similar

From Commandant to Captive

occurrences possible especially since it had become our responsibility to determine the number and names of the escapees. The POWs did, in effect, try to hamper or at least slow down the investigation to give their comrades a bigger lead before systematic search measures were enacted. Luckily, it did not turn into an open rebellion.

The notification of the train station officer and the station police in Sagan was made because experience had shown that escaped POWs went to the station at Sagan, only 1200 meters away, to catch a train (preferably D-train) and put a greater distance in a short time between themselves and Sagan. Extensive preparations had been made with the station officers and the various sections of the Reich's rail system in cases like these. Not only the ticket counter at Sagan was closed but train stations were notified where a train having left Sagan earlier might now be, and sharp controls were undertaken. Emergency measures also had been rehearsed with the units of the tank force stationed around Sagan. The systematic search of the station area as well as the many kilometers of forest around Stalag 3 also was accomplished with the help of all available search dogs.

In the meantime, the trackers of Counterintelligence were busy determining the course and entrance of the tunnel by crawling through it from the exit. They found the shaft under the entrance, climbed up, but were unable to open it. Heavy knocking also was not audible, so one of them crawled back and described the possible location of the entrance. It was then possible to remove the stove in Room 23, Barracks 104, but not without using extensive force. The tracker who had remained in the tunnel could then be freed. He was half unconscious and close to suffocating. The tunnel was at a depth of 7 meters and 123 meters long.

As expected, the identification of the names of the escapees was met with difficulties and took many hours. The ones who stayed behind wished to give their comrades a big enough lead by slowing down the identification process. They exchanged places during roll call, gave wrong names, etc., so that it became necessary to identify about 1100 men individually based on their personal card with picture. The result was earth shaking, 76 were missing. For me personally, the biggest realization was the fact that my warnings given during the last six weeks to the individuals responsible for the camp had been thrown to the wind.

Already during the morning hours, various individuals connected to the POW system administration had arrived on the basis of our phone calls. On orders of the Supreme Commander of the AF, Hermann Göring, Colonel Walde came from the AF Inspection XIII of the Reich Ministry, and on orders from the General Inspector of the POW system and special envoy of Adolf Hitler, General of the Infantry Roettig, his Chief of Staff, Colonel Müller, came. From the political authorities, we saw Kriminalrat Brunner (criminal counselor) with Kriminal Kommissar Dr. Absalon as well as his two detectives, Scholz and Hansel. These gentlemen, however, did not get in touch with me at first. Counselor Brunner departed already the next day and left behind Commissioner Absalon and his two helpers who took over the control of Stalag Luft 3 more or less, encouraged by my official representative, Lt. Colonel Cordes. Colonel Walde and Colonel Müller conducted their investigation through the night of 25 March and into the morning of 26 March. Their reports, after having been seen by me, were transmitted to the Supreme Commander of the AF and the General Inspector of the AF, and they then departed around noon on 26 March. They had come to the independent conclusion and had expressed such that all possible steps had been taken to prevent such a mass escape.

After everything possible had been done in 32 hours of uninterrupted searching, at 1400 hours on 26 March two staff officers of Luftgau Command III in Dahlem arrived in Stalag 3. They were in the company of Deputy JAG, Dr. Garbe of the same command.

I have to interject here than since 16 March 1944 Stalag Luft 3 was no longer under the jurisdiction of Luftgau Command III but from that day on under Luftgau Command VIII in Breslau. In addition, as mentioned earlier, almost a year had passed since all administrative matters pertaining to the officers had been given over from the Luftgau Command to the AF Inspection XIII in the Reich's Ministry. Despite all this, I had informed the chief of staff of Luftgau Command III at his request during the late hours of 25 March of the presence of Colonel Walde and Colonel Müller and their findings. Now I was handed by the senior officer of the delegation from Luftgau Command III a writ from the commander of this Luftgau, General of the Flakartellery Hoffmann, to wit:

> "Colonel von Lindeiner-Wildau is hereby relieved of his duty as commander of the POW camp and a court martial investigation is hereby ordered. Colonel von Lindeiner is to remain in the camp at Sagan until the start of the court martial proceedings, command of the camp to be taken over by the next senior officer."

The unusual physical strain of the last 36 hours, without rest and food, but more so the deep emotional trauma caused by the events had shaken me in such a way that I did not realize that such an order was without authority (judgment of higher authorities, misplacement under wrong authorities, etc.). I pointed out Lt. Colonel Cordes as the ranking officer and went to my quarters. Later on that evening, the representatives of the commander in Luftgau III visited me for a short interview after having spent the day questioning my subordinates but not me. On 27 March, he returned and submitted a writ of our conversation from the previous evening for my approval and signature. I complied and added the following points:

1. The Commander of Luftgau III has no authority to release the order of 25 March 1944 against me, since Stalag Luft 3 is not under his jurisdiction but under that of Luftgau Command VIII at Breslau since 16 March 1944.
2. To support my claim under (1) above, I introduce that the Luftgau Command III, now intervening, did not once on their own volition find it necessary to inquire into the security and countermeasures for the entire length of my 23 months of command at Stalag Luft 3.
3. In all personnel matters, I am under the jurisdiction of the AF Inspection XIII in the Reich's Air Ministry since summer 1943. I had directed to them on the morning of the 25 March 1944 my

request for the convening of court martial proceeding against me for neglecting my supervisory duty. This was rejected since the findings of Colonel Walde and Colonel Müller from 25 and 26 March 1944 had shown no cause for such an action.

My personal opinion was that the order against me from Luftgau Command III stemmed from the fact that through fast intervention they were trying to save their own necks. The commander must have known about a similar incident which happened at an army camp where immediate steps against the camp commandant were not taken and that particular commander regretted his oversight very much. In my particular case, Dahlem must have overlooked the jurisdiction change and also that an investigation had been completed.

The two staff officers of Luftgau III returned to Dahlem on 27 March 1944. Deputy JAG, Dr. Garbe, remained in Stalag Luft 3 to conduct further questioning, excluding me however. On 29 March, I suffered a total collapse with acute heart palpitations mainly caused by the terrible humiliation inflicted on me and only the swift intervention of the doctor living a couple of rooms away saved me. Dr. Garbe left Sagan on the 4th of April after the first preliminary trial investigation, but still without having interrogated me. I received a notification from Luftgau III on 6 April putting me in leave status but mandating that I report any change in domicile should I be needed for interrogation. This was followed on 4 May by my transfer to the Flieger Ersatz Battalion (Pilot Depot Battalion) 3 in Frankfurt on the Oder and the appointment of Colonel Braune to the post of Commandant of Stalag Luft 3. He had been up to then Commandant of POW camp Nr. 6 at Königsberg in the Neumark. My health improved only slowly, so I did not undertake the short trip to Frankfurt on the Oder to report to the Pilot Depot Battalion 3 until 19 May.

Court Martial Investigation and Actual Court Martial

My personal misfortune was rather pleasing to certain people in certain places. From a reliable source I heard that during the meeting of 25 March on the Obersalzberg in Hitler's lair, Heinrich Himmler, rubbing his hands in satisfaction, told the officers present, "Finally I have that Lindeiner. For four years I have tried in vain to catch him." On orders of the Reich's Security HQs, Dr. Absalon and his two criminal detectives who had arrived at Sagan on 25 March were starting to get really active. Absalon first tried to win my confidence by visiting me regularly at my sick bed and telling me that he knew how things had actually been at Stalag Luft 3 and that he was only trying to help. I knew these tactics too well and did not volunteer anything. How correct I was in my judgment I found out really fast when persons whom I had mentioned just casually were called in for interrogation regardless of whether they were camp personnel or lived elsewhere. When Dr. Absalon found out that this did not lead anywhere, he tried to win the confidence of my adjutant and also of my secretary but to no avail.

However, Dr. Absalon did find very faithful coworkers in the Acting Commandant, Lt. Colonel Cordes, in Paymaster Schmidt, as well as in First Lt. of the Reserve Richarts-Wellensieck, a cigar manufacturer in Bunde in Westphalia. The latter had only arrived the beginning of February about five weeks before the Great Escape to be trained in Stalag Luft 3 as counterintelligence officer and, therefore, was lacking any definite experience. Now as the friend of Dr. Absalon he acted as an expert in counterintelligence and was called to testify in this capacity against me beginning October 1944 at the court martial. In actuality, it was he who was fully guilty that the intended escape was not reported to us in time and, thereby, stopped. A few days before 24 March, a German working in the package surveillance division had overheard an English officer of East Compound ask a friend from North Compound, "When are you leaving now?" He in turn replied, "On 24 March." The German soldier reported this important information in the company of a hospital orderly to the Duty Officer, First Lt. Richarts-Wellensieck, who failed to pass on the information. When his tragic omission came to light in November 1944, the incident was covered up by higher-ups. The friendship of Richarts-Wellensieck with the representative of the Reich's Security HQs had paid off.

The three "well affected" gentlemen, Lt. Colonel Cordes, Paymaster Schmidt, and First Lt. Richarts-Wellensieck met regularly in the evenings or late nights in the apartment of Dr. Absalon in Sagan for the consumption of alcoholic beverages that Absalon had confiscated elsewhere. With the blessings of the Acting Commandant, Lt. Colonel Cordes, and with the handy assistance of his detectives, Scholz and Hansel, he also undertook here the penal interrogations of suspect members of Stalag Luft 3 in which the unfortunate ones were rolling around the floor screaming and covered with blood. During all of this, he also undertook extensive trips through Germany to collect information about me. Finally, again with the assistance of Cordes and Schmidt, he submitted a 200-page typewritten report on me to the Reich's Security office. This report was to be the basis of the accusations in the court martial ordered by the Reich's tribunal as the highest authority.

Eleven weeks passed after 24 March before I was actually officially interrogated by the military examining magistrate, Deputy JAG, Dr. Garbe. Dr. Absalon was present at my request. As a result of this interrogation and that of other persons, I was notified that Deputy JAG, Dr. Garbe, saw no evidence to convene a court martial. This time, 14 weeks passed during which I lived rather undisturbed at my residence, Jeschkendorf Manor, about four kilometers west of Sagan. It should be clear that I was still shadowed by the Gestapo. I had also learned that the order had been given to transfer my dossier to the Reich's Military Tribunal.

On 16 September 1944, around 2200 hours, I heard loud knocking on our house door. When I opened it, I was face to face with one of my loyal co-workers from the stalag who said with a sigh of relief, "Thank God you are still here. We were afraid you had been picked up already. You have to get away immediately!" When I asked why I had to leave, I was told, "An order was signed this afternoon at 1:30 p.m. at the Reich's Military Tribunal in Berlin-Grunewald demanding your immediate arrest and incarceration at the military prison, Berlin Kruppstreet." I thanked my messenger and asked him to leave immediately lest he be hanged with me. This message was an indication, though, as to how well news travelled in our circles despite the efforts of the Gestapo.

A flight to safety would have been possible due to my contacts with the counterintelligence authorities at O.K.W. However, I had visions of "kin incarcerations." Furthermore, I had the burning desire to publicly confront the scandalous methods of these items with their numerous violations. I, therefore, said nothing to my wife, packed a small suitcase with necessary items, and awaited the things to come.

The Gestapo would appear in cases like this one in the early morning hours, before daybreak. The night of the 17th of September, however, was uneventful. Only on the second of October while in Sagan an acquaintance asked me, "When are you going to Guben?" To my counter-question, "What would I do in Guben?" he replied that that was where the court martial against me would be held on 5 October. Twenty-one witnesses had been called from Sagan alone. In addition, experts from numerous Reich offices and administrators as well as a number of high-ranking officers were ordered in as spectators. I was now confronted with the question whether I should show up in Guben punctually, invitation or not. I decided to show up at the trial even without an invitation. First of all, it was my duty not to get those persons in trouble who had failed to pass on the arrest order. Second, I still had the desire to release some of the pent up indignation which I felt. And third, I did not wish to subject myself to a sentencing of "in contumacium." [obstinate refusal to appear in court] As I learned later, Guben was chosen only because it had the closest and biggest courtroom available.

So at 9:00 a.m. on 5 October I was in the courtroom in Guben on the bench for the accused together with two officers, Captains Pieber and Broili, two first-rate duty conscious gentlemen, seven soldiers of various ranks, and a civil servant, all of whom worked at Stalag Luft 3. Since I had neither received a bill of accusations, nor a summons, I received them from the presiding judge upon the opening session. I had also not been able to notify my counselor and presently refused one since I did not want to delay the proceedings, especially since no one was as familiar with the POW system as myself.

The course of the trial brought up some rather startling incidents. The first witness for the prosecution was Paymaster Schmidt. At the end of his testimony, the presiding judge asked him: "You are telling me that you cannot uphold the accusations against Colonel Lindeiner?" Answer: "No." Reply from the judge: "Then take your seat." A second witness for the prosecution did not fare any better, and the judge asked him whether he held a grudge against me, Colonel von Lindeiner. Reply: "No, not against Colonel von Lindeiner but against all officers." The official representative of the O.K.W., a colonel, was then asked for his opinion on a certain point of the accusation. He replied, "Mr. President, if this is a point for the prosecution then all I can say is that this is going to make the chicken laugh." This rather honest expression of his feelings later cost him four weeks room arrest for disorderly conduct in court. When another question was presented to my successor as Commandant of Stalag Luft 3, Colonel Braune, he replied, "Mr. President, if this can be used as a point for the prosecution, then I request to take a seat next to Colonel von Lindeiner on the bench."

The trial portion which I was required to attend lasted five days and was conducted in a factual and honorable way according to the military principles governing such trials. Understandably though, it was rather nerve racking for me personally. The prosecution asked for demotion and 18 months prison. The verdict handed down on 9 October was 12 months confinement in a fortress. An appeal against court martial verdicts was not possible during war. The accused had only the right to comment on his sentence before it was submitted for approval to the supreme convening authority. The supreme convening authority was then Heinrich Himmler, a rather dismal prospect for me. He was authorized to void a sentence not suitable to him and order a second or even a third trial in the same matter. I was too well aware of a case during Himmler's regime where an accused, after three trials, was finally convicted and given a sentence agreeable to Himmler – death by hanging.

On 9 October, I returned to Sagan where I was greeted warmly by some of my former co-workers. During the latter part of October, a medical commission arrived on orders from certain military authorities accompanied by a renowned psychiatrist who diagnosed an advanced stage of mental disturbance and ordered my admittance to the psychiatric neurological division of Reserve Hospital I at Görlitz. I never received a written copy of the sentencing of 9 October, therefore, a commentary on my part was never submitted.

Back in Sagan

On 25 January 1945, the chief medical officer of the Reserve Hospital I, Medical Councilor Dr. Engelhardt, revealed to me that the hospital was being moved westward because of the approaching Russians. He also explained that since I was completely rehabilitated, he could not take me along. When I asked what I should do, he replied that I should return home to Sagan.

The distance from Görlitz to Sagan was about 46 kilometers, POVs were not available, movement of fast and express trains had been halted since 20 January 1945, and commuter trains were run on demand only. At 6:30 a.m. on 27 January 1945, I, therefore, sat in the waiting room of the Görlitz train station hoping for a train which would go in my direction of travel. One finally appeared at 11:00 a.m. By way of various interconnections including repair trains I reached the station at Sagan at 9:30 p.m. The trip of 46 kilometers had taken 15 ½ hours. The next day I reported to the Bober River Sector, Sagan, commanded by the former Austrian, Colonel Hepke, and he made me his deputy. When Colonel Hepke died in combat on 9 February near Sagan, I moved from our residence outside Sagan to within the city limits.

The Battle Commander, Sagan, had at his disposal seven companies made up of retreating soldiers who had been stopped at check points, moved to the garrison, and grouped in companies of 100 men under the command of an officer. They had been issued a weapon and 65 shots of ammunition. The behavior of these people, for the most part, was exemplary and was influenced greatly by the personality of each of the officers in charge.

In the early hours of 12 February, I made a reconnaissance trip on motorcycle into the northern battle section accompanied by another officer. When the early fog lifted, we could see occasional Russian guards on the eastern shore of the Bober. Approaching the village of Greisitz, situated on the river, believing it occupied by German troops whom we had telephoned before our departure, we received Russian fire at close range. I was hit in the shoulder and foot causing me to fall. The Russians thought me dead and pursued my escort officer. By crawling through a barn, a stable, and a deep iced-over trench, I was able to reach the edge of the woods, cross through them, and reach Sagan with my last strength after a three-hour grueling march. The bullet was removed from my right foot, and I was properly bandaged. In the evening, a high staff officer took over my command. A heavily-damaged armored scout brought me, on 13 February 1945, via Soran [sic] Sorau-Kalau-Luckau-Torgau and Eilenburg to Leipzig to Reserve Hospital IV St. Georg. On 5 April, I was transferred to the Reserve Hospital at Blankenburg in the Harz and became there a POW of the Americans and then of the English.

My Own POW Captivity

The kind of treatment I received in captivity until I arrived in London on 12 August was in no way comparable to the treatment we had given the Allied Forces. When I complained several times, I was told that with the total capitulation of 8 May the Geneva Convention no longer applied to us. Requests to the doctors who were treating me to release and return me home were refused on the grounds that my name was on a list for special interrogation.

On 7 August 1945, I was moved by special transport under the supervision of one officer and two sergeants to the infamous intern camp, Stanmühle (Nr. 92 Camp VI), where I spent 48 hours in special barracks Nr. 33 on a bare board and without eating utensils. The trip continued on 10 August, this time in handcuffs, chained together with a young civilian by the name of Behrens who had been beaten up pretty badly by the British liberators so that he could only sit or move with extreme pain. The trip by truck, again heavily guarded, went from Paderborn via Münster-Werst-Kaldenkirchen-Brussels to Ostende. During the passing of a border crossing into Holland, a large crowd tried to pull us out of the vehicle with cries of, "Get them out, hang them high!" Only the intervention of our guards prevented these philanthropists from getting their way. On 23 August, we reached Eastend [sic] [East End] on the Thames where we two helpless individuals were picked up by a brigadier general and ten soldiers for the trip to "London District POW Center," or as it was called by the Germans, "London Cage," located in Kensington Gardens, London W8.

The reception there and the accommodations were rather shameful in the beginning. The captain who met me replied to my protest in reference to the Geneva Convention by saying, "I know how to treat Germans." My first interrogation was already the next morning; it lasted, save short interruptions, from 1000 hours to 1700 hours. After some more interrogations, I was finally getting treated a little better. The famous chief of the "War Crimes Unit," Colonel Alexander Paterson Scotland, requested my transfer back home. After this request was denied, a medical commission recommended my admission to a hospital. This was also turned down by higher authorities. The transfer of my beaten up young travel companion, Behrens, to London turned out to be a mistake, as often happened in those times. The occupation force had published lists of persons to be arrested, and some unfortunate ones with the same name were picked up. As the example with Behrens proved, these persons could go through some real bad experiences.

I, myself, was transferred with appropriate guards on 20 August from London Euston Station, via Derby-Grewe- [sic] (Crewe) Warrington-Preston-Lancaster to Shap, a small town in Westmoreland, 68 kilometers south of Carlisle, for admission to the POW camp Nr. 13, Shap Wells, otherwise known as the "Intelligence Camp." The camp strength at that time was about 180 German officers, mostly retired. Our quarters and treatment were adequate. We were living in a hotel in the middle of the wild and bare hills of Cumberland populated by half-wild sheep herds. The owner of this area had constructed the hotel for the avid hunters of red grouse who were paying, aside from lodging and food, one pound sterling for each grouse. Golf and tennis courts as well as trout ponds were installed but lay unused. This extremely isolated hotel had been selected shortly after the beginning of the war as a POW camp for German officers. When I arrived, the barbed wire fence had already been removed, and English guards were no longer posted there so the POWs put up more or less of a guard on their own. Mornings and evenings there was a short roll call, and in between we could take walks in the unspoiled surroundings. This was based on a monthly written word of honor system. A curriculum was set up, and courses were held to break the monotony. Knowledgeable officers taught courses in English, French, and Spanish, as well as English history. High civil servants taught political law, and a professor from a college in Münster even taught logic. We had many evenings where interesting discussions took place, even with Englishmen from the surrounding area. Certain gentlemen narrated the news taken from English, French, and German newspapers. Our religious life was full, and we had among us four clergymen of both confessions. A weekly trip was made to Penrith to buy supplies for the mess. The kitchen was run by German orderlies under the supervision of a cook from the Kempinski Co. in Berlin. An architect among us built a bakery where bread soon was baked, even for the English units stationed in the area. We had our own tailors and cobblers. A clock repair shop started by younger officers also deserves special mention since even the English from all around were using the shop. Parts were procured through the camp administration in London. The POWs also had started a camp library which contained more than 4,000 volumes when the camp was closed in 1946. Here also the requested books were graciously provided by the English camp and administration. Sports were actively practiced and the care of the gardens, which must have been extremely beautiful at one time, was for us Germans a natural thing to do.

The English authorities kept a kind of master file about all German POWs which contained their past as well as their political convictions. Based on this file, the POWs were divided into three categories: Category A, completely harmless; Category B, doubtful characters, gray sheep; Category C, black sheep. To make new classifications or update old ones two officers, Wing Commander Ruffey and Squadron Leader Sullivan from the RAF, appeared at certain intervals in the camp. They were the gentlemen who enjoyed an excellent reputation and were held in high esteem by the Germans. To our dismay these two gentlemen were replaced after some time by an official of the English Foreign Office, Mr. Philip Rossitter. He behaved purposely as the hostile Englishman and gave the impression that he especially wanted to brand young and inexperienced officers as black sheep. Years later, the German press discovered that this "Mr. Philip Rossitter" was none other than Philip Rosenthal, heir to the well-known china factory at Rosenthal in Selb. Interrogation of the older POWs like myself was carried out by Mr. Otto John since the fall of 1944 also employed by the English Foreign Office. After the war, he became the president of the West German Office for the Protection of the Constitution in Bonn and became well known for his temporary stay in the Soviet Zone and his subsequent trial in Karlsruhe.

By September 1946, the occupation strength in the camp at Shap Wells had sunk to 106; it therefore was closed, and the POWs transferred to POW camp Featherstone Park Nr. 18. It was situated on the Tyne near Halt Whistle [sic] [Haltwhistle] about half way between Newcastle in the east and Carlisle in the west. With a maximum strength of about 6,000 POWs, it now had dropped to about 2,400, half of whom had found work in the area and were living nearby in so-called hostels. Our life there followed more or less the same routine as in Shap Wells, and the treatment was also quite adequate. Added to this was the fact that this surrounding afforded us a better insight into the lives of the English.

Ending – My Return Home and Final Words

In early May 1947, the hour of my return home had come after I had promised to take up residence in the British sector should I be needed for possible interrogations at a later time. The trip was by train via Leeds to Oldham, a city adjoining Manchester in the center of the textile industry. In November 1946, a so-called repatriation camp had been opened in one of the idle factories consisting of four huge halls packed with about 1,000 officers and enlisted men each. Due to ill health, I was put up in the sick bay. About 300 German soldiers were employed here to take care of the many repatriation formalities, 34 of whom were engaged to young English ladies after only six months. Every evening around 5:30 p.m., a long line of POVs drove up and English citizens picked up members of the permanent German staff. Our temporary personnel were able to observe from concealed areas the happenings in a nearby English military drill pad. The author of the book, *08/15,* could have found here more material for his penny dreadful literature with which he tried to harm Germany's image after 1945, even more than other Germans had done before him. On our rather extensive walks, we were always treated with friendliness here as in many other places especially from persons ostensibly from the middle class or lower walks of life.

On 4 June, we were transported to the port of Hull and sailed from there on board a liberty ship to Cinehaven [sic] [Cuxhaven] and further on to the Münster camp. Here again, a long stay ensued before we were brought to Münster in Westphalia on 14 July where bus transports were waiting in a garrison to bring us to the district cities of our respective home areas. On 17 July 1947, I finally arrived at my relatives in the Wittgensteiner Land which I had given as a temporary address for my stay in the British Zone.

In November 1947, I received permission from the British occupation force to move to the place of residence of my wife which was 62 kilometers away but situated in the American Zone. After her escape from Silesia, with only a small suitcase, she had been vegetating there for 2 ½ years keeping herself barely alive by giving lessons in English and French and teaching music. Being of Dutch ancestry didn't help much either. Our property in Silesia was in Russian or Polish hands, our apartment in Berlin bombed to the ground, and our extensive land holdings in the Netherlands confiscated as enemy property despite the teachings of Hugo de Grout.

After WWI we had lived in the Netherlands until about 1931. My wife was known as a raving anti-Nazi and had escaped incarceration in a concentration camp only by a hair on several occasions. Now, finally ten of the highest officials in the Netherlands were vouching for my wife. I personally had excellent references from the highest British as well as American authorities, [and] had been court martialed for interceding on behalf of Allied POWs, 23 of whom were alive because of my intervention and were able to return to their homeland. Among them were the Dutch Flight Lt., Bob van der Stock, as well as the British Group Captain Massey who otherwise would have been court martialed for instigating mutiny. I have never heard from them. My wife and I also were very much involved in keeping up the well being of young Dutchmen who were forced to work in Germany during the war. It took more than ten years before at least my wife received a life annuity from the Dutch government. Our property was never returned.

The German POW returning home in the summer of 1947 really found his people and country in a deplorable state of distress and misery. Five years of a merciless war, the implementation of the Allied resolutions of Teheran, Yalta, and Potsdam, as well as the basic concepts of the Morgenthau Plan, had created conditions equal to those at the end of the Thirty Years War. A major portion of the residences were destroyed or seized by the occupation authorities, work places were idled because of the disassembly of industrial plants, transportation and information media were interrupted, forests were decimated by afforestation, tens, yes, even hundreds of thousands of women were raped and even more men, especially in the east, were killed like wild animals. The vegetating German population was threatened by plagues like typhoid without having the necessary antibiotics at their disposal, and into this already overcrowded area were pushed the 12 million expatriates from the provinces east of the Oder and Lausitz [sic] [Lausitzer] Neisse, despite the much acclaimed Atlantic Charter of 1941. Their forefathers had not conquered this land 750 years before but came as settlers on virgin land and brought it to a high culture. The British Prime Minister, however, had declared that Poland could expand to the west, and the Germans should just make room like good soldiers maybe who just step aside. If one stepped on some German toes in the process, then this could not be helped. The most honorable gentleman just forgot that it involved at least 12 million people, but then they were "only" Germans. One is tempted to ask what the allies would have done after 8 May 1945 if Adolf Hitler at the height of his power in June 1940 had forced the non-fascist Dutch and Belgians to move to France with only 72 hours notice taking along only 25 kg of belongings to make room for Germany's excess population. Joseph Stalin, Russia's dictator, had already at Yalta been declared, "Dear Old Joe" and "Protector of Democracy" for east and central Europe, despite his repeated declarations that the goal of Russian politics is conquest of the whole world by communism. To help him in this endeavor the borders of his domain were moved from the Memel and Weichsel to the Lower Elbe and Weser, about 600 kilometers westward. The misery of many people in West Germany was heightened by a so-called currency reform which put respectable savers and pensioners in the poor house but made pushers and hoarders into wealthy people.

Three further decisive actions on the part of the allies against Germany were the destruction of Prussia, the defamation of the soldier corps, and the so-called "reeducation" of the German people. Prussia, looked upon by Adolf Hitler as poor and square - Prussia, which resisted the longest against his doctrines, was wiped from the map as a refuge of reactionism and militarism. This was the same Prussia which had been considered up to then as a bastion of honesty, of faithfulness to duty, of self-sacrifice, and social care, or which, it was said, should be created in Europe, if it did not already exist.

Germany's enemies rightly saw German militarism as an educational tool for the large masses, the backbone of German efficiency, something which had to be wiped out to prevent an economic recovery of Germany. When in 1919, the most shrewd politicians and economists of the world got together and debated how to make a revival of Germany impossible, they also reduced the German armed forces to an unimportant entity, thereby preventing the education of dedicated young men to dutiful workers. It would be hard to prove that before 1914, German military leaders intervened in German politics for the purpose of war. In the ensuing 14 ½ years, 26 ever-changing Reichschancellors with 122 ministers tried in vain to ease the sufferings of a great but starving people brought on by the conditions imposed by the Versailles edicts. Their tries were in vain; a desperate nation, especially the middle and lower classes, turned to Adolf Hitler. Somebody said, and rightly so, "Without Versailles, no Hitler, and without Hitler, no Second World War." Even the armies put up by Hitler were not eager for war; their leaders knew too well what a war could do. No class in Germany had opposed Hitler's war intentions as much as German soldiers such as General Beck and Freiherr von Fritsch. But Hitler said, "I have to use whips to get my generals to go to war," and in March 1939, standing on the Hradschin, he explained, "I could have stood here last year if I had not been surrounded by cowards." After 1945, the officers were stripped of their civil rights and were even refused employment in the civilian sector because they were regarded as the representatives of warmongers. Young people were excluded from studies at universities, others rejected as workers in those factories that were still operating, and young marine officers were refused employment as simple seamen on trade vessels or even mine sweepers. If these young men did not succeed in getting forged papers to get a job, there was still the blooming black market or enlistment in the Russian army where they were gladly taken. Higher ranks had it much more difficult. In the Second World War, 963 generals and admirals lost their lives for people and country, not for Adolf Hitler. They were operating on the English principle, "right or wrong, my country," though this sometimes required surmounting serious scruples. Now, they had to be thankful to earn their and their families' keep as night watchmen, and common workers; every immature boy had the right to insult them without fear of reprisals.

Right in step was the "reeducation" of the German people. Adolf Hitler already had mentioned in his book, *Mein Kampf,* that he wanted to give the German people not only a new religion but also a new upper class; his paladin, Robert Ley, regretted later and publicly that the blue-blooded pigs had not been disposed of during the takeover. After 1945, the destruction of the feeling of obedience and respect for fathers, forefathers, and educators was undertaken by branding them as criminals who had to be gotten rid of to build up a new era. Lord Vansittard, [sic] [Vansittart] the long-time head of English foreign politics, wrote already in 1941 in his book, *Black Record,* "Charlemagne waged war every year in his quest for world domination; in the next hour and years the Germans have remained true to themselves. Hitler is the bred-true creature of this race." Frederick the Great became the father of aggression, the same ruler who called himself the first servant of his state and of his people, whom Goethe called, "the north star around which the world turns." One must not forget to mention the wars Louis XIV waged 100 years before. First Bismark [sic] [Bismarck] became "Hitler I" and a Prussian bully.

How was it with Germany's participation in wars, supposedly instigated by the war-loving German military? An American professor has found that in the years 1800-1940, a 140 year period, 178 wars were fought on earth with the following participation: England 28%, France 26%, Russia 23%, and Prussia/Germany 8%. After 1945, the German youth were made to believe otherwise. A German youth leader was heard preaching to his compatriots that we had to prevent the "Prussian military" from ever again violating the soil of France as they did in 1813, 1815, 1870, and 1914. This knowledgeable young man apparently lacked the most primitive knowledge of history. Reputable international historians have, in the meantime, concluded that no other country ever gave lesser cause for a war like WWI than the Germans. Do these brave men want to run away when the enemy approaches and threatens to destroy their homeland and rape their mothers, wives, and sisters? Certain circles seem to forget that at one time in history the deepest shame of a free man was to be denied the use of the weapon. Many believe the term "Fatherland" is outmoded, but despite European unification wishes, it upholds the love for one's country. This term lives on in the Russian phrase, "Mother Russia," and is still sacrosanct to them. Articles were published in Germany, mostly in shoddy journalism, which propagated distortions under the headings, "What Really Happened?" Such sensationalism seems to find a steady circle of readers, especially if the material deals with princely persons and/or if it has sexual overtones. Even in other countries things happen which might be considered dirty linen but at least they wash it in their own home and not out in front for the whole world to see. If it is a disgrace to be a German, then no one can lift this guilt from any individual no matter how hard he may try to renounce his heritage. Excesses such as those the "Third Reich," unfortunately, brought forth, are not denied. They were, however, the deeds of a group of terrorists who can never soil the greater history of the people, the thinkers, and the poets. They can only serve as a deterrent. May each German show for the good of the community that the threatening spirit of materialism and egoism is being replaced again by one of obligation and not only because communism threatens.

The final act of the Stalag Luft 3 drama began on 1 August 1947 in Hamburg when the biggest war trial convened by the English opened. It dealt with the shooting of the 50 escaped officers, and I had been called as a witness. Accused were 18 members of the Gestapo and the criminal police. Of those, 17 were simple people, among them two chauffeurs who had driven the trucks in which the condemned had been brought to their place of execution. Nr. 18 was the chief of the criminal police in Breslau (not of the Gestapo), 64-year old Councilor Wielen. The tribunal was made up of a major general as president, an air commodore, three colonels of the army, and two group commanders of the RAF. The legal advisor was JAG, C. L. Stirling, the prosecutor was Colonel Halse, and his assistant was Capt. Nicolson. The 18 accused had 14 defense lawyers at their disposal. My own interrogation lasted a full day. I could only talk about one of the accused known to me, Councilor Wielen. Other than that, I answered questions dealing with the general nature of the German POW system. I knew nothing of the circumstances surrounding the shootings. Councilor

Wielen, according to my impressions, had always been an official of the old school, and I could not see him commit atrocities. In my dealings with him, he was always rather obliging; his participation could only have extended to possibly releasing some kind of lists. His sentence was life imprisonment, a punishment which, according to English law, is paid up after 21 years. He could enjoy freedom again at age 85, towards the end of 1968. From the other 17 accused, the two chauffeurs received ten years prison each. The other 15 were condemned to die; one of them had his sentence commuted to life imprisonment while the execution of the others took place in February 1948. Three additional lesser officials of the Gestapo were tried by an English court martial in October 1948 (also in the Kurio-Haus in Hamburg) in connection with the same incidents. Two of the accused had to be set free, the third received the death sentence which was commuted to life.

A much more important, but not decisive, role in the events which led to the shooting of the 50 officers could be attributed to the chief of the Gestapo in Silesia, Councilor Dr. Scharpwinkel, but he was in Moscow. The English request for extradition was refused; therefore, Capt. Cornish of the English army went to Moscow to interrogate him. It is my impression that Dr. Scharpwinkel implicated Councilor Wielen during these interrogations more than necessary. Informed sources have it that Scharpwinkel occupies a rather important position in Moscow. For an adequate picture of his mentality and those of other people, whose deeds seem incomprehensible to us, I would like to recount an incident that happened during an official meeting in his office in Breslau in the fall of 1943. I have to add that Dr. Scharpwinkel gave the impression of a well-bred and rather intelligent man living a spotless life. During our conversation, the telephone rang and a conversation ensued of which I, naturally, was able to hear only one side and which ended with Scharpwinkel's words, "Will be liquidated." To my question what they meant, he replied, "This man will not see the sun go down today!" To my added question, whether it did not bother his conscience to snuff out the life of a human being over the phone, whose reasons for committing the act he did not know, and who might have a mother, wife, or children, he answered, "Three years ago I was thinking just like you now. When I was confronted with that type of situation for the first time, I argued like you and did not sleep for several nights. In the time that passed since then, I have come to the conclusion, however, that the life of a single human being cannot play a role if the destiny of the whole German race is at stake." Aside from persons like Dr. Scharpwinkel and their particular way of thinking there were in the ranks of the Gestapo an increasing number of people who, their feelings and senses dulled, were resembling beasts in their behavior. Unfortunately, I had to deal with some of these people, and one look into their fanatically glowing eyes gave you the creeps. They were relatively few in number, though, compared to a total population of almost 80 million Germans, who, even though they themselves were oppressed, abhorred such persons and their deeds as much as anybody anywhere else. Thus the word "SS" became one of terror associated with the Gestapo, and their views and actions were made synonymous with the "Waffen SS" which was created much later and for an entirely different purpose.

The term "SS" originally referred to the "Security Squad" or auditorium guard created in the 20s for the protection of Nazi speakers at big rallies against dissident spectators. Their creator and leader was Heinrich Himmler, a teacher from upper Bavaria devoted to Adolf Hitler and his teachings until the end of 1944. He renounced a life of luxury for himself and his subordinates in contrast to some of the other "party greats," and in all material things he was meticulously clean. I had repeatedly pointed out to the Gestapo excesses of party greats which became known to me. I always received the answer, "Against these golden pheasants, we are powerless." His subordinates were well cared for in case of sickness or if they got into trouble through no fault of their own.

In his apparent struggle for absolute power, Heinrich Himmler orchestrated the gradual disabling of the Reichswehr (armed forces). He based this action on Röhm's [Ernst Julius Günther Röhm] experiences, when Röhm tried, around 1933-34, to align the armed forces under his command and infiltrate it with Nazi leaders from the SA. Adolf Hitler was then still abiding by his promise given to Reich President Hindenburg never to touch the armed forces. Röhm's opposition to this was the cause of his quarrel with Hitler. This fact was exploited by third parties to give Hitler the impression that Röhm wanted to topple him. This, then, led to the terrible events of 30 June 1934. ["Night of the Long Knives" - the political murders including that of Ernst Röhm, leader of the SA]

After Heinrich Himmler had achieved almost total control of the domestic politics and also the economy of Germany, he tried during the war to gain gradual control of its military might. He received Hitler's permission to set up divisions that in disciplinary and administrative matters were totally under his control. At least during the war years, they were not supposed to be used for tasks concerning domestic policies. Rather cleverly, the budding youth of Germany was won over for duty in the Waffen SS. Qualified persons toured the schools of the Reich, and after some introductory speeches in the upper classes, bound the older pupils to enter voluntarily into the Waffen SS. It was rather apparent after a short while that not only the army and navy, but especially the air force, was suffering from a lack of replacements. Their protests filed with Hitler remained unsuccessful. The army divisions were in the process of slowly burning out, due not only to lack of replacements, but also because in the delivery of weapons, armament, and materials, the Waffen SS was favored. In the last year of the war, Himmler even tried to set up his own AF, but here he ran into difficulties because of a lack of trained technicians. He did succeed in the last days of the war, however, in setting up a few squads of liaison and commercial airplanes.

At the end of WWII there were 32 divisions of the Waffen SS serving in the field. They were elite troops who fought well in combat and did not deserve to be identified either with the Gestapo or the political SS.

Poems from German POWs that End the Memoirs

Evening prayer of a POW, who after the capitulation, was stripped of all rights (the German as he once was):

The sun in going down, the world goes silently to sleep.
Our thoughts are going to you, Lord and Helper.
Be the sun of our hearts, remain the world's bastion.
Let us listen to your all mighty word in humility!
Our loved ones far way, who are separated from us,
We commend them to thee, who knows misery.
To thee, who knows sorrow, to thee who healeth the wounds,
To thee who blesseth all around you,
Forgive us our sins, and erase our guilt.
Cover our lives in perfection and give us your grace.
Let us and our loved ones be protected in you.
Let your light shine in our misery.

From Camp Chaplain, E. Friedel

Spring 1946 (The Realist)

Here you sit and mend your underwear.
Your legs are dangling in the air.
The one below you has lost the will to live,
And the stove pipe is rather crooked and loose too.
From an old box, your wife is looking at you.
How far have you carried this picture, and how far has it carried you?
In one corner sit three who are consulting the pendulum,
And there's a lot of noise in here again.
Someone is taking a drag from the last cigarette.
Patience and smoking come towards the end.

As if in prayer, somebody is folding his hands,
Doesn't this life ever end?

> From the camp newspaper
> "The New Way," POW Camp Nr. 167

A Returnee from 1947

Welcome liberator!
You took our eggs,
The milk and the butter,
The livestock and also the fodder,
Watches and rings
And all kinds of things
Wagons and tracks
Went all on the trip.
From all this rubbish you have liberated us.
We are crying with joy, how nice you are to us.
How bad it was then, and how good we got it now.
Welcome liberators! You beautiful people.

Recommendations for the Returnee Beginning 1948

He, who loves life today,......................................pushes.
He, who has honesty in his blood,..............exchanges.
He, who can't do either of the above, ... steals.
He, who gets everything the honorable way, ... dies.

Germany, Germany, without anything, without butter, without bacon,
And the little bit of marmalade is being eaten by the administration.
The prices up, the borders tightly closed,
Misery marches with quiet, steady steps.
The people are all starving.
The Big Ones are only starving in sympathy.
Fold your hands.

Bow your head.
Always think of unity.
Come Wilhelm, be our guest
And give us what you have promised,
Not only beets or cabbage
But what you eat with Otto Grotewohl.
Nothing on the floor, nothing in the cellar,
Nothing on the table, nothing on the plate,
We don't even have toilet paper.
S.E.D. we thank you.

[The Socialist Unity Party of Germany (German: Sozialistische Einheitspartei Deutschlands, SED) was the governing party of the German Democratic Republic from its formation in 1949 until it was dissolved after the Peaceful Revolution in 1989.]

Col. von Lindeiner's Court Martial - Trial Summary and Judgment – May 10, 1944

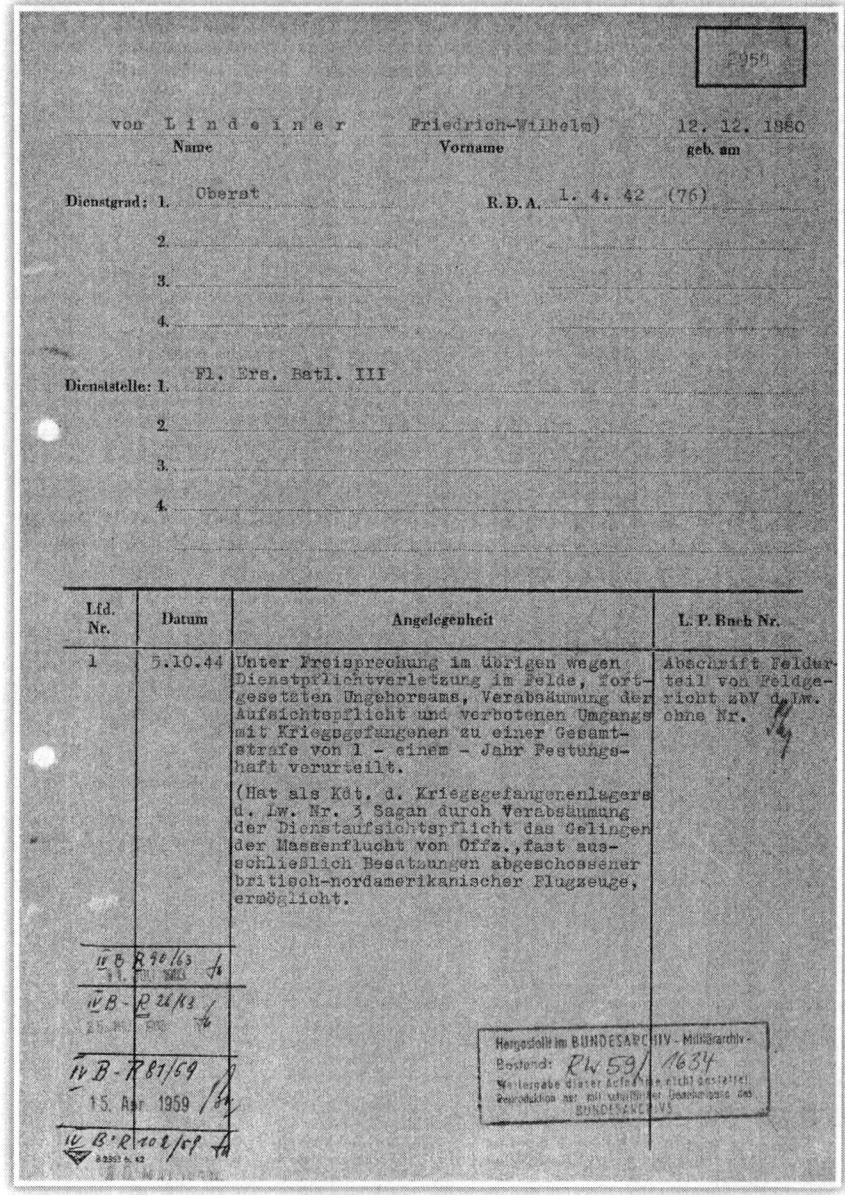

Courtesy Alex Wittenberg
Translation by Kurt Muellenberg

The summary states a failure in the field to apply discipline as commandant of the camp. In addition, von Lindeiner was found guilty of constant disobedience and prohibited contact with the prisoners of war, resulting in a one year penalty.

The second paragraph states that as commandant of the prisoner of war camp, Lw. Nr. 3 Sagan, because of slack application of his duty, von Lindeiner enabled the success of the massive escape of officers, almost exclusively crews of downed British and North American airplanes.

The note on the right side names the court as a Feld Gericht v.b.V. In German "zur besonderen Verwendung", i.e. v.b.V, loosely translated means for special usage outside the usual channels of command.

Commandant von Lindeiner speaking with a visiting German general

Von Lindeiner observes kriegie transfer, probably to Schubin. Arrow marks POW P/O William F. Ash, future author of *Under the Wire*.
Courtesy Imperial War Museum – A/C Charles Clarke – RAF Ex-POW Association

Col. von Lindeiner and Maj. Simoleit, Camp Adjutant, with visiting Protecting Power representative and British officers

Main entrance to Barrack #2 German Compound (Kommandantur) – Oberst (Colonel) von Lindeiner, foreground, and Maj. Simoleit with other Luftwaffe officers during a visit by a German general from the High Command in Breslau

Courtesy Imperial War Museum – A/C Charles Clarke – RAF Ex-POW Association

Von Lindeiner speaks with a British POW at an open air show.

Senior American Officer, Col. Charles Goodrich, to the left of von Lindeiner and Senior British Officer Group Capt. Harry "Wings" Day on the right at an open air show

German officers discover a tunnel entrance in a barrack.

British POWs conferring with German officers - Group Capt. Massey, standing, looking at Maj. Simoleit

German officer inspecting camp guards

German orderly room

RAF officer greeting German officer upon arrival of Red Cross parcels

POW billet – Hauptmann (Capt.) Hans Pieber visits the POWs.

Hauptmann Pieber looks at camera film with British POWs.

POW Peter Butterworth, later to become a famous London actor, inspects a model ship at a display of kriegie arts and crafts.

Messy bookstore in the camp

POWs bringing in wood for fuel in the camp

POW clotheslines in the camp

RAF POWs pose with a cat. Back row, man on the left is S/Ldr Tom Kirby-Green. To the right is F/Lt Pawluk. Both were murdered after the Great Escape. Front row, left, F/Lt Weir and F/Lt Libbey holding the cat. Note adult cat in lower left corner.
Courtesy Colin Kirby-Green

1945 – Ice hockey in the camp

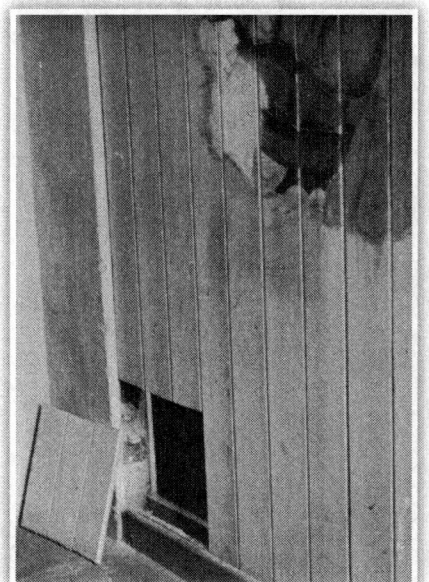
Hole in the bottom of the door in the cooler where a POW was trying to escape

Humorous sign posted by POWs in the camp

German guard stands alone.

Wire cutters

View from a goonbox on a cold winter day

Confiscated KLIM (milk spelled backwards – sent in Red Cross parcels) cans used in escape attempts - The Germans had two barracks filled with confiscated contraband items and called the buildings "their museum," where guards were sent for training.

From Commandant to Captive

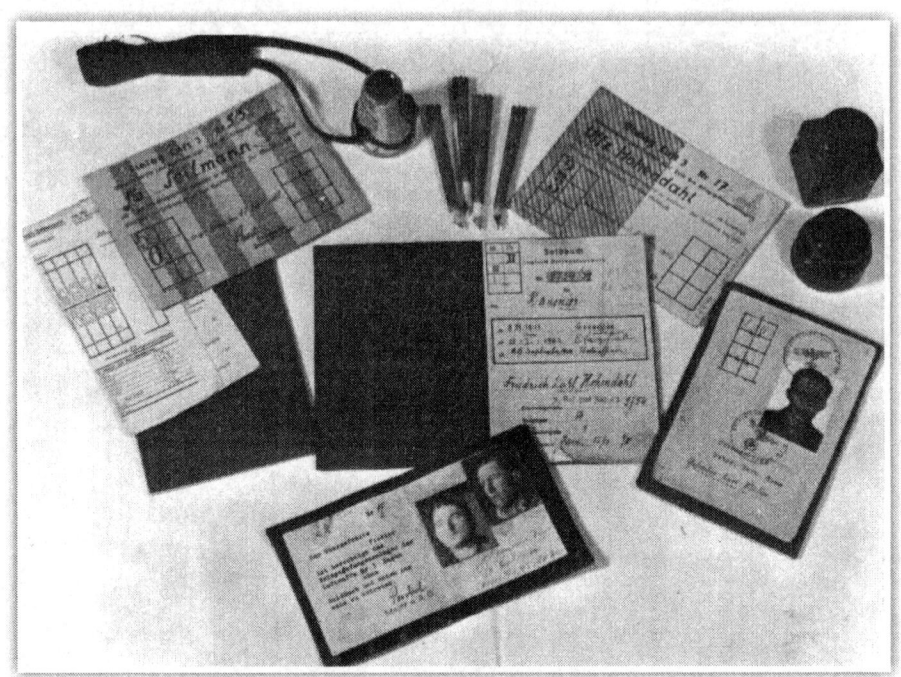

Confiscated forged identification cards and passes

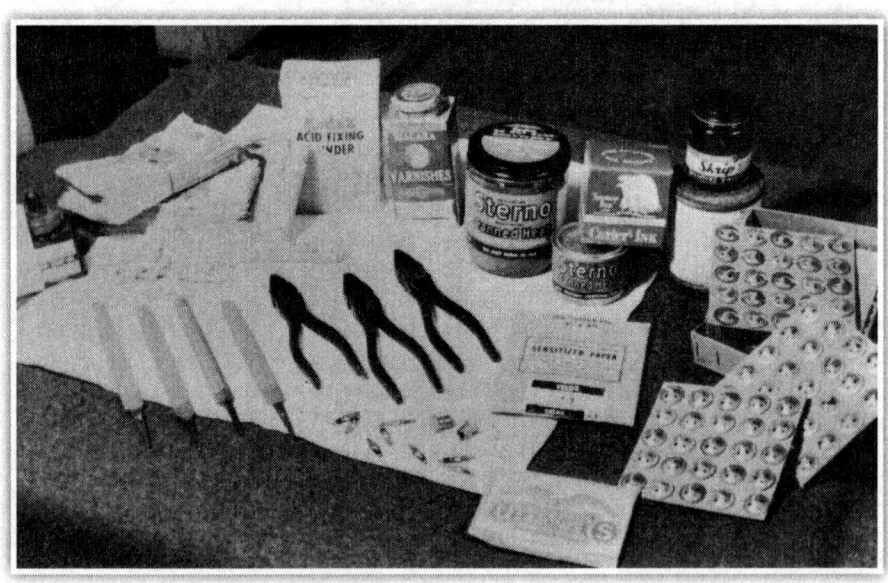

Clandestine equipment, ink, photographic paper,
and chemicals for developing pictures
Courtesy Imperial War Museum – A/C Charles Clarke – RAF Ex-POW Association

Chapter 3

Von Lindeiner Correspondence with POW Senior Officers – Stalag Luft III

Vermin

Oberst v. Lindeiner 　　　　　　Sagan, den 22. Januar 1943
Kommandant d. Kgf.Lagers Nr.3 d.Lw.
Sagan - Carlswalde.

　　　　　　An den
　　　　　　　　Lagerältesten des brit. Offizierlagers
　　　　　　　　Herrn Group Captain MASSEY
　　　　　　　　Stalag Luft 3.

　　　Das Auftreten von Ungeziefer in einzelnen Räumen des von brit. Offizieren belegten Lagers und die infolgedessen vorgenommenen Ermittlungen haben ergeben, dass bei der im allgemeinen herrschenden Unsauberkeit und Unordnung das Auftreten von Ungeziefer fast selbstverständlich sein muss. Eine Ausnahme in Bezug auf die festgestellte Unsauberkeit machen die von Offizieren der U.S.A.A.F. und Offizieren der R.A.F. polnischer Nationalität bewohnten Räume. Der Mangel an Reinigungsmaterial wird als Grund nicht anerkannt, er ist bei dem nötigen Trieb zur Sauberkeit auch mit geringsten Behelfsmitteln zu überwinden.

　　　Ich ersuche Sie, eine gründliche Reinigung der Räume zu veranlassen.

　　　Am Mittwoch, den 27. ds.Mts. wird eine Besichtigung des Lagers durch mich und den Lagerarzt stattfinden, bei der sämtliche Offiziere auf ihren Stuben anwesend sind.

　　　　　　　　　　　　　　　　　Oberst und Kommandant.

See other side for translation

Letter from von Lindeiner to Group Capt. Massey, Senior British Officer

Translation of von Lindeiner's letter

The presence of vermin in certain rooms in the camp occupied by British officers and subsequent searching has proved that uncleanliness and disorder reign in general. The presence of vermin naturally follows. An exception to this proved dirtiness can be made of the officers of the U.S.A.A.F. and those rooms occupied by officers of the R.A.F. of Polish nationality. The lack of cleaning materials will not be admitted as a reason for this, for where there is a will to be clean it is possible with a bare minimum of cleaning materials.

I ask you therefore to have these rooms thoroughly cleaned.

On Wednesday the 27 of this month the camp will be inspected by myself and the camp doctor, during which all officers are to be in their rooms.

Insubordinate Behavior

Oberst v. Lindeiner
Kommandant d. Kgf.Lagers Nr.3 d.Lw.
Sagan - Carlswalde.

Sagan, January 24th 1943

To the
    Senior British Officer
    Senior American Officer
    Senior Officer of Polish nationality
    Senior Officer of Czech nationality.

    During my 8 1/2 months' stay at this place I always endeavoured to treat the R.A.F. Officers as officers and gentlemen and to make the life in this camp endurable. This was sometimes rendered difficult by obstinate behaviour of a few thoughtless elements. I believed that these were young and uneducated people who want peace-time education.

    Events of yesterday's evening and night, however, proved that conceptions regarding behaviour of officers may be different in the Luftwaffe and younger members of the R.A.F. More than a few officers used expressions against the German guards that are absolutely unusual in German officer circles - expressions to be perhaps heard occasionally among coloured dockworkers.

    It would be for the first time indeed that during my more than 40 years military service the respect due to my command could be endangered - and I shall take care that this will never happen. It is to my regret, if quite a considerable number of most honourable officers have to suffer in consequence of the measures to be taken, especially the U.S.A.A.F. officers and British officers of Polish and Czech nationalities who distinguish themselves by decent manners. I hope that it will be possible in future to billet the reasonable elements in a Special Compound.

    Firstly I ordered that barracks in the Officers' Compound will be closed at 17.30 o'clock (G.t.) henceforth. The towers round the Officers' Compound will get reinforcement and mechanical weapons. Everybody will be shot at without warning who leaves barracks after 17.30. Should a stray bullet get into a hut, this would be to the debit of those who cannot submit to a discipline which is beyond question for officers according to German ideas.

    Further steps are under consideration.

    The special measures remain in force, until the names of those officers are brought to my knowledge, who shared in the riots and the unqualifiable injuries against the German guards.

Oberst und Kommandant.

Original letter of reprimand from von Lindeiner to the British POWs
Courtesy USAFA McDermott Library, Stalag Luft III Collections

Translation

Oberst v. Lindeiner Sagan, January 24th 1943
Commandant d. Kgf. Lagers Nr.3 d.Lw.
Sagan – Carlswalde.

To the
Senior British Officer
Senior American Officer
Senior Officer of Polish nationality
Senior Officer of Czech nationality

During my 8 ½ months' stay at this place I always endeavoured to treat the R.A.F. officers as officers and gentlemen and to make the life in this camp endurable. This was sometimes rendered difficult by the obstinate behavior of a few thoughtless elements. I believed that these were young and uneducated people who want peace-time education.

Events of yesterday's evening and night, however, proved that conceptions regarding behavior of officers may be different in the Luftwaffe and younger members of the R.A.F. More than a few officers used expressions against the German guards that are absolutely unusual in German officer circles—expressions to be perhaps heard occasionally among coloured dockworkers.

It would be for the first time indeed that during my more than 40 years military service the respect due to my command could be endangered—and I shall take care that this will never happen again. It is to my regret, if quite a considerable number of most honourable officers have to suffer in consequence of the measures to be taken, especially the U.S.A.A.F. officers and British officers of Polish and Czech nationalities who distinguish themselves by decent manners. I hope that it will be possible in future to billet the reasonable elements in a Special Compound.

Firstly, I ordered that barracks in the Officers' Compound will be closed at 17,30 o'clock (G.t.) henceforth. The towers round the Officers Compound will get reinforcement and mechanical weapons. Everybody will be shot at without warning who leaves barracks after 17,30. Should a stray bullet get into a hut, this would be to the debit of those who cannot submit to a discipline which is beyond question for officers according to German ideas.

Further steps are under consideration.

The special measures remain in force, until the names of those officers are brought to my knowledge, who shared in the riots and the unqualifiable [sic] injuries against the German guards.

[hand-written signature]

Oberst und Commandant.

Black Saturday

The Wooden Horse escape from East Compound occurred the night of Oct. 29/30, 1943, when three POWs escaped from a tunnel dug under a vaulting horse in East Compound. After escapes, Allied prisoners typically caused disturbances at appel (roll call) to occupy the German staff, thus giving the escapers the benefit of a head start away from the camp even before it was discovered they were missing. On October 30th, during appel, one of the most disruptive and chaotic displays by the POWs was staged, followed by severe German repercussions. That day became known as Black Saturday. In the letter that follows, von Lindeiner addresses the events of Black Saturday.

Stalag Luft 3
Commandantur
Sagan, 1st November 1943

To the Senior British Officer
East Camp
Group Captain. R. KELLETT

In connection with the incidents on Saturday, 30th October 1943, the S.B.O. G/C Kellett asked the Kommandant for an interview for him and Group Captain Willetts. The Kommandant also ordered the following six Ps.O.W. officers below from the East Camp to be present:

W/Cdr. R. COLLARD	P.O.W No.	568	S.L.3
W/Cdr. R. MAW	"	740	"
P/O W. POULTON	"	207	"
P/O RUFFEL	"	3792	Ofl. XC
P/O WALTERS	"	714	S.L.2
1st/ Lt. G. HALLER	"	1424	Ofl. IX A

The Kommandant then made the following statement which was translated into English by Major Dr. Simoleit.

"On the morning of Saturday, 30th October, 1943, incidents took place in the East Camp which could easily have led to very serious consequences. The cause of these incidents was that the Ps.O.W did not behave in the manner which must be required of them.

German soldiers do not tolerate provocative and mocking behavior. On Saturday, the German soldiers showed extraordinary self-control when they were greeted as they marched into the camp with extremely improper shouts. Certain Ps.O.W. tried to mock us on our own soil. This behaviours [sic] shows a totally wrong-headed outlook. I expect neither liking nor sympathy, but I do expect a military bearing and respect for German soldiers and for the German uniform. In his own mind, each one of you may think as he likes, but in his behavior he must conduct himself respectfully and in accordance with his circumstances.

I cannot understand how Senior Staff Officers can encourage their junior comrades to play football during Appel or to run across the Parade Ground from one block to another. W/Cdrs. Collard and Maw may hate us Germans and our country as much as they like, that does not interest me in the slightest; I do not seek their friendship, nor do I need it. But while they are Prisoners of War they will learn what we Germans expect above all from an officer, namely correct, respectful, behavior in accordance with the German ideals of officership.

On Saturday we arrested 7 men who expressed their bravery, their heroism and their good up-bringing by grinning, shouting, and whistling. Behaviour of this kind is only possible if their attitude is totally misguided. I believe I can be certain that at least 95% of the officers in this camp have the same officer-like attitude as we have but a small proportion appear to desire to make the relations between the detaining power and the Ps.O.W. as strained as possible.

I wish to warn these gentlemen and to advise them for the last time to avoid stirring up trouble amongst their comrades.

After the attempted escape on Friday, we discovered that the entrance to the tunnel was on the Sports Field in the Golf Course and that sand had been dispersed on the Golf Course. The tunnel had to be filled in as quickly as possible and the leveling of the ground was absolutely essential in order to maintain security.

I myself saw as we entered Blocks 68 and 69 that the lights were extinguished and that they came on again as we left the barracks. In order to prevent this kind of mockery during the night, I had the light bulbs removed from both barracks.

The escape on Friday took place from the Northern part of the sports field between 1920 and 2120 hours. The Ps.O.W. must therefore have been outside the permitted area at this time, having left their barracks by a route not allowed. As a result, I must take all Security measures to see that no-one leaves barrack blocks after the circuit lighting is switched on, and having the window shutters closed all night.

I will now repeat the quintessence of my remarks:

1. I urgently advise the avoidance of any stirring up by underhand propaganda on the part of some of the prisoners, and any sympathetic reception of it by the rest.
2. I expect no sympathy and I will use all the force at my command to ensure that due respect as well as absolute obedience is paid to the Detaining Power and its representatives.

(Signed) von Lindeiner
Oberst and Kommandant

Discipline of POWs Climbing Fences – Christmas 1943

Sagan 27th December 1943

Stalag Luft III
Commandantur

To the Senior Camp Officers

Group Captain H.M. Massey North Camp.
" " A. H. Willets East Camp.
Colonel C.G. Goodrich South Camp.

On my return here I have [illegible] with regret that in spite of my most earnest admonitions, the trust which was placed in the Ps.o.Ws, the way in which the requests were met half way and the special concessions given to the Ps.o.W. over the Christmas holidays have led to intolerable incidents.

1. Nine British Ps.O.W. of North camp climbed the barbed wire fence separating North and South Camps in the night of the 25/12/43.
2. In the night of the 25 - 27/12/43, 15 Ps.o.W. of the U.S.A.A.F. climbed without permission the barbed wire fence separating the South from the North Camp.
3. In the night of the 25 - 26/12/43, 3 British Ps.o.W. of East Camp climbed the barbed wire fence separating East and Centre without permission.
4. On the night of the 25th inst. [Latin for "instante mense," meaning a date of the current month] instead of the allowed number of five Staff officers and 75 P.O W. Officers (i.e. 80 Ps.o.W. in all) 81 officers went from East to North.

5. I am punishing the officers concerned in [illegible] 1 and 2 each with 14 days close Stuben-Arrest. [confined to barracks] The sentences to begin on 28/12/43.
6. The special privileges allowed in connection with the close of the year are hereby withdrawn. Closing of barracks and appels will take place on the days of the week in the usual way.
7. The possession and use of drinks containing alcohol is forbidden effective from today, instead of hitherto ordered with effect from 4/1/44. Existing alcohol will be confiscated and destroyed.

For information:

Colonel D. T. Spivey, Centre Camp

(Signed) von Lindeiner
Colonel and Kommandant.

South Compound's Response to von Lindeiner's Insistence on a Clean Camp

```
                                        South Compound
                                        Stalag Luft 3
                                        Sagan, Germany
                                        May 15, 1944
```

Memo To: All Block CO's.
Subject: Sanitary Regulations.

    1. Block CO's will initiate a "spring buck-up" in sanitary standard of their Blocks. The following specific instructions will be brought to the attention of all POWs living in your Block and will be rigidly enforced.

    a) Area of Block responsibility - Everything within 15 feet of your block.
    b) All rooms and hall to be swept daily and living rooms to be mopped at least once every two weeks.
    c) Latrine to be kept clean, dry, and odourless.
    d) Kitchen floor adequately drained.
    e) Wash basins in wash room cleaned daily.
    f) No trash or dirty water to be thrown out of windows.
    g) No solids down block drains.
    h) Trash, cans, and garbage to be sorted _in_ living rooms and properly disposed of.
    i) Communal pots kept clean.
    j) Hall water tubs to be kept full and clean. Dust covers will be provided.
    k) Area around block within 15 feet policed once a week. Raked and wood stacked.
    l) No raw vegetables or peelings in Aborts.
    m) No unconsumed Reich rations visibly disposed of.

    2. You are reminded that the rate of Dysintary and skin disease will go up when the flies arrive unless we make it impossible for them to breed here.

    3. Block CO's will inspect all rooms in their blocks at 11 A.M. each Saturday morning at which time they will require rooms to be clean and orderly.

    4. Cols. Stillman and Clark will accompany Block CO's on their inspections from time to time.

    5. Capt. Smithwick 135/9 is Camp Sanitation Officer and as such is responsible for outside sanitation. He will need your cooperation.

    By Order of Senior American Officer.

    R. M. Stillman   A. P. Clark
    Lt.Col., U.S.A.A.F.   Lt.Col., U.S.A.A.F.

South Compound
Stalag Luft 3
Sagan, Germany
May 15, 1944

Memo To: All Block CO's.
Subject: Sanitary Regulations.

1. Block CO's will initiate a "spring buck-up" in sanitary standard of their Blocks. The following specific instructions will be brought to the attention of all POWs living in your Block and will be rigidly enforced.

    a) Area of block responsibility - Everything within 15 feet of your block.
    b) All rooms and hall to be swept daily and living rooms to be mopped at least once every two weeks.
    c) Latrine to be kept clean, dry, and odourless.
    d) Kitchen floor adequately drained.
    e) Wash basins in wash room cleaned daily.
    f) No trash or dirty water to be thrown out of windows.
    g) No solids down block drains.
    h) Trash, cans, and garbage to be sorted in living rooms and properly disposed of.
    i) Communal pots kept clean.
    j) Hall water tubs to be kept full and clean. Dust covers will be provided.
    k) Area around block within 15 feet policed once a week. Raked and wood stacked.
    l) No raw vegetables or peelings in Aborts.
    m) No unconsumed Reich rations visibly disposed of.

2. You are reminded that the rate of Dysintary [sic] and skin disease will go up when the flies arrive unless we make it impossible for them to breed here.
3. Block CO's will inspect all rooms in their blocks at 11 A.M. each Saturday morning at which time they will require rooms to be clean and orderly.
4. Cols. Stillman and Clark will accompany Block CO's on their inspections from time to time.
5. Capt. Smithwick 135/9 is Camp Sanitation Officer and as such is responsible for outside sanitation. He will need your cooperation.

By Order of Senior American Officer.

R.M. Stillman A.P. Clark
Lt. Col., U.S.A.A.F. Lt. Col., U.S.A.A.F.

All letter material courtesy USAFA McDermott Library, Stalag Luft III Collections

Chapter 4

Interrogation/Interview Summaries - Col. von Lindeiner Regarding the Killing of 50 POWs from Stalag Luft III London Cage – August, 1945

After the war, German officers suspected of war crimes, or who might be called as witnesses at postwar trials, were arrested and sent to the United Kingdom and held at various places, most notably the London Cage. Nine other "cages" were established from southern England to Scotland, with the London Cage being an important transit camp. The London Cage, located in a fashionable part of the city, had space for sixty prisoners and was equipped with five interrogation rooms. Col. von Lindeiner arrived there August 7, 1945.

While the term, "cage," conjures up the image of a metal cage enclosure, in actuality the term came into common usage when the United Kingdom systematically interrogated all of its prisoners of war in 1940 in each command area of the UK. The nine cages were visually quite different. For example, one cage used a portion of the town's race track as a camp, while two others were in bare fields.

Besides the interrogation of von Lindeiner, Lt. Col. Alexander Scotland, the head of Prisoner of War Interrogation Section (PWIS) of the Intelligence Corps, participated in the investigation of the SS and Gestapo men who murdered fifty escaped prisoners from Stalag Luft III in 1944 in the aftermath of the Great Escape. Scott later wrote a book entitled, *London Cage*, in 1950, but it was not published until 1957.

The summaries that follow document the proceedings when Col. von Lindeiner was interrogated. He was held at the London Cage until August 29th, 1945, and was then sent on to the first of several prisoner of war camps in England before being returned to Germany.

Report on interrogation of PW LD 757

Oberst Fried. W. von LINDEINER-WILDAU

KILLING OF 50 RAF OFFICERS ESCAPERS

FROM STALAG LUFT III – MARCH 1945

This Pw, who was Commandant of Stalag Luft III during the period before the escape, was immediately placed under room arrest after this event and finally, in Oct 44, was sentenced to one year fortress detention for his slackness of control of the Camp which contributed to the success of the escape.

Pw is extremely friendly to the British and his information is supplied willingly. He will make a reliable witness should his services be required in the case.

PW was arrested in the evening of 25 Mar 44 and had to rely on second hand reports as to what transpired. On hearing that 16 escaped PW from Stalag Luft III were being held by the Police in SAGAN, Oberst LINDEINER, realizing the danger these Officers were in, so long as they were retained by the Police, endeavored at midday, 25 Mar 44, to get a call on the telephone to the head of the Kripoleitstelle, ABSALON at GOERLITZ, the special investigating Officer appointed to deal with this case, to have the escaping PW returned to the camp.

Oberst LINDEINER was then told that as he had been superseded by Oberstlt CORDES, no instruction from him would be accepted.

Oberst LINDEINER heard that on the night of 26 Mar 44, the 16 PW were transferred to GOERLITZ. He also heard that Buergermeister KORN of HERMSDORF nr SAGAN had later boasted that they had all been 'laid out' that same night.

Oberst LINDEINER knows nothing of the details of further happenings to the remainder of the escaping PW. He had heard of the delivery of urns with ashes back to the Camp.

In his view, the members of the German Kripo Services who must know all the details concerning this crime, are:-

1. Chief of the R.S.H.A. KALTENBRUNNER
2. Chief of the Kripoleitstelle BRESLAU, O'Reg Rat WIELEN
3. Special Kripo Agent ABSALON, whom he described as being:

Aged	33 to 36 years	Height	1.78 m
Hair	Blonde	Face	oval
Nose	straight and thin	Figure	slim

Good German type with polished manners. The perfect drawing-room criminal.

THE MURDER OF 50 BRITISH

R.A.F. OFFICERS AT STALAG

LUFT III IN SAGAN

This is a translation of various documents found on POW LD 757 Oberst von LINDEINER-WILDAU, Commandant of Stalag Luft III, SAGAN, at the time of the murders. The documents consist of:

1. Draft – report of a meeting of Security Officers of Air-Force PW Camps, held in the PW Camp No 3 of the Air-force in SAGAN.
2. Agenda of the meeting.
3. Minutes of the meeting.
4. Lists of personnel present.
5. Notes by Oberst von LINDEINER-WILDAU for his speech and notes taken during the meeting by him.

The meeting, it should be noted, was the last meeting to be held prior to the attempted escape by the 50 R.A.F. Officers. Immediately after the attempted escape, Oberst von LINDEINER-WILDAU was put under arrest (report no.: PWIS(H)/LDC/774).

The original, typewritten manuscript in German, of which the following is a translation, contains a number of underlinings, which have been omitted in the translation, and a number of penciled notes. These are given in the translation, but enclosed in '_____'.

London District Cage,
16 Aug 45

DRAFT

Report of a meeting of Security Officers of Air-force PW Camps, held at Air-force PWS Camp No 3 at SAGAN from 15 to 17 Mar 44.

An agenda of the meeting has been appended. Alterations of the original times states, due to travelling difficulties of non-resident participants at the meeting, may be seen on the agenda.
A list of personnel present is appended as enclosure 2.
Report of the meeting on 15 Mar 1944.

The Commandant of Air-force PW Camp No 3, Oberst von LINDEINER, opened the meeting at 0900 hours, by welcoming the participants. He gave a brief outline of the objects of the meeting: 'Exchange of Experience' and 'New Developments in Security'.

The number of new PW taken at present amounts to 2000 men per month. As PW Camps are enlarged or newly built, the demand for Security Officers increases. At present, it is impossible to give them an extensive training, particularly in theoretical matters. Security Services in Air-force PW Camps requires broad-minded, energetic and active Officers, who like their work, and who are in full possession of their physical and spiritual capacities. Experience, being the best teacher, should be supplemented by visits to similar establishments and discussions with comrades, occupying similar positions in different Camps.

The tasks of a Security Officer in Air-force PW Camps with British and U.S. flying Officers and Sjts [sic] [Sgts.] differ widely from those of Security Officers in PW Camps of members of other nations. For the British and American personnel the following amendment of the Geneva Convention applies: 'Officers and Sjts [sic] of the British and American Air-force are not required to work' (…kommen nicht zum Arbeitseinsetz).

The special position enjoyed by captured flying Officers of those powers, who are still at present at war with Germany, is due, in the first instance, to the desire for information. Army PW Camps for Ors [Other Ranks] should, properly speaking, be empty, as their inmates are supposed to work. In Air-force PW Camps, nobody should be unaccounted for, as the missing person is likely to have escaped. The prevention of escapes is to be ensured through preventive measures; as far as a PW Officer is concerned, being afraid of being punished or even being shot dead is only a deterrent. All measures are to take into account the esprit de corps, prevailing in particular within the British Air Force.

MEETING

Of Security Officers of the Air-force PW Camp from 15 – 17 Mar 1944 in Air-force PW Camp No. 3, SAGAN-CARLSWALDE

15 Mar 1944

0900 hrs	Welcoming the participants and introduction to the meeting	Oberst v. LINDEINER
0920-1020 hrs	~~Organization of PW affairs, in particular as far as Security Officers are concerned~~. / Security affairs in general; principal points in PW affairs/	Hptm SALEWSKI, O.K.W.
1020-1120 hrs	Objects, organization and methods of the Intelligence Services	Ast VIII / Hptm Dr KOEHLER
1120 1200 hrs	Discussion	
1215 hrs	Lunch.	

Interval

1400-1445 hrs	Propaganda among Prisoners of War	~~Hptm KUNTZEN, O.K.W.~~ /Oberst v. LINDEINER/
1450-1515 hrs	Regulations concerning the keeping of secret documents (Air-force regulation 99, new edition)	Ast VIII/Hptm Dr KOEHLER/
1515-1545 hrs	Military correspondence (Air-force regulation 30)	Ast VIII/Hptm Dr KOEHLER/
1600-1620 hrs	Discussion	

16 Mar 44

0700 hrs	Presence at duty-allocation of Security Officers.	Gp III
0800–0900 hrs	Employment of Intelligence formations	Hptm BROILI
0900–1000 hrs	Experiences of Security Officers in Air-force PW Camps	Major PESCHEL
1000–1030 hrs	Correspondence of PW	O'Lt v. MASSOW
1035–1200 hrs	Discussion	
1215 hrs	Lunch	

Interval

From 1400 hrs onwards	Visit to the Escape Museum. Censoring parcels. Censoring books. Duty in the M.I. room. With discussion of Security Officers about these matters.	O'Feldw SCHOLZ Hptm BROILI O'Lt v. MASSOW

17 Mar 1944

0900–0945 hrs	Police-search for wanted persons in war-time (Kriegsfahndung).	Kripoleitstelle, BRESLAU
1000–1045 hrs	Dealings with PW	Stapoleitstelle, BRESLAU
1045–1200 hrs	Discussion and concluding speeches.	
1215 hrs	Lunch.	

Meeting of Security Officers of Air-force PW
Camps, from 15 to 17 Mar 1944 in

Air-force PW Camp 3 SAGAN-CARLSWALDE

On 15 Mar 1944, at 0900 hrs, the Commandant of Air-force PW Camp No. 3, SAGAN, Oberst von LINDEINER, opens the meeting and welcomes the participants. He briefly outlines the reason for the meeting; All that is new within the sphere of Intelligence work is to be assimilated, and experiences are to be exchanged. Proper, lengthy training of Security officers is rather difficult, due to lack of time, created by the monthly increase of 2000 Air-force PW. The monthly increase of PW at the present time, amounts to approximately 2000 men, and the demand for Security officers increases correspondingly. Consequently, an intensive training _____. The establishment of special Air-force PW Camps is supposed to be due to the Reichsmarschall through a "Fuehrer' Order. It is said that one of the reasons for the establishment of special Air-force PW Camps was the fact that Intelligence about enemy Air-forces was best obtained from enemy airmen PW.

Subsequently, Oberst v. LINDEINER introduces the speakers for the following days and their topics. Passing to questions concerning security, he underlines the importance of the GENEVA convention in Camps with British and U.S. inmates. Flying Officers PW are not to be put to work, as they are sure to commit acts of sabotage. Officer PW are not deterred from trying to escape by being afraid of punishments or of being shot; prevention of escapes can only be achieved by preventative measures. A particular difficulty in the treatment of PW arises from the Espirit de Corps prevailing amongst them.

The first speaker is Hptm Dr KOEHLER of Ast VIII, who chooses the topic: 'Objects, organization and methods of the Intelligence Services.' Until HITLER's coming to power, the organization of the Intelligence Services was insufficient, both from the personal and from the material side. Their objects were counter-espionage, sabotage and gathering information.

The re-organisation effected after HITLER's coming to power resulted in an immediate establishment, sufficient from a material and a personal point of view. Today, the tasks are divided into active Groups (Group I + II) and a passive Group (Group III). The active tasks consist of gathering Intelligence and the secret signal service; the passive tasks comprise counter-espionage, sabotage and subversive activities (Zersetzung). The operational units at home are the Abwehrstellen (Ast), on the Eastern Front the Intelligence officers and 'Abwehrtrupps,' respectively 'working squads.' The 'Geheime Feldpolizeistellen' (F.S. posts) serve as executive authorities in combat zones. The principal executive authority at home is the Gestapo. The Group III applies the annual regulation (Jahresverfuegung) of 1941/42.

By giving two examples, the speaker illustrates carelessness and lack of security at some army offices. It is, consequently, highly necessary to extend the Intelligence organization. Mental training is the best weapon against subversion.

Group II requires special knowledge of foreign nationalities and mastery in the art of leading men. Where it is a question of surprises, special 'K' (battle) troups or sabotage troups must be employed. As long as there exists confidence the establishment of local national units has proved of value.

Group I comprises the secret signals service; it is particularly important that the work is carried out inconspicuously. Units working in combat areas must distinguish between areas in the immediate zone and those further behind, and reconnaissance in depth. From all what the signals officers knows and gleans, he must be able to draw the correct conclusions, he must be capable of inferring from preparation to facts.

In the course of the discussion, Hptm MALSBENDEN (LODZ) draws attention to the importance of getting to know how enemy PW have been instructed to answer questions in the event of capacity, and particularly what they were supposed to answer to questions most likely to be asked.

In this connection, Hptm KOEHLER gives information about training of 'V-men' (SP), who are trained in special training squads. Oberst v. LINDEINER contributes some practical suggestions on how to induce S.Ps., how to train and how to use them, in particular in Russian PW Camps. Hptm MALSBENDEN asks to be told of experiences with men who give themselves out to be special Germanophiles. Oberst v. LINDEINER believes that it is not possible to issue general directives for such contingencies.

Major Dr. PESHEL talks on: 'Experiences of Security Officers in Airforce PW Camps'. The composition of prisons in Air-force PW Camps is different; such Camps consist primarily of intelligent prisoners, who were issued with two Commandments: To escape, and not to fraternize with Germans. Indoctrination along German lines appears to have no effect as the prisoners are under severe internal control. The fact that they cannot be put to work increases the incidence of 'barbed-wire nerves' and 'simulating madness. The speaker gained his experiences mainly in HEYDEKRUG, which is very similar to the SAGAN Camp, although there are no officers there. Difficulties arise through the geological features of a Camp (sand---) and a situation near railway stations, the sea, or near a frontier. A security officer's main concern are attempts of escape. A favoured method of escape is by means of a tunnel; prisoners go to no end of trouble in order to obtain material for the construction of tunnels. A preventative ditch filled with water up to 1 ½ foot, situated in the danger area (Warnzone), has proved effective. The support given to the guard at the gate by the interpreter on duty is very valuable in order to prevent escapes in camouflaged dress. Prisoners are very keen to manufacture pliers and wire-shears, which will help them in the escape. The switching off of the surrounding searchlights in case of an air-raid leads to an increase in the number of attempts to escape. A 'trip-wire' is very successful against such attempts. To avoid other faults in the electricity supply each camp should possess its own power unit. Going beyond his original topic, the speaker touches once more on matters of cultural welfare (theatres and sports grounds), questions of communal feedings, the parcel department; the use of Russian PW for fatigues, the attachment of a special C.I.D. official (Kriminalbeamter) to the camp and on activities of a field court-martial in case of attempts to escape.

In the ensuing discussion, Oberst von LINDEINER underlines the danger of private parcels and, as far as SAGAN is concerned, denies the necessity for the services of a specially attached C.I.D. official. Hptm Dr. KOEHLER mentions the proposal for the establishment of so-called 'free camps,' in which all fatigues are to be carried out by the prisoners themselves and thus save camp-staff. Hptm BROILI reports that in several cases Swedish skippers were induced through being bribed to help escapers. Oberst v. LINDEINER makes it clear that to inform the field court martial of attempted escapes is rather awkward but must not be avoided. Hptm v. MILLER reports on the supply of escape material to prisoners through the 'Lancashire-Penny-Fund'. [A scheme by which money and maps, hidden in Christmas crackers sent by an imaginary "Lancashire Penny Fund" direct to the German Camp Commandants was successful in a large number of camps. A letter with the crackers requested the Camp Commandant in each case to pass them to the S.B.O. or Camp Leader to help brighten their Christmas Party. 50% of these got through.]

Oberarzt Dr. LECHTKEN deals in detail with 'depression mania' prevalent with prisoners behind barbed wire and about means for a cure.

Hptm SALEWSKI, of the department 'Foreign Intelligence' (Amt Ausland/Abwehr) at the O.K.W. talks about: 'Security Affairs in General and Principal Points in PW Affairs'. The Amt Ausland/Abwehr consists of 4 main departments:

1. Foreign Intelligence, dealing with political questions.
2. 'Intelligence 1' comprises the secret espionage service with the sub-depts 'economy' and 'technical army affairs'.
3. 'Intelligence 2', the Intelligence department proper, has, among others, the following sub depts.: 3 c, supervision of human traffic, 3 f, espionage and counter-espionage, 3, PW affairs. Since autumn 43 the Intelligence Depts. increased beyond the 'red memorandum'. In view of that and, considering the lack of personnel it was found necessary to concentrate work on a few main points, such as: a) the penetration of enemy signals service into PW camps. b) Battle against Communist propaganda which is at present the main task of the security personnel. Danger spots will be found in some Wehrkreisc (Command areas), mainly in those adjoining the Czechoslovak frontier. c) The question how PW are going to react when the 'A-hypothesis (2nd front) arises. It may be assumed that they, in any case the British and Americans, will only start to take part after they have been supplied, perhaps through the air, with arms and ammunition. As far as Communist propaganda is concerned, there is a possibility of using Eastern workers who are liable to influence PW as well as the German staff. The starting point is the formation of cells, either from below or from above (directly conducted from MOSCOW). It is also possible to use the Political Intelligence service as a means to spread Communist propaganda. The propaganda disseminated by DE GAULLE is now also under Communist influence. As a preventative it is considered necessary to stop all unnecessary letter-writing. For the Intelligence Services it is considered necessary to work decentralized down to the smallest cells. Russian propaganda is particularly active in PW Camps containing Germans. To avoid these men spreading disruptive propaganda, a 'Returned PW Camp' has been established in LISSA. It is of great importance to evaluate mail from the point of view of conditions in Great Britain and U.S.A. Intelligence gathered must be divided into political, military, and economic information. To obtain S.P.'s,

collaboration with members of foreign powers is required. These S.Ps, often employed in foreign countries, are in possession of secret information and as such are to be sealed off. There are 3 groups of them: a) Those permanently in possession of secret information, who have been sealed off until the end of the war. b) Persons who have been trained, but who do not appear to be suitable. They have to be vetted in good time. c) Those with a grouse, who, provided they do not fall under category a) have to be housed separately. These bearers of secret information are increasing, especially now, after the reverses on the Eastern Front; they are mainly Ukrainians, who may be used again against Poles. The escape-'graph', which always shows a peak in July and August, is now led by Russians, who mostly join the partisans. The resistance movement which exists for instance in France, increases the dangerous consequences of an escape to a degree far surpassing that following an escape in 1943 or earlier. The concentration on major points, whilst neglecting minor matters, is more decisive than ever for a success.

Prior to the first speech in the afternoon, some individual subjects were discussed:

Reports on articles of any kind found in Red Cross parcels are to be made to L.Insp.XVII (Air Force Directorate).

1. The withdrawal of full military honours at burials and permission to put wreaths on the graves led to a serious state of mind among the PW.
2. The 'radio-letters', transmitted in the 'Germany calling' programme, are to be preferred from a point of view of propaganda, to short news bulletins and telegrams, which are sent through the corresponding Embassy in BERNE. Telegrams to the Red Cross are to be reduced to the utmost. Until a final

decision has been reached such telegrams are to be forwarded through the German Red Cross.

Hptm Dr. KOEHLER reports on: 'The New Regulations Concerning the Keeping of Secret Documents'. They are contained in army and air-force orders 99 (Heeres- & Luftwaffen Dienstvorschrift) and deal with security and Intelligence matters in respect of army correspondence. The new regulation came into force on 25 Nov 43. A new development is the division between matters to be kept under lock and key, i.e. correspondence and documents. Such matters are also sub-divided into: 'For official use only'; 'Secret'; 'Top Secret' matters ('N.f.D.Sachen'; 'Geheim-sachen'; 'Geheime Kommandosachen'). A special note applies to civilian authorities how they have to deal with documents in order to keep them secret. Furthermore the new regulation also classifies documents into 'open' or 'secret'. Complete distribution lists must only be appended to the original. The administration of all matters kept under lock and key, too, has been altered. Security instructions concerning matters under lock and key must be renewed w.e.f. a day to be appointed. The intelligence services are to investigate cases of loss or other infringements and, if necessary, will have to issue amendments to the regulations. The question of up-grading of matters to be kept under lock and key within a garrison area or beyond, has also been newly clarified. These regulations are orders or prohibitions, issued by the Government in the interest of National Security; all regulations beyond the original ones are to be kept at a minimum.

Afterwards, Hptm Dr. KOEHLER reports on 'Military Correspondence'. Army order (air-force order) 30 of 1 Nov 39 applies. An instruction, issued in connection with it by Wehrkreis VIII deals mainly with the form of the letter and with abbreviations to be used (date, place, subject matter, reference, address, underlinings, no need for separate 'appendices'). All letters are to be addressed to the ultimate recipient (without intermediate channels) with the addition 'a.d.D.' through official channels). Instead of full pages, only half – or quarter pages are to be used.

During the discussion Hptm SALEWSKI maintains that even in such letters one's own opinion should not be left out and economy in paper should not be overdone.

In the following talk, Oberst v. LINDEINER treats the subject of: 'Propaganda among Prisoners-of-War'.

The camp staff in air-force PW Camps must never forget that the prisoners are men on a high intellectual level. The speaker answers the question whether propaganda is desirable at all, with 'Yes', provided that there is a chance of maintaining German dignity. The prisoners themselves do not mind propaganda at all. However, the instructions from 'O.K.W. press department' do not always coincide with those about treatment of PW. In consequence, most of the propaganda must be left to representatives of the O.K.W. press department. The speaker considers as objects of propaganda: 1) Awakening of the conviction that Bolshevism spells danger; 2) Instructions on Jewry and its morale; 3) Gaining of understanding for the German Reich and its aims, as well as the National Socialism represented in it. Only those can be employed in propaganda work, who admit their national consciousness in a dignified manner when undertaking propaganda. A difference must be made between British and American personnel. The former are more easily influenced by matters of fact, the latter through ideological subjects. This could, for instance, be used to shake their attitude towards Bolshevism. Nothing can be done with regard to the Jewish question; but there are important differences among British personnel in their attitude towards Russia and therefore we can find an Ally among old enemies of Bolshevism.

How is propaganda work to be conducted? Among PW there is always distrust against anything specially printed for them, but there is great interest in German newspapers. Those who want to know something about us are most easily susceptible to personal influence without obtrusive propaganda. Success depends entirely on the person conducting the work; he must have tact and must also show it towards the German guards, as otherwise they are liable to become confused through his attitude towards the PW. Proper conduct of propaganda obliges the British to reciprocate correctness and it will be found that they will usually observe it.

During the discussion, Maj Dr. SIMOLEIT, Hptm SALEWSKI, and Hptm SCHULZ considered whether propaganda is to be undertaken at all and, if so, how it can best be carried out. Hptm SALEWSKI expounds the official attitude, namely that there is no official objection against relations with PW for the purpose of propaganda; he is going to get further information from the O.K.W.

Oberst v. LINDEINER expresses his thanks to Hptm Dr. KOEHLER and SALEWSKI for their speeches which found undivided attention from all participants.

On 16 Mar the participants started with being present at a duty-allocation of the security group. Afterwards, Hptm BROILI talks about: 'Employment of Intelligence Formations'. He starts with the duty interpreter (D.v.L.) who controls the outer compound gates together with the guards and who must keep a sharp eye on the passes. Counterfeit passes often lead to 'gate-escapes'. To avoid this, die-stamping of passes was found to be very useful. The reverse side of the passes must be carefully checked as well. Attempts have been made to counterfeit paybooks. The D.v.L. must check all vehicles, as they have often been used by PW in an escape. After sunset, the D.v.L. must issue metal chits to all personnel entering the camp. Small transports may be quartered for a night in the camp cells, which can also be employed for searching PW who are changing from one part of the camp to another. On such occasions, papers may sometimes be found. Rations, books, and laundry can be searched in the cells.

Normally, searchers are employed during day-time in the camp itself, sometimes, when large transports arrive or when a whole barrack has to be searched, they must be employed wholesale. Observation of the camp by means of spies can be done from the surrounding woods as they are thus not exposed to the PW's view. Dog-leaders, of which camp SAGAN has 20 at present, are employed between 2100 and 0700 hrs in the camps. Dogs are also used for tracking and when new transports arrive. The listening installation of the camp is at present in process of reconstruction.

During the ensuing discussion, Oberst v. LINDEINER refers to the disciplinary powers of the camp commandant, which he considers too narrow. He draws attention to the difference between ordinary arrest and detention; during the latter PW receive only German rations and are not permitted to smoke. Prisoners protest without success against the award of detention of staff officers. Ordinary arrest, however, is hardly considered a punishment by them. Hptm KLUGE asked for a copy of the punishment regulations as applying to SAGAN, for camp BELARIA.

In reply to a question Maj. PESCHEL informs the participants that the packing material of Red Cross and ordinary parcels, in particular card-board boxes, are to be taken away from the prisoners. Oberst v. LINDEINER asks the camp officers to make sure that each cardboard box is withdrawn from the camp. Hptm Dr. KLUGE is of the opinion that the PW take good care that the Germans cannot use the boxes again. The necessity for a listening installation if underlined by various speakers (Oberst v. LINDEINER, Maj PESCHEL, Hptm MALSBENDEN). Maj HUEHNEMOERDER describes a case where PW managed to declare a wrong number present for several weeks, whilst one PW had escaped. Oberst v. LINDEINER admits the possibility for such manoeuvres in view of the prevailing overcrowding and the lack of sufficient personnel during roll-calls. If at all possible, such personnel should know the inmates of 1-2 barracks personally. Maj PESCHEL suggests exchange of unsuitable camp-staff with the Landesschuetzen personnel.

Oberleutnant von MASSOW starts his talk on 'Postal Censorship' with the remark that the censorship in Air-force PW Camp 3 differs from that in all other camps as all mail for flying personnel is censored here. This not only centralizes evaluation, but also leads to similar procedure throughout. Censorship must be mainly concerned with the following points: Incoming mail must be checked in particular for prohibited articles, maps, codes, etc.; outgoing mail for everything in connection with escape attempts, Military information can mainly be gleaned from mail of new arrivals; the same applies to information on transfer of squadrons, political and economic information, such as strifes and short supplies. All these matters are correlated in a monthly report which is sent to 3 offices. A card-index is being maintained of all inhabitants of the occupied territories who correspond with PW. Censorship also deals with examination papers. The card-index in camp SAGAN is constantly being checked against the central card-index in OBERURSEL.

During the ensuing discussion, Maj HUEHNEMOERDER raises the question of registering comrades from the same squadron and the correlation of all information sent monthly to the evaluation centre at OBERURSEL. Oberst v. LINDEINER does not consider that the establishment of a second censorship office would serve any real purpose. Maj HUEHNEMOERDER believes that a re-organisation of the censorship organisation can hardly be avoided, considering that PW are transferred directly from Italian Camps to German Camps without passing through Dulag Luft. Oberst v. LINDEINER draws attention to the danger of eye-trouble among persons constantly employed in postal censorship. Hptm MALSBENDEN would like to know with what type of persons correspondence is permitted and what army forms have to be used. Oberleutnant v. MASSOW explains the 'short news bulletins' and, together with Maj PESCHEL, clarifies the problem of sending on examination papers and that of stopping and sending on under separate cover the mail of 'suspects.'

At the end of the morning session, the participants pay a visit to the escape museum; in the afternoon the parcel censorship is visited, as well as book-censoring and finally a visit is paid to the M.I. room.

At the beginning of the speeches on 17 Mar, Oberst v. LINDEINER welcomes Oberst v. FLOTOW from the PW Camp MAEHRISCH-TRUEBAU and the representatives of the RSHA (Central Government Security Department); he underlines the important of collaboration with these departments; the meeting would like to learn from these gentlemen the art of observing and judgment.

Kriminalrat BRUENNER of the RSHA (Kriminalpolizeileitstelle BRESLAU, i.e. C.I.D. district HQ), speaks on: 'Police search for Wanted Persons in Wartime'.

Following the outbreak of war, the C.I.D. entered new fields, increasingly so after the arrival in Germany of foreign workers and enemy PW in increasing numbers. Untrained personnel may, now and then, make a mistake, but 'It is better to do too much, than to be neglectful in a decisive moment'. According to a decree issued by the RFSS and Chief of the German Police of 5 Nov 42, the C.I.D. (Kripo) is responsible for searching for wanted persons in wartime within Germany, whilst the Gestapo takes over this duty in frontier zones. The principal methods of search are the following: 1. Railway searches. Conducted by numerous squads operating in the train itself, it is mainly concerned with checking civilians, especially men liable to call-up. In principle, military personnel are only checked in case of special suspicions. However, C.I.D. personnel are competent to check numbers of the Armed Forces, as otherwise cases of forgery are able to slip through. The paybook must be shown to a detective inspector; we welcome the fact that it now bears a photograph. Judging purely from numbers, railway searches for foreign workers is the main task. It has been found that foreign workers strive to return home in increasing numbers after air-raids. 2. Street-traffic search. This is carried out by ordinary police (Orpo) personnel, but specially appointed NSKK men also participate. 3. Sealing-off searches (Riegelfahndung), consisting mainly of blocking large rivers or canals. 4. Police-raids, conducted in public houses or in the private homes of suspects. In the case of mass-escapes of PW, the C.I.D. uses 3 degrees of police raids: Alpha, Beta and 'large-scale search'

('Grossfahndung'). The first is an ordinary search; at the second the county constabulary joins in. Mass-raids are conducted jointly with the Labour Service (R.A.D.), party organisations, the voluntary Fire Service (N.S.F.), etc. and during such raids, whole streets are roped off. Britishers and Russians conduct themselves quite differently during an escape: The former always try to use vehicles, even aircraft; on the other hand, Russians march on foot for days and even weeks. Russians contribute to a large extent to the increase of petty crimes in the country districts. As far as such searches are concerned, some 1000 arrests are being made monthly within the area of the Kripoleitstelle BRESLAU. The speaker underlines what Oberst v. LINDEINER had said before him: 'Prevention is better than cure'. He asks for support of the military authorities for the work of the Kripo. This is mainly applicable to Britishers who try their utmost to make the work of the Kripo difficult. Reports of escapes must be made as quickly as possible. In the manufacture of escape material, such as counterfeit passes, British and American Flying Officers lead the field. The output of work by PW in civilian industry has greatly decreased. Severe supervision appears to be called for.

In the discussion, Oberst v. LINDEINER deals with the practice of searches in Camp 3. He reminds listeners that the 'escape season' is approaching. In case of searches, first information is given to the appropriate railway authority and to the Kriminalpolizeileitstelle by telephone. Major PESCHEL deals with immediate measures following the escape from HEYDEKRUG. As the camp is near a frontier, the customs authorities are informed first, to be followed by the railway and police authorities. Hptm MALSBENDEN asks how it is best possible to detect a false detective inspector. Krim. Rat BRUENNER advises to ask for the badge and to be shown the pass bearing the photograph. Oberleutnant Dr. SCHMID asks for a discussion on escape attempts during transports. Oberst v. LINDEINER makes it clear that the card indices in possession of the transport leader should enable the authorities to establish the identity of the escaper. The consequences of the lack of personnel which exists at present and will be aggravated in the near future, will soon become ever more apparent. Maj Dr. SIMOLEIT believes that if fixed seats were allotted to PW during transport on the railway it would make control much easier.

Oberleutnant SCHMID announces that special railway cars for such transports are being manufactured and some are already in use.

Kriminalkommissar LAEUFER reports on: 'Prohibited Traffic with PW'. The law prohibits any traffic with PW, unless it is required 'officially', as for instance in the case of employers. 'Prohibited relations and careless talks in the presence of PW may have dangerous consequences. Secret relations of German women with PW was particularly noticeable in rural areas. The consequences of such relations can be of serious nature and may lead to a decrease in the fighting spirit of the armed forces. Employers do not always attend sufficiently to their duties of supervision. Another consequence of prohibited traffic with PW are crimes. Too often German women helped PW during an escape. Although it did not happen within the area controlled by the Kripoleitstelle BRESLAU, yet cases are known of high treason on behalf of PW. Relations between PW and their own compatriots should not be allowed as they would find help there in the first instance. The Gestapo knows that illegal organisations exist in all PW Camps, comprising all enemy powers under Soviet leadership. Many attempts are made at self-mutilation or simulating illness, in order to escape from working. It appears important to introduce S.Ps in PW Camps, in order to detect traces of such forbidden activities. Collaboration in this sphere between armed forces and Gestapo proved to be extremely fruitful.

During the discussion, Maj HEUNEMOERDER reads a list of questions, which, however had almost all been touched upon previously, or, alternatively, had to be considered in a smaller meeting. Oberst v. LINDEINER draws attention to the fact that the PW of PW Camp 3 SAGAN hardly ever go outside the Camp, therefore the principal danger is removed. Strict discretion when dealing with PW, when talking to them or among one another in the presence of PW, is of utmost importance and must be impressed on the German camp staff repeatedly. Another difficulty in PW Camps is the problem of how to keep foreign workers away.

In his concluding words, Oberst v. LINDEINER thanks the speakers who spoke today. He underlines once more that we, too, desire a friendly collaboration. 'To understand one another is everything.' Similar meetings, of which this is the first, are to be repeated from time to time in other camps. Expressing the hope that all participants will keep the meeting in good memory, Oberst v. LINDEINER concludes the meeting.

3. PARTICIPANTS AT THE MEETING OF SECURITY OFFICERS FROM 15-17 MAR 1944

Oberst	von FLOTOW	MAERISCHTRUBAU
Major	Dr. HUENEMOERDER	Lw In 17
Major	PESCHEL	HEYDEKRUG
Major	Dr. KLUGE	BELARIA
Hptm	Dr. KOEHLER	Ast VIII
Hptm	MALSBENDEN	LITZMANNSSTADT
Hptm	SALEWSKI	O.K.W.
O'Lt	HOELLERER	WOLFEN
O'Lt	Dr. SCHMID	DULAG LUFT
Hptm	von MILLER	BARTH (only on 15 March)
Kriminalrat	BRUENNER	Kripoleitstelle BRESLAU
Kriminalkommisser	LAEUFER	Gestapo BRESLAU
Oberst	von LINDEINER	SAGAN
Oberstleutnant	CORDES	SAGAN
Major	JACOB	SAGAN
Major	KLAMT	SAGAN

Major Dr.	SIMOLEIT	SAGAN
Major	STEHLE	SAGAN
Major	WIDMANN	SAGAN
Hptm	BAUMAN	SAGAN
Hptm	BROILI	SAGAN
Hptm	FEHMER	SAGAN
Hptm	SEIFERT	SAGAN L.S. (Guard Coy)
O'Lt	GRALKA	SAGAN
O'Lt	von MASSOW	SAGAN
O'Lt	ROSKE	SAGAN
O'Lt	WELLENSIEK	SAGAN
O'Arst	Dr. LECHTKEN	SAGAN
O'Feldw	DIEKERS	SAGAN L.S.
O'Feldw	HATTWIG	SAGAN L.S.
O'Feldw	KRACHT	SAGAN
O'Feldw	ROELKE	SAGAN L.S.
O'Feldw	WICHMANN	SAGAN
Feldw	ILLING	SAGAN L.S.
Feldw	MEYER	SAGAN L.W.
Uffz	SCHREIBER I	SAGAN

4. Notes by Oberst von LINDEINER-WILDAU for his speech and notes taken during the meeting.

1. Internal Propaganda is desired.
2. Internal Propaganda is possible.
3. Internal Propaganda is permitted.
4. How can Propaganda be conducted?

To start with:

> The difference between Air-force PW Camps and other PW Camps, which was specially referred to this morning, is most noticeable in Propaganda matters. The difference

in _____ accentuated in Officer Camps as against OR Camps. Here are 5000 of the most intelligent Officers, therefore, other ways and methods from Camps of Russians, Serbs, French.

Propaganda through printed matter. Always distrust. Nobody likes to hear those deeds belittled that one has learnt during one's youth as great achiever.

Sepoy revolt.

Egypt.

If I start to tell the Britisher your Government is a crooked lot of Jewish Criminals, I immediately antagonize him. To start with, I have to approach him in a different manner.

Pamphlet: How odd of God.

Private letters from SCHULLING to BEAUTMANN. Of his letter of 1 Feb 44. It would have been correct to let me know.

Propaganda methods: Newspapers, pamphlets, leaflets, posters, etc. German lessons. Talks about Germany.

The description: "Terror-flyers', murderers, gangsters.

On 29 Feb. SCHILLING sent a letter, circumventing this postal censorship, from Lt. Col. KLOCKO through Uffz MEIER to Lt. Col. STEVENSON.

List of newspaper ordered for here.

Which pamphlets reach us at present?

Films.

Theater and musical shows.

Loudspeakers in the British parts of the Camps.

British transmissions, Blue network (CALAIS, BREMEN, LUXEMBOURG, FRIESLAND)

1415-1445 hrs and 1830-1845 hrs. Switch off German transmitters during those times.

Small film projects.

Klangfilm type No. 20-151

Ufa small film distributors and O.K.W.

Normal film 'Bringing up Baby' shown on own projector.

Shall We Dance. [film]

Officers do not mind overcrowding and other personal discomforts so much; they are hurt by matters touching their honour such as refusal to bury with full military honors or legal punishments.

MURDER OF 50 R.A.F. OFFICERS

ESCAPERS FROM STALAG LUFT 3

(Mar/Apr 1944)

This report should be read in conjunction with reports:

PWIS(H)/LDC/774 and PWIS/(H)/LDC/777).

Further interrogation of PW LD 7 5 7 –

Oberst Fried. W. von LINDEINER-WILDAU

Comd Stalag Luft 3. May 42 – Mar 1944.

PREAMBLE:

This PW has now recovered from the shock of finding himself in a PW Camp and his statements are more comprehensive and apparently reliable.

He is in the right frame of mind now to face up to Oberregierungarat WIELEN or any other PW connected with this case.

10 May 42	Oberst v. LINDEINER took over the position of Commandant of Stalag Luft 3 from Oberst STEPHANI. At this time Maj PESCHEL was Abwehr officer No. 1 and Hptm BROILI was Abwehr officer No. 2
Jun 43	Maj. PESCHEL was transferred as Abwehr officer to the new camp for R.A.F. Sergeants at HEYDEKRUG. BROILI was then made Abwehr officer No. 1 at Stalag Luft 3.

The camp at Stalag Luft 3 was for Abwehr purposes divided into 5 sections, in each of which there were 4 or 5 O.Rs allocated for detail duty, making BROILI'S staff directly under his control a total of about 20 O.Rs. BROILI should have had 2 other officers on his staff, but because of the difficult manpower situation at this time he was alone. BROILI reported to his superiors through the Commandant, who exercised a certain amount of censorship over his (BROILI's) comments.

The organization of the chain of control is given in Appendix 'A', attached hereto. This shows that the immediate Chief of the Commandant was the O.C. of the Luft Inspektion and the Chief of the Abwehr Service at the Camp was the O.C. Abwehr in BRESLAU, Oberst WEISE. At no time was the camp security staff or the Commandant in contact with the Gestapo.

Summer 43　　In the summer of 1943, following the period of insecurity caused by the frequent attempts to escape and the successes of escapers, the Comd was instructed to contact Kriminalrat BRUNNER in BRESLAU on matters of security.

BROILI's Monthly report on parcel inspection and escape attempts continued to be sent regularly to Abwehr Wehrkreis Kommando VIII, who were responsible for passing on these reports to Major SALEWSKI at Abwehr III.

Nov. 43	In Nov 43 Oberregierungarat WIELEN, accompanied by Kriminalrat BRUNNER and 10-12 security police officials, carried out a special inspection of Stalag Luft 3 without obtaining any effective results.
Feb 44	In Feb 44, Oberst v. LINDEINER wrote to BRUNNER, asking for advice on his difficulties in the matter of the camp security and also asked BRUNNER to visit the camp and carry out a special inspection. BRUNNER visited the camp, talked with BROILI and then left. He did not carry out the special inspection requested by v. LINDEINER.
Mar 44	In Mar 44 v. LINDEINER presided at an Abwehr officers' meeting. A translation of the transactions of this meeting is published in report: PWIS(H)/LDC/777.
24/25 Mar 44	On Mar 24/25 Mar the expected outbreak took place in foul weather and at 0420 hrs)
24 Mar 44	Oberst v. LINDEINER was informed by Hptm BROILI that the breakout had taken place and that the adjoining railway station had been warned. Oberst v. LINDEINER immediately inspected the camp and found that the remainder of the escape party was in hut No. 104, and ordered a count (roll-call) to establish who was missing.

Meantime the report of the outbreak was being telephoned to the 42 points which had to be warned:

Luft Gau Kdo III
Luft Inspektion XVII
Abwehrstelle VIII BRESLAU
Kripoleitstelle BRESLAU

                    All Flieger Horste
                    All neighbouring railway stations
                    All near police stations

0800 hrs   Oberst v. LINDEINER reported personally by phone to Luft Inspektion SVII and requested that the normal legal proceedings against him following the break-out should be immediately instituted.

1330 hrs   Oberst WAELDE of Luft Inspektion SVII arrived at the camp and made investigations.

1400 hrs   From Kripoleitstelle BRESLAU there arrived :

                    Kriminalrat BRUNNER
                    Dr. ABSALON
                    Kriminalsekretaer SCHOLZ
                    Kriminalsekretaer HAENAL

                    Oberst v. LINDEINER did not see anyone of this party. BRUNNER returned to BRESLAU that evening, the others remained the night at the camp.

1730 hrs   Obstlt MUELLER, from the special security section of the Kriegsgefangenenwesen arrived at the camp to study the method of the escape plan. WAELDE's report went to Field Marshall GOERING; the report produced by MUELLER was sent to his General and it would then be passed on direct to HITLER.

26 Mar 44   WAELDE and MUELLER left the camp before mid-day.

1200 hrs   Oberst v. LINDEINER was called to appear before Oberst DANNEMEYER, a Major and Kriegsgerichtsrat Dr. GARBE, all from Luft Gau Kdo III, when he was ordered to consider himself under arrest and await examination.

10 May 44   Oberst v. LINDEINER remained in his quarters at Stalag Luft 3 (2 rooms) and on 10 May 44 proceeded to his wife's home in JESCHKENDORF near SAGAN. During the period 26 Mar – 10 May 44, Dr. ABSALON called twice to obtain from v. LINDEINER information to prepare his prosecution.

GESTAPO:

During the period v. LINDEINER was at Stalag Luft 3 members of the Gestapo only once visited the camp and this was only in connection with a suspected case of insecurity at the camp among the German staff. The origin of this trouble were letters found on a woman in VIENNA from Stalag Luft 3, which had not passed through the censorship. Those letters, parcels and money had been sent by the woman's husband, PW RADAMICE. Gestapo personnel came to investigate the case, which was dropped when it was found that the PW had permission to send his wife letters, parcels, and money from the camp.

Prior to the mass escape of 24/25 Mar 44, about 100 planned escapes were known and had been laid on by PW and about 200 PW had left the camp. Up to then, the drill had been that when PW were recaptured the holding unit phoned the Comd for an escort which brought the escapers back to Stalag Luft 3 without fail. Oberst v. LINDEINER insists that he knew that the Kripo was at his disposal to assist in camp security duties and that he could call on them at any time. He did not call them in until he felt it polite so to do in order to save his own position.

He is positive that at no time did he have connections with Stapo elements and knows nothing about local agents of this force. Curiously enough, when discussing the crimes, he automatically uses the terms 'Gestapo' or 'Stapo' forces as those responsible. When questioned and asked to explain, he responds with reference to Kripo as the agent although Gestapo may have provided the killers.

LINDEINER now adds Kriminalrat BRUNNER to the list of senior officials in the Kripo who can supply positive information as to who killed the R.A.F. officers. He insists also that although some may have been killed in other centres, WIELEN must have been informed of the circumstances of their destruction.

London District Cage
18 Aug. 45

Chapter 5

Goering Testimony Regarding Great Escape and von Lindeiner

Hermann Goering
Courtesy USAFA McDermott
Library, Stalag Luft III Collections

When Reichsmarshall Hermann Goering, former head of the German Luftwaffe, was prosecuted at the War Crimes Trials in Nurenberg, Germany, from November 20th, 1945 to October 1st, 1946, he offered testimony, which included brief references to von Lindeiner, and exonerated him from any responsibility for the murders of the fifty British prisoners of war murdered after the Great Escape.

Mug shot of Hermann Goering
Courtesy USAFA McDermott Library,
Stalag Luft III Collections

Excerpts of the Testimony of Hermann Goering

[Testimony on 3/20/46]

SIR DAVID MAXWELL-FYFE (British prosecutor): I want to ask you first some questions about the matter of the British Air Force officers who escaped from Stalag Luft III. Do you remember that you said in giving your evidence that you knew this incident very completely and very minutely? Do you remember saying that?

GOERING: No-that I had received accurate knowledge; not that I had accurate knowledge-but that I received it.

SIR DAVID MAXWELL-FYFE: Let me quote your own words, as they were taken down, "I know this incident very completely, very minutely, but it came to my attention, unfortunately, at a later period of time." That is what you said the other day, is that right?

GOERING: Yes, that is what I meant; that I know about the incident exactly, but only heard of it 2 days later.

SIR DAVID MAXWELL-FYFE: You told the Tribunal that you were on leave at this time, in the last period of 3/1944, is that right?

GOERING: Yes, as far as I remember I was on leave in March until a few days before Easter.

SIR DAVID MAXWELL-FYFE: And you said, "As I can prove." I want you to tell the Tribunal the dates of your leave.

GOERING: I say again, that this refers to the whole of March--I remember it well--and for proof I would like to mention the people who were with me on this leave.

From Commandant to Captive

SIR DAVID MAXWELL-FYFE: What I want to know is, when you were on leave.

GOERING: Here, in the vicinity of Nuremberg.

SIR DAVID MAXWELL-FYFE: So you were within easy reach of the telephone from the Air Ministry or, indeed, from Breslau if you were wanted?

GOERING: I would have been easily accessible by phone if someone wanted to communicate with me.

SIR DAVID MAXWELL-FYFE: I want you to help me with regard to one or two other dates of which you have spoken. You say: "I heard 1 or 2 days later about this escape." Do you understand, Witness, that it is about the escape I am asking you, not about the shooting, for the moment; I want to make it quite clear.

GOERING: It is clear to me.

SIR DAVID MAXWELL-FYFE: Did you mean by that, that you heard about the actual escape 1 or 2 days after it happened?

GOERING: Yes

SIR DAVID MAXWELL-FYFE: Did you hear about it from the office of your adjutant or from your director of operations?

GOERING: I always heard these things through my adjutant. Several other escapes had preceded this one.

SIR DAVID MAXWELL-FYFE: Yes, that's right. There had been a number of escapes from this camp.

GOERING: I cannot tell you exactly whether they were from this camp. Shortly before several big escapes had taken place which I always heard of through the office of my adjutant.

SIR DAVID MAXWELL-FYFE: I want you to tell the Tribunal another date: You say that on your return from leave your chief of staff made a communication to you. Who was your chief of staff?

GOERING: General Korten was chief of staff at that time.

SIR DAVID MAXWELL-FYFE: Can you tell us the date at which he made this communication to you?

GOERING: No, I cannot tell you that exactly. I believe I discussed his incident with my chief of staff later, telling him what I had already heard about it from other sources.

SIR DAVID MAXWELL-FYFE: Who was the first to tell you about it? Was it your chief of staff who told you about the shootings? Do you mean that someone else had told you about the shooting?

GOERING: I cannot say exactly now whether I heard about the shooting from the chief of staff, or from other sources. But in any event I discussed this with the chief of staff.

SIR DAVID MAXWELL-FYFE: What was the date that you talked about it with your chief of staff?

GOERING: I cannot tell you the date exactly from memory, but it must have been around Easter.

SIR DAVID MAXWELL-FYFE: That would be just about the end of March, wouldn't it?

GOERING: No. It might have been at the beginning of April, the first half of April.

SIR DAVID MAXWELL-FYFE: And then you had an interview with Himmler, you have told us?

GOERING: Yes, I talked with Himmler about this.

SIR DAVID MAXWELL-FYFE: Can you fix that?

GOERING: Of course I cannot establish this date with certainty. I saw Himmler, and, at the first opportunity after I had heard about this incident, spoke to him about it.

SIR DAVID MAXWELL-FYFE: So that you can't fix the date in relation to your coming back from leave, or the interview with your chief of staff, or any other date, or Easter?

GOERING: Without any documents it is, as I said, impossible for me today to fix the date. I can only mention the approximate period of time; and that I have done.

SIR DAVID MAXWELL-FYFE: You said the other day that you could prove when you were on leave. Am I to take it that you haven't taken the trouble to look up what your leave dates were?

GOERING: I have already said the 28th or the 29th of March. I cannot tell you. For proof of that perhaps can fix this date more definitely. I know only that I was there in March.

SIR DAVID MAXWELL-FYFE: Witness, will it be perfectly fair to you if I take the latest of your dates, the 29th of March, to work on?

GOERING: It would be more expedient if you would tell me when Easter was that year, because I do not recall it. Then it will be easier for me to specify the dates, because I know that a few days before Easter I returned to Berchtesgaden in order to pass these holidays with my family.

SIR DAVID MAXWELL-FYFE: A few days before Easter you went back to Berchtesgaden?

GOERING: Yes.

SIR DAVID MAXWELL-FYFE: So you had come back on leave some day before that. Before you went to Berchtesgaden you had come back from your March leave?

GOERING: Berchtesgaden was then at the same time the headquarters of the Fuehrer. I returned from my leave to Berchtesgaden and with my return my leave ended, because I returned to duty. The return to Berchtesgaden was identical with the termination of my leave.

SIR DAVID MAXWELL-FYFE: Well, I can't give you Easter offhand, but I happen to remember Whitsuntide was the 28th of May, so that Easter would be early, somewhere about the 5th of April. So that your leave would finish somewhere about the end of March, maybe the 26th or the 29th; that is right, isn't it?

Now, these shootings of these officers went on from the 25th of March to the 13th of April; do you know that?

GOERING: I do not know that exactly.

SIR DAVID MAXWELL-FYFE: You may take that from me because there is an official report of the shooting, and I want to be quite fair with you. Only 49 of these officers were shot on the 6th of April, as far as we can be sure, and one was shot either on the 13th of April or later. But the critical period is the end of March, and we may take it that you were back from leave by about the 29th of March.

I just want you to tell the Tribunal this was a matter of great importance, wasn't it? Considered a matter of great importance?

GOERING: It was a very important matter.

SIR DAVID MAXWELL-FYFE: General Milch--I beg pardon--Field Marshal Milch has said that it was a matter which would require the highest authority, and I think you have said that you know it was Hitler's decision that these officers should be shot Is that so?

GOERING: The question did not come through clearly.

SIR DAVID MAXWELL-FYFE: It was Hitler's decision that these officers should be shot?

GOERING: That is correct; and I was later notified that it was Hitler's decree.

SIR DAVID MAXWELL-FYFE: I want you just to remember one other thing, that immediately it was published, the British Foreign Secretary, Mr. Eden, at once said that Great Britain would demand justice of the perpetrators of these murders--do you remember that?

GOERING: I cannot remember the speech to the House of Commons given by Eden. I myself do not know the substance of this speech even today. I just heard that he spoke in Parliament about this incident.

SIR DAVID MAXWELL-FYFE: I want you to tell the Tribunal just who the persons in your ministry involved were. I will tell you; I think it would be shorter in the end. If you disagree you can correct me.

The commandant of Stalag Luft III was Oberst von Lindeiner of your service, was he not?

GOERING: That is quite possible. I did not know the names of all these commandants. There was a court martial against him and that was because the escape was possible. He was not connected with the shootings.

SIR DAVID MAXWELL-FYFE: No, but he was commandant of the camp, and I suppose you had to review and confirm the proceedings of the Zentralluftwaffengericht which convicted him and sentenced him to a year's imprisonment for neglect of duty. That would come to you, wouldn't it? Wouldn't that come to you for review?

GOERING: No, only if larger penalties were involved. One year imprisonment would not come to my attention. But I know, and I would like to certify, that court proceedings were taken against him for neglect of duty at the time of the escape.

SIR DAVID MAXWELL-FYFE: In 5/1943, Inspectorate Number 17 had been interposed between the Luftwaffe and the Prisoners of War Organization of the OKW, the Kriegsgefangenenwesen; do you remember that?

GOERING: I do not know the details about inspection nor how closely it concerned the Prisoners of War Organization of the OKW, or how it was otherwise.

SIR DAVID MAXWELL-FYFE: I want to remind you of who your own officers were. You understand, Witness, that your own officers are involved in this matter. I want to remind you who they were.

Was the head of Inspectorate 17 Major General Grosch of the Luftwaffe?

GOERING: Major General Grosch is of the Luftwaffe.

SIR DAVID MAXWELL-FYFE: You told the Tribunal the other day--I am quoting your own words--that you knew from information, you knew this incident very completely and very minutely. You are now telling the Tribunal you don't know whether Major General Grosch was head of Inspectorate Number 17 of the Luftwaffe.

GOERING: That is irrelevant. I told the High Tribunal that I heard an accurate account of the incident of the shooting of these airmen, but that has no connection with General Grosch and his inspectorate, for he did not participate in the shooting.

SIR DAVID MAXWELL-FYFE: I will show you that connection in one minute if you will just answer my questions. Was Grosch's second in command Oberst Welder; do you remember that?

GOERING: I do not know the particulars of the organization for inspection of prisoner-of-war camps, nor the leaders, nor what positions they held. At least not by heart. I would like to emphasize again, so that there will be no confusion, that when I said I knew about this matter, I mean that I knew how the order was issued and that the people were shot, that I came to know all about this but not as far as this was related to inspections, possibilities of flight, et cetera.

SIR DAVID MAXWELL-FYFE: And did General Grosch, as head of Inspectorate 17, have to report to General Forster, your director of operations at the Luftwaffe Ministerium?

GOERING: That I cannot tell you without having the diagram of the subordinate posts before me. General Forster was, I believe at that time, head of the Luftwehr, or a similar designation, in the ministry. I concerned myself less with these matters, because they were not directly of a tactical, strategic, or of an armament nature. But it is quite possible and certain that he belonged to this department.

SIR DAVID MAXWELL-FYFE: I put it to you quite shortly, and if you don't know I will leave it for the moment. Did you know Major General Von Graevenitz was head of the Defendant Keitel's department, the Kriegsgefangenenwesen, that dealt with prisoners of war?

GOERING: I first heard about General Graevenitz here for this department did not directly concern me. I could not know all of these military subordinate commanders in their hundreds and thousands of departments.

SIR DAVID MAXWELL-FYFE: So I take it that you did not know Colonel, now General Westhoff, of the department under Von Graevenitz?

GOERING: Westhoff I never saw at all, and he did not belong to the Luftwaffe.

SIR DAVID MAXWELL-FYFE: I am not suggesting that Von Graevenitz and Westhoff belonged to the Luftwaffe. I wanted to make it clear that I was suggesting they belonged to General Keitel's organization.

GOERING: I did not know either; and I did not know what posts they occupied.

SIR DAVID MAXWELL-FYFE: Up to that time you still had a considerable influence in the Reich, didn't you?

GOERING: At this time no longer. This no longer concerns 1944.

SIR DAVID MAXWELL-FYFE: But you were still head of the Luftwaffe and head of the Air Ministry, weren't you?

GOERING: Yes, I was.

SIR DAVID MAXWELL-FYFE: And you had, as head of the Luftwaffe and head of the Air Ministry, been responsible for six prisoner-of-war camps for the whole of the war up to that time, hadn't you?

GOERING: How many prisoner-of-war camps I do not know. But of course I bear the responsibility for those which belonged to my ministry.

SIR DAVID MAXWELL-FYFE: To the Air Force?

GOERING: Yes, those which were subordinate to the Air Force.

SIR DAVID MAXWELL-FYFE: You knew about the general plan for treatment of prisoners of war, which we have had in evidence as the "Aktion Kugel" plan, didn't you?

GOERING: No. I knew nothing of this action. I was not advised of it.

SIR DAVID MAXWELL-FYFE: You were never advised of Aktion Kugel? [a secret decree (*Geheimbefehl*) issued by Nazi Germany in March 1944 stating that escaped Allied POWs, especially officers and senior non-commissioned officers, should be handed over to the Sicherheitsdienst who should execute them in concentration camp Mauthausen.]

GOERING: I first heard of Aktion Kugel here; saw the document and heard the expression for the first time. Moreover no officer of the Luftwaffe ever informed me of such a thing; and I do not believe that a single officer was ever taken away from the Luftwaffe camps. A report to this effect was never presented to me, in any case.

SIR DAVID MAXWELL-FYFE: You know what Aktion Kugel was: That escaped officers and noncommissioned officers, other than British and American, were to be handed over to the police and taken to Mauthausen, where they were shot by the device if having a gun concealed in the measuring equipment when they thought they were getting their prison clothes. You know what "Aktion Kugel" is, don't you?

GOERING: I heard of it here.

SIR DAVID MAXWELL-FYFE: Are you telling the Tribunal that you did not know that escaped prisoners of war who were picked up by the police were retained by the police and taken to Mauthausen?

GOERING: No, I did not know that. On the contrary, various prisoners who escaped from my camps were caught again by the police; and they were all brought back to the camps; this was the first case where this to some extent did not take place.

SIR DAVID MAXWELL-FYFE: But didn't you know that Colonel Welder, as second in command of your ministry's inspectorate issued a written order a month before this, in 2/1944, that prisoners of war picked up by the Luftwaffe should be delivered back to their camp, and prisoners of war picked up by the police should be held by them and no longer counted as being under the protection of the Luftwaffe; didn't you know that?

GOERING: No. Please summon this colonel to testify if he ever made a report of that nature to me, or addressed such a letter to me.

SIR DAVID MAXWELL-FYFE: Well, of course, I cannot tell whether your ministry was well run or not. But he certainly issued the order, because he says so himself.

GOERING: Then he must say from whom he received this order.

SIR DAVID MAXWELL-FYFE: I see. Well, he says that he issued this order, and you know as well as I do that prisoners of war is a thing that you have got to be careful about, because you have got a protecting power that investigates any complaint; and you never denounced the Convention and you had the protecting power in these matters all through the war, had you not? That is right, isn't it?

GOERING: That is correct, but I take the liberty to ask who gave him this order, whether he received this order from me.

SIR DAVID MAXWELL-FYFE: Well, he would not get it direct from you. I do not think you had ever met him, had you? He would get it from Lieutenant General Grosch, wouldn't he?

GOERING: Then Grosch should say whether he received such an order from me. I never gave such an order.

SIR DAVID MAXWELL-FYFE: I see. So you say that you had never heard--this was 3 1/2 years after the beginning of the war and you had never heard that any escaped prisoners of war were to be handed over to the police. Is that what you ask the Tribunal to believe?

GOERING: To any offenses or police, I believe gave any order the extent that escaped prisoners of war committed crimes, they were of course turned over to the [word omitted]. But I wish to testify before the Court that I never said that they should be handed over to the police or sent to concentration camps merely because they had attempted to break out or escape, nor did I ever know that such measures, were taken.

SIR DAVID MAXWELL-FYFE: This is my last question: I want to make it quite clear, Witness, that I am referring to those who had escaped, who had got away from the confines of the camp and were recaptured by the police. Didn't you know that they were handed over to the police?

GOERING: No. Only if they had committed crimes while fleeing, such as murder and so on. Such things occurred.

[Testimony on 3/21/46]

Morning Session

SIR DAVID MAXWELL-FYFE: Witness, do you remember telling me last night that the only prisoners of war handed over to the police were those guilty of crimes or misdemeanors?

GOERING: I did not express myself that way. I said if the police apprehended prisoners of war, those who had committed a crime during the escape, as far as I know, [they] were detained by the police and were not returned to the camp. To what extent the police kept prisoners of war, without returning them to a camp I was able to gather from interrogations and explanations here.

SIR DAVID MAXWELL-FYFE: Would you look at Document D-569? Would you look first at the top left-hand corner, which shows that it is a document published by the Oberkommando der Wehrmacht?

GOERING: The document which I have before me has the following heading at the top left-hand corner: "The Reichsfuehrer SS," and the subheading: "Inspector of Concentration Camps."

SIR DAVID MAXWELL-FYFE: It is a document dated the 11/22/1941. Have you got it?

GOERING: Yes, I have it now.

SIR DAVID MAXWELL-FYFE: Now, look at the left-hand bottom corner, as to distribution. The second person to whom it is distributed is the Air Ministry and Commander-in-Chief of the Air Force on 11/22/1941. That would be you.

GOERING: That's correct. I would like to make the following statement in connection with this...

SIR DAVID MAXWELL-FYFE: Just for a moment. I would like you to appreciate the document and then make your statement upon it. I shall not stop you. I want you to look at the third sentence in Paragraph 1. This deals with Soviet prisoners of war, you understand. The third sentence says: "If escaped Soviet prisoners of war are returned to the camp in accordance with this order, they have to be handed over to the nearest post of the Secret State Police, in any case."

And then Paragraph 2 deals with the special position--if they commit crimes, owing to the fact that: "...at present these misdemeanors on the part of Soviet prisoners of war are particularly frequent, due most likely to living conditions still being somewhat unsettled, the following temporary regulations come into force. They may be amended later. If a Soviet prisoner of war commits any other punishable offense, then the commandant of the camp must hand the guilty man over to the head of the Security Police."

Do I understand this document to say that a man who escapes will be handed over to the Security Police? You understand this document says a man who escapes will be handed over to the Secret police, a man who commits a crime, as you mentioned, will be handed over to the Security Police. Wasn't that the condition obtained from 1941 up to the date we are dealing with in 3/1944?

GOERING: I would like to read the few preceding paragraphs [so] that no sentences are separated from their context.

SIR DAVID MAXWELL-FYFE: My Lord, while the witness is reading the document, might I go over the technical matter of the arrangement of exhibits? When I cross-examined Field Marshal Slecking I put in three documents, UK-66, which becomes Exhibit 274, D-39, which becomes GB-275; TC-91, which becomes GB-276; This document will become GB-277. (Turning to the witness) Have you had an opportunity of reading it, Witness?

GOERING: Yes, I have.

SIR DAVID MAXWELL-FYFE: Then I am right, am I not, that Soviet prisoners of war who escaped were to be, after their return to the camp, handed over to the Secret State Police. If they committed a crime, they were to be handed over to the Security Police, isn't that right?

GOERING: Not exactly correct. I would like to point to the third sentence in the first paragraph. There it says, "If a prisoner-of-war is in the vicinity, then the man who is recaptured is to be transported there."

SIR DAVID MAXWELL-FYFE: But read the next sentence, "If a Soviet prisoner of war is returned to the camp"--that is in accordance with this order which you have just read--"he has to be handed to the nearest service station of the Secret State Police." Your own sentence.

GOERING: Yes, but the second paragraph which follows gives an explanation of frequent criminal acts of Soviet prisoners of war, et cetera committed at that time. You read that yourself; that is not connected with this Paragraph Number 1. But this order was given by itself and it was distributed to the Army, the Air Force, and the Navy. And I would like to give the explanation of its distribution. In this war there were not only hundreds, but thousands of current orders which were issued by superiors to subordinate officers and were transmitted to various departments. That does not mean that each of these thousands of orders was submitted to the Commander-in-Chief; only the most decisive and most important were shown to him. The others went from department to department. Thus it is, that this order from the Chief of the High Command was signed by a subordinate department and not by the Chief of the High Command himself.

SIR DAVID MAXWELL-FYFE: This order would be dealt with by your prisoner-of-war department in your ministry, wouldn't it?

GOERING: This department, according to the procedure adopted for these orders, received the order, but no other department received it.

SIR DAVID MAXWELL-FYFE: I think the answer to my question must be "yes." It would be dealt with by the prisoner-of-war department-- your ministry. Isn't that so?

GOERING: I would say yes.

SIR DAVID MAXWELL-FYFE: It is quicker, you see, if you say "yes" in the beginning; do you understand?

GOERING: No; it depends upon whether I personally have read the order or not, and I will then determine as to my responsibility.

SIR DAVID MAXWELL-FYFE: Well now, the escape...

THE PRESIDENT: You were not asked about responsibility; you were asked whether it would be dealt with by your prisoner-of-war department.

SIR DAVID MAXWELL-FYFE: Now, the escape about which I am asking you took place on the night of the 24th to the 25th of March. I want you to have that date in mind. The decision to murder these young officers must have been taken very quickly, because the first murder which actually took place was on the 26th of March. Do you agree with that? It must have been taken quickly?

GOERING: I assume that this order, as I was informed later, was given immediately, but it had no connection with this document.

SIR DAVID MAXWELL-FYFE: No, no; we are finished with that document; we are going into the murder of these young men. The Grossfahndung--a general hue and cry, I think, would be the British translation--was also issued at once in order that these men should be arrested; isn't that so?

GOERING: That is correct. Whenever there was an escape, and such a large number of prisoners escaped, automatically in the whole Reich, a hue and cry was raised, that is, all authorities had to be on the lookout to recapture the prisoners.

SIR DAVID MAXWELL-FYFE: So that in order to give this order to murder these men, and for the Grossfahndung, there must have been a meeting of Hitler, at any rate with Himmler or Kaltenbrunner, in order that that order would be put into effect; isn't that so?

GOERING: That is correct. According to what I heard, Himmler was the first to report this escape to the Fuehrer.

SIR DAVID MAXWELL-FYFE: Now, General Westhoff, who was in Defendant Keitel's Kriegsgefangenenwesen, in his prisoner-of-war set-up, says this, that "On a date, which I think was the 26th, Keitel said to him, 'This morning Goering reproached me in the presence of Himmler for having let some more prisoners of war escape. It was unheard of.'"

Do you say that General Westhoff is wrong?

GOERING: Yes. This is not in accordance with the facts. General Westhoff is referring to a statement of Field Marshal Keitel. This utterance in itself is illogical, for I could not accuse Keitel because he would not draw my attention to it, as the guarding was his responsibility and not mine.

SIR DAVID MAXWELL-FYFE: One of the Defendant Keitel's officers dealing with this matter was a general inspector, General Rottich. I do not know if you know him.

GOERING: No.

SIR DAVID MAXWELL-FYFE: Well, General Westhoff, as one could understand, is very anxious to assure everyone that his senior officer had nothing to do with it, and he goes on to say this about General Rottich:

"He was completely excluded from it by the fact that these matters were taken out of his hands. Apparently at that conference with the Fuehrer in the morning, that is to say, the conference between Himmler, Field Marshal Keitel, and Goering, which took place in the Fuehrer's presence, the Fuehrer himself always took a hand in these affairs when officers escaped."

You say that is wrong? You were at no such conference?

GOERING: I was not present at this conference, neither was General Westhoff; he is giving a purely subjective view, not the facts of the case.

SIR DAVID MAXWELL-FYFE: So that we find that--you think that--Westhoff is wrong? You see, Westhoff, he was a colonel at this time, I think, and now he finishes as a major general, and he asks that the senior officers be asked about it; he says this: "It should be possible to find out that Himmler made the suggestion to the Fuehrer--to find that out from Goering who was present at the conference." Again and again Westhoff, who after all is a comparatively junior officer, is saying that the truth about this matter can be discovered from his seniors. You say that it cannot.

GOERING: I would not say that. I would like just to say that General Westhoff was never present for even a moment, therefore he cannot say, "I know or I saw that Reichmarshall Goering was present." He is assuming it is so, or he may have heard it.

SIR DAVID MAXWELL-FYFE: What he says is, you know, that Keitel blamed him, as I have read to you, that Keitel went on to say to him at General Von Graevenitz's, "Gentlemen, the escapes must stop. We must set an example. We shall take very severe measures. I am only telling you that, that the men who have escaped will be shot; probably the majority of them are dead already." You never heard anything of that?

GOERING: I was neither present at the Keitel-Westhoff-Graevenitz conversation nor at the Fuehrer-Himmler conversation. As far as I know, General Westhoff will be testifying here. Moreover, Field Marshal Keitel will be able to say whether I was there or not.

Chapter 6

Trial Transcripts - War Crimes Trials - Hamburg, Germany - 1947

For three days in August, 1947, Col. von Lindeiner, directed by the Allies as a witness to a Military Court held at No. 1 War Crimes Court at the Curio Haus in Hamburg, Germany, was examined and cross-examined during the proceedings against eighteen German nationals being tried for their roles in the death of fifty Stalag Luft III POWs murdered after the Great Escape. War crimes prosecutors felt his testimony was relevant to the trial of the charged Germans, some of whom were executed after findings of guilt.

PROCEEDINGS

of

MILITARY COURT

HELD AT

No. 1 WAR CRIMES COURT

CURIO HAUS, ROTHENBAUMCHAUSSEE, HAMBURG

on

MONDAY, 25TH AUGUST, 1947

TUESDAY, 26TH AUGUST, 1947

and

WEDNESDAY, 27TH AUGUST, 1947

upon the trial of

Max Ernst Friedrich Gustav WIELEN AND 17 others German

Nationals in the charge of 9S Group Royal Pioneer Corps

INDEX

		Page No.
FORTY-THIRD DAY (25 August 1947)		
Capt. F.M. Cornish – cross examination by		
	FRAU DR. OEHLERT continued	2
	Re-examined by COL. HALSE	10
	Questioned by the court	10
Lt. COL. A.P. SCOTLAND (recalled)		
	Questioned by the court	18
F.W. von LINDEINER	Sworn, examined by DR. ADLER	20
	Cross examined by DR. OESTMANN	24
	Cross examined by FRAU DR. OEHLERT	24
	Cross examined by COL. HALSE	25
	Re-examined by DR. ADLER	28
	Questioned by the court	29
FORTY-FOURTH DAY	(26 August 1947)	
	Closing address by DR. MEYER LABASTILLE	37
	Closing address by DR. JONAS	68
	Closing address by DR. MOTZ	75
	Closing address by DR. ROTH	97
	Closing address by DR. GRAENER	102
FORTY-FIFTH DAY	(27 August 1947)	
	Closing address by DR. OESTMANN	110
	Closing address von SALDERN	124
	Closing address by DR. LAPPENBERG	133
	Closing address by FRAU DR. OEHLERT	139

THE JUDGE ADVOCATE: Mr. Prosecutor, have we had all the witnesses you want to call?

COL. HALSE: Yes.

THE JUDGE ADVOCATE: Now, as far as I know, this is the only outstanding matter before we can go to the final addresses. Dr. Adler, what have you got to say about the camp commandant?

DR. ADLER: Col. Lindeiner, the former commandant of the Sagan camp is at present in Hamburg. I talked to him and I am of the belief that he would be able to help us in some points. I asked him to attend here for all eventualities. I have just made enquiries and I have been told he has not arrived yet. I presume that he will arrive in the course of this afternoon as I thought that this morning would have been used for the cross-examination of British officers. I would apply to the Court to allow me to call this witness even at this stage.

THE JUDGE ADVOCATE: Where is he at the moment?

DR. ADLER: If he is not in the building I do not know where he is. At any rate he told me that he would stay in Hamburg in case he was wanted for cross-examination.

THE JUDGE ADVOCATE: There is some question that he may be here. Will you clear that up first? Will you look at the man who is just coming into Court and tell us if that is the man you want? Is that the man?

DR. ADLER: Yes.

F.W. von LINDEINER is called in and, having been duly sworn, takes his stand in the witness box and is examined by DR. ADLER as follows:

Col. Lindeiner, since you are not known to the Court would you repeat your personal particulars to them, that is to say, your surname and your Christian name and your place and date of birth? A. Friedrich Wilhelm von Lindeiner, called von Wildau, born on 12th December 1880 at Platz.

THE JUDGE ADVOCATE: You can lead him on this. Let us get along quickly until we get something.

DR. ADLER: (To the witness) You were an active officer in the German Army or the German air force? A. I was re-called in July 1938. Before that I had retired.

Q. In other words you had already been an officer during the First World War? A. I had left the army in March 1919.

Q. And am I right if I say that later on you became the commandant of the prisoner-of-war camp at Sagan? A. On 5th May 1942.

Q. That was after you had been seriously injured? A. Not during this war, I was not injured – before that. I was wounded many times during the First World War.

Q. Were you the camp commandant of this camp during the time of the mass escape, that is to say, the 24th or 25th March? A. Yes.

Q. And, another question, do you know any amongst the accused sitting in the deck? A. Only Chief Inspector Wielen.

Q. Do you know him from his activities in Breslau when he was in charge of the Kripoleitstelle? A. In summer 1943 we, the camp commandants, received the order to contact the respective chiefs of the Gestapoleitstelle in order to discuss with them the technical preparation for the prevention of escapes from camps.

Q. Was the reason for this order the fact that a greater number of escapes from these prisoner-of-war camps had happened? A. I take it to be so. I think I am not mistaken if I say that at Sagan we had 362 escape attempts within two years.

Q. Is it correct that the construction of the tunnel towards the end of March 1944 was preceded by approximately a hundred other attempts, the tunneling in order to help prisoners to escape? A. A tunnel of dimensions large enough to bring about an escape, I think, the last one before this one was the fourth or the fifth but all together I think approximately 99 other tunnels, some of them larger, some of them smaller.

Q. Did Wielen take a personal interest in these escapes? Was he, for instance, ever in Sagan to have a look at these tunnels? A. After the order which I mentioned a moment ago according to which we were to contact the respective chiefs of the Kripoleitstelle, I saw Wielen in Breslau, and he thereupon visited my camp at Sagan to look at things on the spot.

THE INTERPRETER: I am sorry; I think I said "Gestapo" at one time; it should have been "Kripo".

THE JUDGE ADVOCATE: What we want to get right is whether the witness said the discussion was to be both with the Gestapo and the Kripo or only the Kripo, because we have all got rather confused notes on it.

THE WITNESS: I have occasionally also had to deal with the Gestapostellen but this had nothing to do with the prisoners-of-war but

From Commandant to Captive

with the repeated arrests of German personnel at the camp who had been accused of collaboration with the prisoners inside.

THE JUDGE ADVOCATE: That is all right; I think we have cleared up what we want.

DR. ADLER: (To the witness) You told us a moment ago that Wielen and some of his officials had visited your camp at Sagan. How do you remember this visit? Did Wielen show any incorrectness or spitefulness towards either the British officers inside the camp or your German officers during this visit? A. I can say that the attitude of the officials, in particular that of Dr. Wielen, was absolutely tactful.

Q. Did a conference take place with you during which it was discussed how one could either make such future escapes of prisoners more difficult or prevent them all together? A. I believe I can say that our experience with those escapes was far greater than that of the Kripo and that the Kripo repeatedly borrowed from us instruments which the prisoners used to break out as well as forged passports and things of that nature.

Q. Did Wielen suggest in any way that the punishment for those who tried to escape should become more severe? A. No, that was not his business, and I would not have accepted it either.

Q. Or did you rather have the impression that he approved and furthered your attitude towards the British prisoner officers? I believe that your attitude towards them was a very humane one. A. I think I may say that during the few times – I think it was only three times – I met Dr. Wielen during those nine months not a single thought was expressed to the effect that the prisoners should be treated in an inhuman way.

Q. Now, about this escape at the end of March, do you remember telling me that you said that Wielen came to your camp personally to have a look at the tunnel through which the prisoners had escaped after he had been informed about the mass escape? A. The escape through the tunnel was discovered at about 0400 hours in the morning. We were very busy that morning because representatives of the Air Ministry and the General Inspectorate arrived immediately on this morning. I saw from a distance that Dr. Wielen arrived approximately at about lunchtime on that day but I am certain to be able to believe that he left again during the latter part of the afternoon and that he did not return.

Q. Did you ever learn, either by your experience or from your officers, whether Wielen had any interest in this matter, any other interest in this matter, than merely a purely professional and technical one, namely, how it was at all possible that this escape could come about? A. No.

Q. Was a list of the escapees compiled on that day, in particular of those most active among them, the ringleaders, and was this list handed to the accused Wielen on that day? A. The names of the persons who had escaped could only be ascertained by lunchtime. On that day I was still the commandant, and I am convinced that Dr. Wielen could not have been given such a list without my knowledge.

Q. Can you tell us whether in the meantime, that is to say, from that moment until then, up to 29th March, a list was compiled in the camp of the officers who were to be shot? A. I myself was relieved of my post by the commission on the morning of the 26th and at first I was imprisoned, and I remained in imprisonment for a considerable period, but I can say that I was repeatedly visited by officers belonging to my staff, and I may say that the news of the shooting, of the death as it was called at the time, of those prisoner-of-war officers brought about in us an indescribable horror. The number of which I was informed – in the first instance it was only a number and no names – was 21 and at first we believed that it was some kind of a trick in order to deter the remaining prisoners from undertaking further escape attempts. I don't think that any officer would have allowed himself to be used in the compiling of a list of prisoners-of-war who were to be murdered.

Q. Did you hear later on that a selection among those officers who had escaped was carried out in April and that, as a result of this selection, some officers were sent to a special camp and not returned to Sagan? A. As far as I am informed about the regulations enforced this would be impossible because at that time the military authorities had no influence on the fate of these men.

Q. Apart from Wielen did you also have to deal with other representatives of the police – I am thinking of Brunner and Absalon? Did either of these two tell you that he had to take up duties at your place by direct order of the RSHA? A. I had heard that the second class inspector, Brunner, had been ordered directly by the RSHA to deal with the POW matter in the district of Lower Silesia. Our contact was limited to about two or three cases. After the escape, I did not hear his name mentioned anymore, and I assume that he probably too had paid for this escape either with his life or with a serious punishment.

Q. And did you know that Dr. Absalon was sent to the prisoner-of-war camp to carry out further investigations from the Kripoleitstelle at Breslau? A. On the evening or the late afternoon on the day of the escape, Dr. Absalon and one or two criminal secretaries, equivalent rank 2nd lieutenants, arrived at Sagan. They were, it was said, special representatives of the RSHA but mainly they were interested in my own person.

Q. You said that you were then arrested yourself and that proceedings were taken against you. Was that a court martial? A. Yes, a court martial.

Q. If a mass escape came off successfully, was it usually so that proceedings would be taken against the officer in charge or the officer commanding the camp? A. Yes.

Q. In your opinion, did Wielen have anything to do with the institution of these proceedings against you? A. I assumed that Wielen as well as Brunner – but Brunner rather more – had also disappeared as a consequence of those happenings.

Q. You said that Absalon took an interest in your person. Is it known to you that Absalon was also put at the disposal of the German Air Force court martial in order to establish who was guilty of this mass escape? A. He was present as a witness during my trial, but I have the feeling that everything in connection with the Sagan affair was in his hands in his capacity as the special representative of Himmler, the Reichsfuehrer of the SS.

Q. Did you yourself become aware of this so-called Sagan order, that is, the order emanating from superior authorities to the effect that a number of those British officers who had escaped from Sagan were to be shot? A. No, we knew no more than everybody else, namely, what we could gather from the radio and press.

Q. And did you also receive information to the effect that this order had come from Hitler? A. I cannot say anything from what I know from my official duties. We, that is to say, the elder and more senior officers, had only heard that Hitler had had one of his attacks of rage again on that day and had then given this order within a certain smaller circle.

Q. Do you believe that if an order emanated from Hitler that any official in Germany would have been in a position to resist such an order, and may I add was anybody in a position, anybody who had been detailed with the execution of such an order, was he in a position to evade carrying it out? A. During the latter part of the war, even criticisms of the Fuhrer were punished. I experienced such a case with a friend of mine. Failure to carry out a Fuehrer order would mean that the best thing for the person who had failed to carry out this order would be to shoot a bullet through his own head. In that case he would at least not be hung.

Q. Do you believe that an officer or an official could have excused his attitude and the fact that he resisted an order before a court by saying that in his opinion the order was immoral or that it offended against certain established laws? A. I discussed this point in 1943 with my senior officers, namely, the possibility that we could be given certain inhumane orders by way of reprisals, and I said that in the case of such orders I would take my own life.

Q. Could you tell us anything about the general situation in 1944? I mean in how far Himmler exercised complete control over the entire population and how far the possibility existed of getting out of it all together. A. No limits were imposed on Himmler.

Q. Apart from the fear of being placed in front of a court martial, did you also have to fear being made responsible for other authorities without being put in front of a court and to be prosecuted by them? A. Yes, I would like to differentiate in this case between the armed forces and their institutions. At that time, a member of the armed forces still enjoyed a certain measure of protection. I, for instance, was to be demobilized at the beginning of 1945. My military superiors cancelled this order because as a civilian in all probability I would have immediately disappeared in a working camp. For their persons, there existed, in my opinion – I did not experience it myself – plenty of opportunity or plenty of possibilities to disappear somewhere without further ado.

Q. With the last sentence, you meant that if Hitler wanted to Hitler could let any person disappear without the public knowing anything about it. A. We took it to be so. It did not happen to me, but I think it is certain.

Q. Do you know whether official circles of the SS and of the police reckoned, generally reckoned, with those possibilities or can you only tell us about the armed forces? A. No, the discipline – I could almost call it "the terror" – was much more severe in the Kripo and the Gestapo and in the SS because we could intervene there in a more indirect manner.

Q. On more final question. Later on you became a prisoner-of-war and as such you were taken to England? A. Yes.

Q. And were you there every interrogated about the affair which forms the subject of this court? A. The subject of the escape and the deaths of 50 POW officers was repeatedly dealt with at length.

DR. ADLER: I have put down several questions but I believe that they were all already discussed in the course of these proceedings. I am not going to ask any more questions now.

(At 1300 hours the Court adjourns until 1430 hours)

COL. HALSE: May the British witnesses be released now?

THE PRESIDENT: All right.

DR. MOTZ: Mrs. Schimmel asks for permission to be allowed to see her husband, Schimmel.

COL. HALSE: During the break?

THE PRESIDENT: Please.

THE JUDGE ADVOCATE: You had finished, I think you said, Dr. Adler, had not you?

DR. ADLER: Yes.

THE JUDGE ADVOCATE: Now do any counsel wish to cross examine?

Cross-Examined by DR. OESTMANN

Q. One question. Is it correct that at first the proceedings instituted against you were stopped but that they were taken up again by instigation of a liaison officer or liaison man belonging to the RSHA? A. That I cannot know. I only know that the official in charge of the investigations in my case, when I was interrogated about eleven weeks after the incident, applied for the proceedings to be stopped and that all files were forwarded to the Judge Advocate's department of the Wehrmacht.

Q. And they took the proceedings up again in their own initiative and in their own right? A. I assumed that because a special field court martial was detailed to take charge of this case.

Cross-Examined by FRAU OEHLERT

Q. Are you aware, or were you aware, of the circumstances or conditions under which the British officers made their preparation for the escape? A. Well, after all, we had a great deal of experience with this. It was a technique which kept on developing.

Q. It is correct, is it not, that a complete staff was found amongst the prisoner officers in the camp, that various officers were detailed to be responsible for certain matters and that other officers, in their turn, were detailed to work under the leadership of the officers previously detailed? That is how it happened, was not it? A. We knew, of course, that an escape committee was in existence, but we could only make assumptions as to the members of it.

Q. But there were several hundred officers who were to try to escape on this occasion. A. In general, it was intended that 200 officers should escape through one of those large tunnels.

Q. Could one say, taking into consideration the special circumstances of the escape and the way the escape was prepared, that one could call it a military action? A. From our own point of view it is a matter, of course, that any POW will try his utmost to rejoin his troops. We very frequently discussed this with the prisoners-of-war, and we called this the war of brains. Well, there was an agreement between the prisoners and ourselves that we could treat each other in a correct way. The prisoners-of-war said that we must understand that they would try everything to get away from the camp, and I replied that that was their duty but that they in turn would have to understand that it was our duty to see that they would never be able to throw bombs again from England.

Q. Well, if you consider that it is the military duty of those prisoners to try their utmost to rejoin their regiments or their units would you then not answer my question whether you regarded the whole thing as a military operation in the affirmative? A. Well, I never thought about this matter but, after all, we were all soldiers, and any action which we undertake is naturally in the nature of a military operation.

Q. And would you therefore say that one could call this whole affair a military operation?

THE JUDGE ADVOCATE: What are you trying to get at Frau Doktor?

FRAU DR. OEHLERT: There would be a point for the defence counsel if it is a military operation because there are some other points which could be ------

THE JUDGE ADVOCATE: What the witness has said is quite right. It is a part of the duty of an officer, during a war, to try to get away, and it is the duty of the commandant to try and stop them if they try to get away. The only point is there are rules to this game, and it is suggested that your client and the others were not playing to those rules.

FRAU DR. OEHLERT: I have no further questions on this point.

<u>Cross-Examined by COL. HALSE</u>

Q. Did you find that the RAF officers in your charge took a great deal of trouble before they escaped? A. May I ask: "Going to a lot of trouble with respect to the escape?"

Q. Did they not, before they escaped, make certain they had got false papers and sufficient food for the journey and small compasses? A. Yes, it was very well organized, excellently organized. They had their specialists for everything. After all, they were all young flying officers of an average age of about 28 to 29.

Q. But you did not find a flying officer making an escape without making preparations for it? What I mean is, if I could explain myself, you did not find a flying officer just getting out of the camp without having false papers on him or a compass? A. I only remember two among the many thousands when attempts at escape were undertaken spontaneously, but they were what we called mental cases.

Q. Passing to another matter, how many times did you see the accused Wielen in the camp? A. I believe twice.

Q. That was once when he inspected a tunnel, which had been broken, and once, you say, on the day of the escape? A. Once while passing on his way to Neuhammer. That was a short visit.

Q. And the other occasion? A. Once a visit for information purposes when passing through on his way to Neuhammer and on the day of the escape, but I would not swear it on my oath that it might not have happened once more, but it was always only by way of visiting.

Q. You are quite satisfied though that he came to your camp on the morning of the escape, that is to say, on 25th March? A. Not in the early morning exactly; it was between 12 and 1300 hours and when I made enquiries as to his whereabouts later on in the afternoon he had already left again and the only one who was still there was Dr. Absalon.

Q. And did Dr. Absalon tell you where he had gone to? A. No, I did not speak to Absalon at all.

Q. You see, we have not been told anything about this visit to the camp by the accused Wielen at all on the day of escape. Did you speak to him on that occasion? A. No.

Q. And Sagan is on the way from Breslau to Berlin, is it not? A. Yes.

Q. Now, passing to another matter, did you expect serious consequences, as a result of this escape, to yourself? A. Yes.

Q. And you thought that Brunner would also suffer serious consequences? A. Yes.

Q. And you thought Wielen would suffer serious consequences as a result? A. I also believe that, yes.

Q. I think you thought, until you heard that Wielen was alive after the war that Wielen might well have been disposed of by Himmler? A. I did not hear anything about it but it was reasonable to assume that, after those incidents had happened, that he would be removed or be locked up or made to disappear from public life at any rate.

Q. Now, in point of fact, I think you received a comparatively minor punishment? A. I received a comparatively minor punishment because it was established that my behavior and attitude was not responsible for the success of this escape. I was sentenced on other matters.

Q. Now I want to come back with you to the very early days before you were placed in house arrest. You knew, did not you, that there were a number of prisoners-of-war in Sagan gaol on 25th March, that is to say, those that had been recaptured in the vicinity? A. During the first 24 hours I heard only that several prisoners had been brought back, and it was only later that I heard that some of them were also held in the prison at Sagan.

Q. Did you ask Absalon or anybody else for the return of the prisoners to the camp in accordance with the usual procedure? A. I had no longer an opportunity to do that. For instance, I asked to be allowed to settle certain matters on the 26th but even that I was not allowed to do.

Q. Did you know that application had been made for them by the camp staff, for these prisoners-of-war to be returned to the camp? A. I do not know, but I considered it as very probable.

Q. Did you know in whose custody those prisoners-of-war who were held at Sagan gaol? A. They can only have been inside the town in the police prison.

Q. Now there were some prisoners taken back to the camp, were there not? A. That I do not know.

Q. I thought that you said that there were some who came back to the camp? A. Yes those were recaptured immediately on the first day.

Q. Is that the four who went back into the camp? A. I cannot say that because I was held for investigation immediately on the first day and for the entire day, but I think that apart from the four there were several others, but I am not certain.

Q. Those others were not admitted to the camp. Did you know that? A. No.

THE JUDGE ADVOCATE: What is that?

COL. HALSE: Some were taken back to the camp and were not allowed to go in. That is what I am putting to the witness, but he does not know it.

THE JUDGE ADVOCATE: Some recaptured prisoners were taken back to Sagan?

COL. HALSE: Some recaptured prisoners were taken back to Sagan camp, but they were not allowed to be received in the camp. (To the witness) But you do not know anything about that? A. Is this supposed to have happened on the first day?

Q. Either the first or second day? A. Not within my knowledge.

Q. I am not suggesting it was the Wehrmacht who refused to have them back. A. Well, I can only say that if they had been returned to me I would not have handed them back.

From Commandant to Captive

Q. I think you said that after the first day you did not see Brunner again. A. No.

Q. But Dr. Absalon continued the investigations at the camp? A. Dr. Absalon, as far as I know – and I think this is fairly certain – had the order to investigate the whole incident at the camp, apparently by some special order, and he frequently came to me and talked to me and asked me questions about it.

Q. Did you know Absalon was one of the accused Wielen's staff? A. I always assumed that Absalon was a special representative of the Reichsfuehrer.

Q. Now you told the Court you know nothing about the list of these officers who were specially concerned in the escape committee. A. No.

Q. That was not prepared while you were in charge of the camp? A. At any rate not during my time. I would say that I consider it as out of the question that such a list was compiled at the camp.

Q. You see, the accused Wielen has told us that he had to get a list, by orders of Amt 5 RSHA, of those people who were mainly concerned in escaping matters, but you know nothing about that? A. I cannot say anything about this.

Q. Now when did you know, Herr Oberst, that 50 RAF officers had been murdered under orders of Hitler? A. I do not know. A considerable time must have elapsed when one of my visitors told me that information had reached him that a number of officers had been killed either while resisting recapture or because they escaped again after recapture, but the first mentioned number was, I believe, twenty-one.

Q. I am not speaking of attempting to re-escape or of resisting arrest. What I am asking you is when did you first hear of Hitler's order that 50, more than half of the officers who had escaped, were to be killed? You see the difference, Colonel? A. It is very difficult to remember. Since I am under oath, I must think about it carefully. The more detailed circumstances of the conference with Hitler and of the intervention of the General Schuster and Grocht and Field Marshal Milch, those things only became known to me when I was a prisoner-of-war. It would have been unreasonable, of course, if at the time I had not noticed that it was mostly improbable that 50 officers would get shot dead without a single wounded and particularly in view of the fact that I knew the behavior of British and American officers well. A British officer would not run away once he had been identified.

Q. May we take it then that you did not know of the Sagan order – it has been called in this case – until after you became a prisoner-of-war? A. You mean the Sagan order?

Q. Yes. A. I can say with absolutely certainty that we discussed the fact that this was an order given by Hitler at some stage during my stay in Sagan and before I became a prisoner-of-war but when this was and the details I do not remember. I was continually, more or less, shut off from the public, and all I heard was brought to me--was told me from time to time by people who came to see me.

THE INTERPRETER: The Colonel wants to add something.

THE JUDGE ADVOCATE: Well, he must not say it.

Re-examined by DR. ADLER

Q. The learned prosecutor asked you about lists which had been compiled of persons who had been concerned in the Sagan escape.

I regard it as a matter of course that such questions were asked and put in the course of the investigation proceedings as far as it concerned contacts with the German population. Dr. Absalon dealt with it. Do you agree with me on that? A. Dr. Absalon extended the investigations even to German soldiers who had supplied material for escape.

Q. Is it correct to say that such a list could not have been compiled during the first few days but only after some time had elapsed and proper investigations had been carried out? A. I only know that Dr. Absalon made a report to his own authority, a very voluminous report of 210 to 212 typewritten pages, which I did not see myself and which he submitted to his authority in a large number of copies which no doubt formed the basis of the charges against me.

Q. Wielen says that he never got such a list from Absalon nor did he get the result of his investigations but that the list, if such a list was made, was sent directly by post from Absalon to the RSHA, and then Absalon made the report on the request of the Luftwaffe court martial authorities. A. May I ask which list you mean?

THE JUDGE ADVOCATE: Dr. Adler, I agree the prosecutor put this question in the way he did to the witness but I think the court will remember that that is stated in a statement and that Wielen here gave different testimony in the witness box. I do not know if that is the point you are trying to bring out.

DR. ADLER: In that case I would like to draw the attention of the Court to the fact that Wielen altered his written statement here and said at the time he may have mixed up the two lists when he made the written statement.

THE JUDGE ADVOCATE: The Court knew that, I think. I have got a note of that. This witness would not know anything about that. (To the witness) Now you realized, did not you that Hitler was supposed to have got in a frightful rage over this escape? A. I heard this later, yes, whilst I was a prisoner, from the other prisoners.

Q. And however much you may blame the officers who escaped, surely even the most misguided angry man is going to blame more the commandant who let them go, is not he? (No answer) Let me start again; you are not following it. Do not you think that if Hitler was going to be annoyed with the prisoners at escaping he ought to have been more annoyed with you for letting them go? A. He had his own investigation carried out on my case, but it was found that all technical precautions had been taken.

Q. I want to get on. Were you ever court martialed in respect for your dereliction of duty as commandant of this camp? A. My trial was from 5th to 9th October, and I was found guilty not because of any dereliction of duty but because the measures I had taken had been too chivalrous and humane against the prisoners-of-war.

Q. Let us just follow. Were you brought before a Wehrmacht court martial – and do try and answer the questions quickly and shortly or we will be here all day. Now were you brought before a Wehrmacht court martial and what was the charge against you? A. The charge was disobedience to orders whilst on active service in five cases.

Q. And what were the sort of orders you were charged with disobeying? A. That I had not prevented the prisoners from destroying Reich property by utilizing it for their escape to an extraordinarily large extent.

Q. What sort of Reich property is this – the bed boards? A. Bed boards, yes, and things like that.

Q. And what else? A. I had not taken away from them a sufficiently large number of tins.

Q. And all this was, of course, true and you were properly convicted, were not you? A. The points were thought to be impossible to carry out.

Q. Well, were you eventually convicted on those charges? A. I was found guilty of having switched off the listening apparatus at an improper time or to have it repaired. I was found guilty of not having removed a man who was suspected of being in contact with the prisoners-of-war sufficiently early. I was also found guilty of having had too friendly relations with the prisoners – I had sent them a bottle of wine at Christmas or for their birthdays.

Q. And what did you get for these sort of convictions? A. The prosecution asked for two months imprisonment and degradation, and the sentence was, in fact, twelve months imprisonment in a fortress, but it was not confirmed.

Q. So you got nothing. Cannot you answer the questions shortly; you are a soldier.

Q. Did your court martial result in that you got nothing by way of punishment so you cannot complain that you did not have a very proper enquiry into your affair. A. Not as far as the military were concerned.

Q. Do you know that we have been told that exactly the same thing happened to Brunner and Wielen, and nothing happened to them? A. I do not know.

Q. Did you get the impression that in the end the military authorities higher up were rather pleased that you had given the opportunity to shoot these officers and thus create an opportunity of trying to terrorize everybody? A. They did everything to prevent it.

Q. Do you know who it was who decided not to confirm your conviction? A. I think that in the first place it was General Furster of the Luftwaffe who asked me to come and see him.

Q. Do you think, in a court martial of such important as this, you being the commandant of the Sagan camp, that it would have been referred to Hitler? A. I had the impression that the promulgation of the sentence and the confirmation was delayed intentionally because the sentence was not promulgated for three months.

Q. Did anybody ever tell you that somebody high up had intervened and said that sentence should not be confirmed in your case? A. Well, I have been to see him. I went to see him.

Q. And what did he tell you was the reason why you should not have your sentence confirmed? A. It was to be expected. It was expected by everyone that the sentence was not going to be confirmed because it was too mild.

Q. Well, were you tried again? A. There was no appeal with us. I received the promulgation of the sentence after three months. I was given a month to comment upon it or to state what I thought but by that time I had been sent to a clinic for nervous causes.

Q. In the German army you can be tried again, cannot you, or another sentence substituted if the sentence is not considered sufficiently severe; is that right? A. If the convening officer does not confirm the sentence a new court is ordered.

Q. Well, I will not ask you any more about that. Now were you in Sagan all the time after 26th March? A. On the 28th March or 29th, as a result of the excitement and the general upset, I had very serious heart trouble and was severely ill for many weeks after that.

Q. But up to then you were in the camp, were you? A. I was still in the camp during the time when I was in bed ill.

Q. And who was commanding the camp when you handed over? A. Lt. Col. Kordoz. [sic] [Cordes]

Q. A Wehrmacht officer? The Luftwaffe.

(At 1530 hours the Court adjourns until 1545 hours)

THE PRESIDENT: Col. Lindeiner, did you ask the British officers in the camp, before the Sagan escape, not to attempt future escapes because otherwise something dreadful might happen? A. I asked the senior officers, the Air Force padres and the MO's, to come to me and I informed them that the mood of the population was such at that time that no guarantee could be given that in the case of an escape on their part they would go unmolested. I called their attention to the fact that the war might last another year or two. I told them that they were young people, who would be in a position, in a year or two, to render further service either to their country or to their families. I told them I personally could only guarantee their health within the province of the camp itself.

Q. Now had you any notification from higher authority that more stringent measures would be taken against prisoners-of-war if there were further mass escapes? A. I had been informed in February of that year that in future, contrary to general usage as it had been in force up to then, escaped prisoners would not be returned to the camp immediately but would remain for a time in police custody and that the orders for the disposal of those prisoners-of-war would come from the supreme army headquarters. Simultaneously the order was given that larger transports of prisoners would be undertaken in future with the prisoners handcuffed. We discussed without superior authorities, the Air Force Inspectorates, how we could translate those orders into a form compatible with those presentable to offers. We had special transport wagons built in order to avoid the necessity of handcuffing the prisoners during transport. We could do nothing about their being held in custody by the police. In the first instance I did not like it at all, and after careful consideration I asked a larger circle of them, and later on, also the group captains, not to undertake any further mass escapes in consideration of the fact that they knew what my attitude towards prisoners-of-war was.

A MEMBER OF THE COURT: When the officers arrived in your camp, were their identity cards taken away from them? A. Those officers only came to me after they had been to Oussel and to Frankfurt on Main.

Q. Well, had they no identity cards when they arrived? A. I cannot say for certain, but I think they were in possession of the well known large cards containing their photo and their personal descriptions.

Q. Now did you, in your camp, issue any identity discs of any type? A. No.

Q. Nothing at all? A. No; I do not quite understand what you mean by identity discs.

Q. Well, you say the only cards they had were very big cards. A. Yes.

Q. Well, they would not carry those about with them all day, would they? A. No.

Q. Therefore had not they some small identity disc to show that they belonged to the camp? A. No, I do not think so, no.

Q. Well now, an officer escaping would have false papers? A. Yes.

Q. Do you agree there would come a time, if he were recaptured, when he would have to say who he really was? A. Yes.

Q. Well, do you think it is likely that somewhere in his clothing he would have – probably sewn up – some means so that he could readily be identified as an escaped prisoner-of-war? A. I do not know but I do not think so. Practically this case would never arise because, let us say a prisoner was recaptured in Stuttgart then Stuttgart police would ring up our camp and would say: "We hold here a man who says that he is Flight-lieutenant – followed by a name – and then he escaped from your camp; is that correct?" and we would say: "Yes, the man has escaped," and we would arrange for an escort to collect him, and he would be brought back to our camp and locked up for a fortnight.

THE JUDGE ADVOCATE: You said in answer to the president something which was rather interesting to us, and I would like to amplify it. Now what orders did you get in February that you were referring to – was it February 1944? A. Yes, it may have been towards the end of January or the beginning of February 1944 when we were made aware -----

Q. Is it before the escape from Sagan; that is what I want? A. Yes.

Q. Now where did you get those orders from? How did they come to you? A. The commandants of the prisoner-of-war camps were ordered to come to the Air Force inspectorate at Werweldt, and we were informed of those orders or directives verbally.

Q. Were there a number of camp commandants present then? A. Perhaps four or five.

Q. So it looked as if somebody had decided on a policy and was trying to get uniformity with camp commandants; is that right? Was this an order to you or was it an order to four or five different commandants? A. An order direct to all camps of the air force.

Q. And who was purporting to give you these orders? A. We were informed verbally. It was not a direct order but merely verbal information to the effect that in future recaptured escaped prisoners-of-war would not be returned to our camps immediately but would be held in custody.

Q. Now who did you gather was going to hold them in custody, the Kripo or the Gestapo or what? A. Well, the Kripo was out of the question at any rate. The Kripo is only an executive organ of the police but it could happen on that they would be transferred to a stricter camp or to a punishment camp.

Q. Now it is quite likely that a prisoner-of-war would be picked up by some form of police. What was the object of telling you this and why was it necessary to summon you to a conference? That is what I do not understand. Did you gather it was to tell you not to ask for those people back; is that right? A. The reason I cannot give at any rate; I do not know that. I repeatedly asked for POW Air Force members to be returned to my camp; if I knew that somebody was still held in Paris or in Prague I would ask for them to be handed back.

Q. Now can you tell me whether, after you had these instructions, any person escaped from your camp, was recaptured and not handed back to you at all or for a very long time? A. Yes.

Q. Perhaps you have not understood the question. After January or February have you known of any occasion where somebody from your camp, having been recaptured, was not handed back to the camp at all or was handed back for some longer period? A. No escape took place since that time because it was still winter and no escapes took place.

Q. Were you apprehensive about this order? A. I felt uneasy.

Q. Were you envisaging something like what happened in March? Were you envisaging something happening like what actually occurred in March? A. No, impossible.

Q. Why were you uneasy? A. Well, the thought that they might get into difficulties or that they might be sent to a stricter camp, and I meant to protect them from that.

Q. Did you think they might be shot? A. No, impossible.

Q. But the impossible sometimes happens, does not it, and it did happen in this case? A. Yes.

Q. Now who was this higher authority who was going to decide whether the prisoner would come back to you or would not come back when he was recaptured? A. We were told that the decision rested with the supreme command of the armed forces.

Q. Is that Keitel? A. I think so, yes, but there was a department within the supreme command of the armed forces dealing with POW matters.

Q. I gather than, in March, you must have realized that when these prisoners were being held by the Kripo that you had no right to ask for them back at all? A. No longer at that time; no longer after those orders had been given.

Q. So in March you were acting on your orders or instructions that you got in February; is that right? A. Yes; well, I only carried on in my command for one more day.

Q. Well, you know – I think I am right – that some of these prisoners-of-war were picked up at four o'clock in the morning of the 26th not so far away from Sagan? A. I heard no more about it at that time, because I was already undergoing investigation by Col. Welder and Col. Möller.

Q. You said you were not put in house arrest until the 26th. I am talking about four o'clock in the morning of the 26th. A. I heard nothing about people being picked up or anything of the kind. They may have been held by the police, but I did not know.

Q. Did you give instructions on the morning of the 25th that you should be notified the moment one of the escaped prisoners had been picked up? A. Well, it was the general procedure that such things would be reported especially at a moment when there was a great deal of excitement and people were scurrying about everywhere.

Q. Now did you know the grossfahndung was in operation? A. I do not know when it was put into operation, but I would almost assume it.

Q. And did you realize that Wielen had a great deal to do with this rounding-up? A. I do not know who gives the order for a round-up to start.

Q. Were you keeping in touch with Wielen at all in regard to the picking up of these escaped prisoners? A. No.

THE JUDGE ADVOCATE: Are there any questions arising out of what the Court have put?

DR. ADLER: Just one question perhaps. (To the witness) You spoke about Wielen's personal character. I will touch on that in a moment. How long did it usually take in former days until a recaptured prisoner-of-war officer would be returned to your camp from the moment of his being picked up by the police? A. That varied widely. One cannot say. I had some Air Force officers, officers of the Royal Air Force, who lived on one of our aerodromes for a fortnight. I know others who had been living in Prague for six months. I cannot say.

Q. You told us a short while ago that recaptured prisoners-of-war had to be returned immediately to your camp, and you used the word immediately. Now, if this handing back of a prisoner to your camp had taken a few days, would you still regard this as immediately? A. With "immediately" I meant without intervention of any other institution or authority. Sometimes it took days because we were short of men. We did not always have enough men available to send them down to collect them.

Q. Now, about Wielen, if Chief Inspector Wielen had known that those persons had been recaptured, and he had had the possibility of returning them to you, do you think that he would have held up their return to your camp? A. He would not have done that.

Q. Are you aware of the fact that it was not Wielen, who was in charge of the round-up operations, but that it was the representative of the RSHA, who would get his orders and instructions accordingly direct from the RSHA? A. Officially, I did not know but, as far as I know, an overall round-up operation extends over the entire Reich territory and obviously an operation of this extent cannot be ordered by Dr. Wielen.

Q. May I sum-up what you said about Wielen. You say that Wielen took no part at all in the shooting, that it happened against his wish, and that he was drafted into the whole affair against his will and without having a practical possibility of evading being dragged into it? A. I know nothing about the organization of the RSHA and the detailed commitments of the various departments, but I do not think that Dr. Wielen, as an old German official, who was only dragged into this affair by virtue of his position, would have taken part in it on his own will.

(The witness withdraws.)

THE JUDGE ADVOCATE: Now that completes the evidence in the whole case, I gather. Now what is counsels' proposition to the Court in regard to addresses? Would you perhaps indicate what you would like and then the Court will indicate whether or not they agree?

DR. MEYER LABASTILLE: We are, of course, in the position to start our final speeches tomorrow but in view of the fact that Dr. Adler and Dr. Oehlert have not yet completed their speeches as a result of having to take into consideration the final portions of evidence, we would ask that tomorrow it would be adjourned for the whole day.

THE JUDGE ADVOCATE: But, Dr. Meyer Labastille, is there any particular point in Dr. Adler and Frau Dr. Oehlert being in Court while the other counsel address the Court? What I mean, Dr. Meyer Labastille, is that I would have thought – this is entirely a matter for the Court to decide and not for me – that there would have been enough substance in the addresses of the other counsel to probably cover tomorrow and perhaps well into the next day. I do not know. Could you let me have your views on that? If counsel agrees the Frau Doktor could be the last to address us on the Gestapo aspect, and Dr. Adler could be the last of all to address us on the Kripo aspect, Wielen. I do not know how that appeals to counsel, but we do not want to waste a whole day.

DR. MEYER LABASTILLE: Herr Dr. Adler could manage it but perhaps Frau Dr. Oehlert could not.

FRAU DR. OEHLERT: I could manage to speak but the thing is I do not know – because it does not depend on me; it depends on my typist, and it depends on the translation office, and I do not know if the Court can have the copy of my whole speech then when I propose to begin on Wednesday. That is the only thing. I mean, I, myself, could speak – I am very glad to, but I do not know.

THE INTERPRETER: We might be able to help if it is a question of very small bits. We could probably cope with it.

THE JUDGE ADVOCATE: Dr. Meyer Labastille, how long do you think you and other counsel will take?

DR. MEYER LABASTILLE: I, myself, two hours and the others half an hour or one hour. I believe half my colleagues will have finished in one day and the other part in the other day.

THE JUDGE ADVOCATE: I mean, it would run into two days apart from the two counsel.

DR. MEYER LABASTILLE: Yes, with the two colleagues.

THE JUDGE ADVOCATE: No, just confine yourself to yours and all the speeches other than Dr. Oehlert's and Dr. Adler's. How long do you think that should take?

DR. MEYER LABASTILLE: In two days, we are ready, all counsel – one day and a half.

THE JUDGE ADVOCATE: And then I gather that the other two counsel will want a day between them. Dr. Adler said about three hours.

DR. MEYER LABASTILLE: That they will do in one day. Yes, one day will see both of them through.

THE JUDGE ADVOCATE: It looks like two and a half days, and it will give the other two counsel about a day and a half from today.

THE PRESIDENT: Well it seems to me that the answer is that it would not be any use starting to-night, and we should go straight ahead to-morrow morning starting with Dr. Meyer Labastille followed by the other learned counsel concerning charges three to eight and then come on to Frau Dr. Oehlert and then finishing up with Dr. Adler as a separate day if necessary. In other words, having a short adjournment, if necessary, between the two complete cases, but there is no reason, to my mind, why we should not start off to-morrow morning bright and early and get down to this main case, and the other counsel can go straight ahead from there. What do you say to that; is that all right?

DR. MEYER LABASTILLE: Yes.

(At 1630 hours the court adjourns until 09:30 hours to-morrow, Tuesday, 26th August, 1947)

[end of transcript]

Faded correspondence between Col. Delmar Spivey
and Col. Friedrich von Lindeiner
Courtesy USAFA McDermott Library, Stalag Luft III Collections

Chapter 7

Mutual Respect - Postwar Correspondence - Col. Friedrich von Lindeiner and Maj. General Delmar T. Spivey

During his years confined at Stalag Luft III, Major General Delmar Spivey, then Col. Spivey, had worked closely with Col. von Lindeiner on a wide variety of concerns and programs. The German colonel found him easy to work with and always appreciated his professional manner and ability to communicate well with the German staff as well as his fellow POWs. The association of the two men did not end at war's end.

Spivey was a 1928 graduate of the U.S. Military Academy. On August 12, 1943, while serving as an observer on a B-17 of the 92d Bomb Group on a mission to hit the rail marshalling yards at Gelsenkirchen, Germany, Colonel Spivey was shot down. As the USAAF expert on aerial gunnery, he had been on the mission to evaluate and improve the function of gun turrets. Afterward, he became a prisoner of war at Stalag Luft III and served as Senior American Officer in Center Compound, where he had many dealings with von Lindeiner.

"More than once I stood eyeball-to-eyeball with the commandant and demanded our rights under the conventions," said Spivey years after the war, "and sometimes it had to be done in very undiplomatic expressions."

Spivey stayed in the service after the war and in 1956 became Superintendent of the Culver Military Academy in Culver, Indiana. He authored a book in 1984 on his experiences as a POW in Stalag Luft III entitled, *"POW Odyssey."*

Maj. Gen. Delmar T. Spivey
Courtesy Scott Spivey

Several years after the war ended, Spivey wondered how von Lindeiner had fared after the war, so he made the attempt to find him as Germany recovered from the destruction and devastation of the war. Once found, a mutually-satisfying series of letters were exchanged from 1947 to 1963 when von Lindeiner died. The letters clearly show the bond held between the two former enemies that only became stronger after the war. After decades of service to his country, Major General Spivey died in 1982 in Clearwater, Florida.

What follows is the Spivey/von Lindeiner correspondence and related letters in chronological order beginning with the first letter in which Col. Spivey locates Col. von Lindeiner living as a prisoner of war in England in 1947 and the last letter at the death of von Lindeiner. While the two men were former adversaries, a genuine affection and almost dependency on each other is increasingly evident throughout the course of their lives, which could not have been imagined in wartime Germany. All letters, typed as they originally were, are courtesy of the USAFA McDermott Library, Stalag Luft III Collections, Spivey Collection, SMS 699, where they are held, and we are grateful for permission to share them.

HEADQUARTERS
AIR UNIVERSITY
MAXWELL FIELD, ALABAMA

DTS:lw

13 August 1947

No. 141835 Oberst von Lindeiner
Camp 168
Glen Mill Camp
Oldham
Lancs, England

My dear von Lindeiner:

    I have been endeavouring to locate you ever since the war was over but could not find any trace of you until recently. Group Captain Day of the RAF recently made a visit to this country and told me that you were in England and gave me your address.

    I want you to understand that the Americans who were in Stalag Luft III feel that they owe much to you for the manner in which we were treated. I have consistently told our authorities that you were an officer and a gentleman in the true sense of the word in all of my dealings with you. I fully understand what a difficult job you had and the troubles you encountered when you tried to make our surroundings and life more pleasant, and I sometimes wonder that the SS and the Gestapo allowed you so much freedom as they did in dealing with the English and Americans, when their treatment of other nationalities was so bad.

    I appreciate the courtesies you showed us and the opportunities which you gave us to live in a manner which enabled us to keep well and sane. I hope that you are soon repatriated and that you can find your family. I hope that you and they are well and can help get your country and people back into the family of nations quicker than most

Germans believe at this time.

I have recently had a letter from Major Simoleit and have had the pleasure of writing him in order to assist him in finding suitable work for himself. I have also had letters from Sgt. von Schilling and from several other members of the German Staff at Luft III. I would like to find the whereabouts of Captain Shultz and Sgt. Strangherner. [Wilhelm Stranghörner]

Please let me know your address in Germany as I would like to send you a small package.

Sincerely yours,

DELMAR T. SPIVEY
Colonel, Air Corps

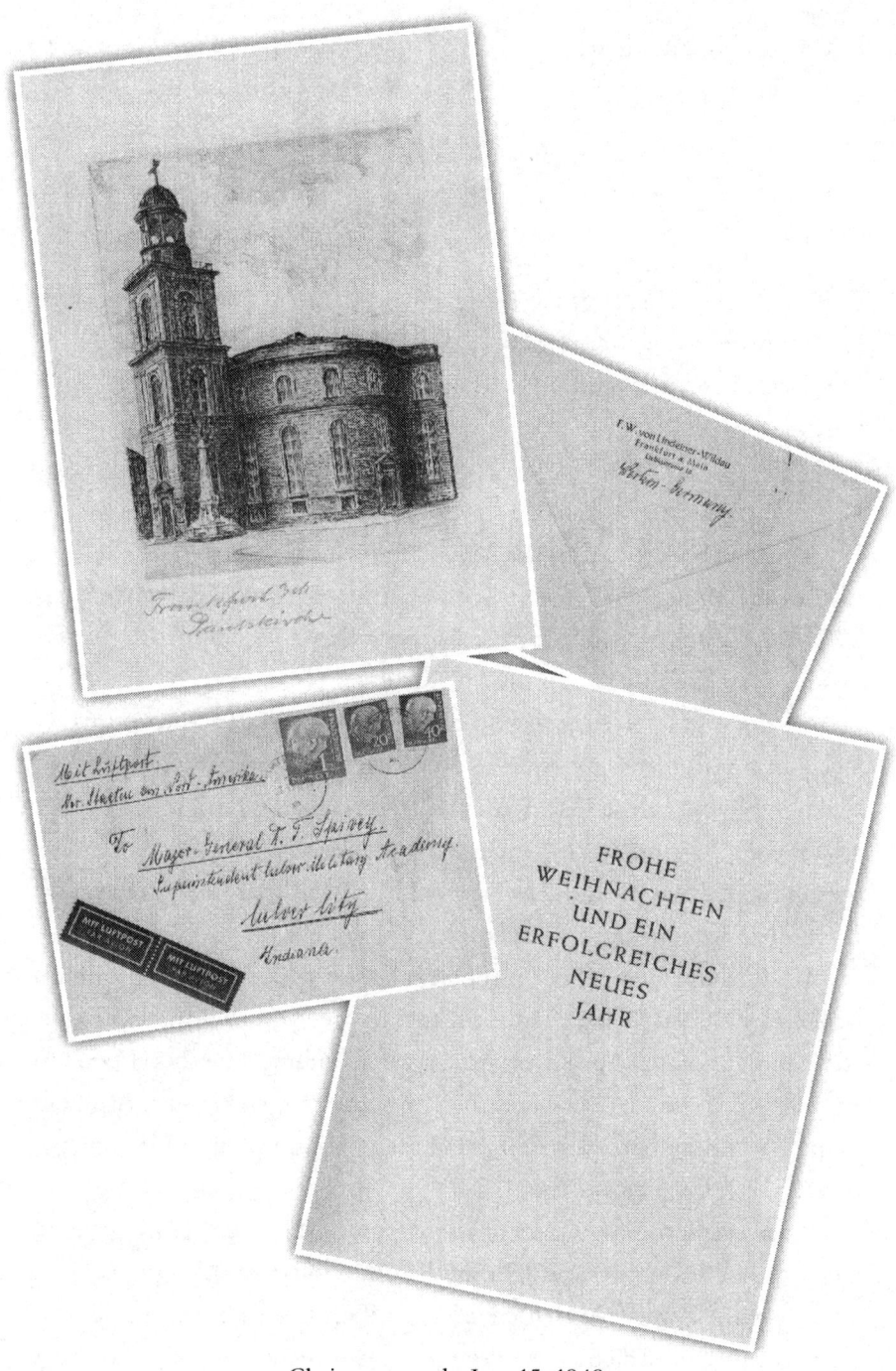

Christmas card - Jan. 15, 1948

F.W. von Lindeiner gen. Hermannstein über Wetzlar. (16).
von Wildau. Wetzlarer Strasse 194.
Gross-Hessen. Deutschland.
Amerikanische Zone
Den 15. January 1948

Colonel, Air Corps, Delmar T. Spivey.
Headquarters Air University.
Maxwell Field, Alabama.
U.S.A.

Dear Mr. Spivey:

Your letter dated from the 18th of August but stamped by the post-office Montgomery the 16th of December arrived here by Air Mail the 30th of the latter month. I should have answered you immediately, if not just in those days I had lost my only brother.

To-day I wish to express you my sincere gratitude for your missive and for all you say in it. If I succeeded in my endeavourings to make the living of the U.S.A.A.F. officers in Stalag Luft III as pleasant as possible, I owe that for a great part to your valuable assistance. The members of my staff know in how far I realized that then already and therefore I wish to thank you emphatically.

Being a German officer and permanently shadowed by two members of the Staff it was very difficult for me, to give you a clear view of the rapidly growing boundless cruelty of Germany's tyrants. I tried to calm down the most active members in some camps, but unfortunately in vain. Within the barbed wire I warranted life and sanity of the POWs, outside of it I was powerless.

The escape of 76 officers of the RAF on March 25, 1944, gave to Himmler the opportunity for my annihilation, for which he had longed since 4 years. I was told that he said: Endlich habe ich den Lindeiner, jetzt kann ich ein Exempel statuieren!" I was dismissed, put under court-martial and a special commission of the Gestapo charged with an investigation about all my doings since my re-enlistment in November 1938. The sentence pronounced in October 1944 was not confirmed for being too indulgent. I am convinced that I owe my life to some friends, who brought me in a neurotic establishment. There I remained up to the Russian invasion.

In 1946 in London a book was published written by 2 officers of the RAF, who were once in Stalag Luft III. They say that my prosecution was due to my buying of provisions in the occupied countries and piling them up in the camp. The existing documents prove the incorrectness of the [sic] these statements. They show, that I was exclusively prosecuted for treating POW's too indulgently and with too much chivalry. After having saved life and sanity of many members of the RAF by saving them from the Gestapo, I was disappointed when reading this description.

It would take too much of your precious time to describe you the manifold and grave events of my life during the following years. In July 1947 I was repatriated to the British Zone, as I was still needed as a witness in certain trials. There I was placed in Category V by the Public Safety Special Branch and cleared by the German Denazification Court. In October 1947 I got the permission to join my wife, who is living as a fugitive for nearly three years at the above address in the U.S.A. Zone.

My own and my family's situation is very serious. Our house in Berlin is destroyed. All our German possessions were in Silesia and are taken by the Poles. Our house and farms in the Netherlands and my my [sic] wife's there invested considerable fortune are seized by the Dutch Government. For manual work, I am too old and notwithstanding my knowledge of 5 languages as well as some twenty years of experience in foreign countries and trade, it is nearly impossible for me to get a job, as the suitable positions were taken when I was a PoW. So we are without a home and more or less penniless. You were so kind as to announce me the sending of a small package and I thank you already now for your very kind intentions. Please don't regard me as too immodest, if I put the following question before you: I should very much like to work as an employe [sic] with the U.S.A.-Military Government, even in a subordinate position. I know that a great number of Germans are occupied there. I see no means to come into touch there and ask you, if you could recommend me to your authorities at Wiesbaden or Wetzlar. If you see no way to do so, please forget my question.

It was very kind of you to help Mr. Simoleit, I am convinced that few people deserve that more than he does. The address of captain Schulz [Schultz] is unknown to me. Mr. Wilhelm Stranghörner is living in Herford in Westfalen (21), British Zone, Benter Weg 21.

I think that every well-minded German fully and thankfully realizes the great aid of the powerful U.SA. given to his country. The way for recovering will be very long and toilsome, but one must not loose [sic] hope for a better time. In any way I thank you once more for your very kind letter, which did me so much good.

With my best regards I remain, Dear Sir,

Yours truely, [sic]

[hand-written signature]

UNITED STATES AIR FORCE
HEADQUARTERS
THE AIR UNIVERSITY
MAXWELL FIELD, ALABAMA
MONTGOMERY, ALABAMA

21 May 1948

Colonel F.W. von Lindeiner
Hermannstein über Wetzlar. (16).
Wetzlarer Strasse 194.
Gross-Hessen.
American Zone
Germany

My dear Colonel von Lindeiner:

    I have been trying to find a way to get employment for you with the U.S. Government but as yet I have not found a solution. More than a year ago I began to use what little influence I have in order to find employment for Simoleit but to date I have not succeeded in getting him anything to do other than with the YMCA. There seems to be a regulation which prohibits the American Government from employing former party members. I have written to my good friend, Major General Hall, who is in charge of the Armed Forces Division of the Office of Military Government for Germany and asked him to see if he could help you in some way to obtain employment. It appears to me that the best solution would be for you to act as instructor in the German language to a group of adult Americans in Wiesbaden. I would be very happy for you to take this letter and present it to the American Military authorities as identification and as a recommendation for employment. I can state without hesitation that you possess all those fine qualities of honesty, integrity, alertness, and intelligence which we admire in an officer and a gentleman. There was never any question in my mind nor in the minds of those of us who were the Senior Officers in your camp concerning your ability as an administrator and as a linguist. We felt assured that you would do your duty towards us regardless of pressure from Gestapo and SS leaders. I would consider it a personal favor on the part of myself and the other 10,500 Americans in your camp if you could find employment by the Government of the United states.

Mrs. Spivey and I have sent you two small packages containing some food and some clothes. I hope that these reached you and that you have been able to use some of the clothes and that the food has helped a little. I shall never forget the courtesy which you always extended me when I had to report to your office for conferences concerning the prisoners, how you would rise and remain standing until I was seated even through you were many years my senior in age and rank, and were the Kommandant of the prisoner of war camp; nor will I forget the offer by you of cigars and cigarettes whenever you smoked. I hope that you have been able to obtain some cigars since I know how well you like them. I would send you some but it is prohibited to send them in private parcels. Maybe I shall be able to visit Germany sometime this Fall and if I do I shall bring you a few.

I would greatly appreciate your comments on your experiences after the British prisoners of war escaped in March 1944. If you have an opportunity to set them down on paper I know that I and many of my friends would be most happy to have them. I have received quite a full report from Major Simoleit and from two German doctors connected with the prisoner of war work in Berlin. I hope that you and your wife are well and that your daughter and her family are all right.

Sincerely yours,

DELMAR T. SPIVEY
Colonel, USAF

19 June 1948

Colonel F.W. von Lindeiner
Hermannstein uber Wetzlar. (16).
Wetzlarer Strasse 194.
Gross-Hessen.
American Zone
Germany

Dear Colonel von Lindeiner:

    I have recently received a letter from Colonel Delmar T. Spivey, enclosing a copy of a letter which he had previously sent to you. To make certain that you receive a copy of this letter I am enclosing one herewith.

    Col. Spivey has been a close personal friend of mine for twenty-three years, and I, therefore, join him in his expression of appreciation to you for your kindness and courtesies to American air prisoners of war who were under your control.

    If I can be of assistance to you I hope you will feel free to establish communication with me.

Sincerely,

WILLIAM E. HALL,
Major General, USAF
Director

Enc

Office of Military Government for Germany (U.S.)
Armed Forces Division
Berlin, Germany APO 742

19 June 1948

Colonel Delmar T. Spivey
United States Air Force
Headquarters, Air University
Maxwell Air Force Base
Montgomery, Alabama

Dear Del:

Enclosed is a copy of a letter which I have just forwarded to Colonel von Lindeiner. If he gets in touch with me I will be glad to be of assistance to him.

I am sorry you missed your trip to Germany as all of us here would have enjoyed seeing you.

Tell Bob Harper for all of his friends here that we are delighted with his new assignment and wish him well.

Best wishes.

Sincerely,

WILLIAM E. HALL
Major General, USAF
Director

Enc.

F.W. von Lindeiner gen.
von Wildau.

                                              Hermannstein über Wetzlar. (16.)
                                              Wetzlarer Strasse 194.
                                              Gross-Hessen, Deutschland.
                                              Amerikanische Zone.
                                              Den 22 Juni 1948

Colonel Air Corps Delmar T. Spivey.
Headquarters Air University.
Maxwell Field, Alabama.
U.S.A.

Dear Mr. Spivey,

    Please allow me to thank you very sincerely for all your kindness, first of all for your so very kind letter and then for the two lovely parcels. The first reached me on the 21rst of April, then I received your letter of May the 21rst on the 29th of the same month and on June the 8th your second parcel arrived. Very many thanks for everything and please transmit my wifes [sic] hearty thank [sic] and mine to Mrs. Spivey. I would have written much sooner, had not my health been so bad of late, in consequence of which I had to go to the sanatarium [sic] Hohe Mark at Oberursel near Frankfurt. Now the devaluation of the Reichsmark and our resulting proletarisation obliges me to leave this place and to return to Hermannstein.

    The contents of your parcels surpassed all expectations. The underwear and the pants fit beautifully, the shoes are too small, but I shall try to barter them at the "Tauschzentrale". What a very great [sic] the tins with eatables [sic] are, I can hardly describe. The soup too is almost an unknown luxury for us. I am not such a passionate cigar-smoker as you seem to think, my great joy are cigarettes, but these may not be sent.

    I now want to express my special thanks for the way you judge my way of having treated the POW's – I have tried to do justice to my parents [sic] education as well to that of the old Prussian Army. Therefore I tried also to impress upon the German staff, that an unworthy conduct towards defenceless POW's [sic] was cowardly und [sic] once dishonorable. I reminded each of my inferiors or subordinates of the fact; that each POW had a mother or a wife or children, who were anxious about him, that not one individual waged war against the other because he had happened to be born under another flag, but that his government obliged him to fight, often against his will. The increasing instigation made it very difficult for me to keep up my principles and procured me much enmity, but I am aware of having been faithful to the doctrine of both my parents and teachers.

Your observations concerning an employment with the U.S.A. Military Government interested me very much. Dr. Simoleit had already let me know, how kindly you helped him. Some months ago he asked me to give him a certificate for his liberation from nacism. [Nazism] When I followed his request I wrote under other items:

> "In the court martial against me (Lindeiner) I was reproached of
> "having removed all the reliable members of the party. Without
> "refuting this I must confess, that I would not have made Dr. Simo-
> "leit to one of my most intimate collaborators, had he shared the
> "opinions of Germany's tyrants. ……In 1941 Dr. Simoleit
> "already refused one of the highest positions in the administration
> "of the occupied Eastern territories, as he was not willing, to
> "follow the instructions of the there [sic] ruling people…….. I
> "became thoroughly acquainted with Dr. Simoleit and knew him to
> "have a very noble and – I should like to say – a very clean cha-
> "racter, who impitiably rejected every idea of injustice and viole-
> "ce, but who defended justice and humanity." –

As to myself, I opposed the penetration of nacism in the many clubs and societies of which I was either a president or a member of the board in the Netherlands, during my stay there from 1919 till 1932. After my return to Germany I refused every connection with the party till 1937, although it inflicted commercial disadvantages upon me and that I was removed from the upper German sport-board on that account. Only in spring 1937 my notification to the party as an "Anwärter" [Nazi party member candidate] ensued, as I belonged to the central-staff of the Firm "Schenker & Co. G.m.b.H.", which had been swallowed by the German Government. I do not know, whether I was a real member. I left the firm at the end of 1937. When I accepted an appointment in the Airforce Ministry [sic] in 1938 I was influenced by a wish to get rid of my connection with the party.

Within my office I soon found several people sharing my opinion condemning the actions of the reigning clique. From 1940 onwards leading men from other ministeries [sic] joined our circle, among them several who paid later for their conviction by being strangulated, well known people like envoy Kiep, navy captain Kranzfelder, colonel Hansen. I myself was transferred to Sagan in May 1942. These, able to judge of the circumstances, think I owe my life to the general breakdown. –

Having returned from my imprisonment to the British Zone on the 10th of July 1947, I was ranged into Category V as seen as the 25th of the same month by the British Public Safety Special Branch in Westfalia. [sic] [Westphalia] I notified my return immediately to the competent German committee for the liberation of Nazism and militarism which on the 2nd of October 1947 certified, that I had been cleared under the provisions of Military Government No. 79.

In November 1947 I was allowed to move into the American Zone where my wife was living. There, after nearly 5 months, on the 23rd of April 1948, in opposition to the clearance in the British Zone, I was declared a "Mitläufer" (Category IV) [party member following blindly and enthusiastically] and put to a penance of Rmk. 2.456 by the German court for denazification at Wetzlar. I do not consider myself as a "Mitläufer" but on the contrary as "persecuted by the Nazi regime", so I brought an action against it, with the result, that the first decision was annulled and the British clearance acknowledged. Never asked for the acknowledgement as having been persecuted by the Nazi regime, as I did not want to be rewarded by higher rations and other advantages at the cost of suffering countrymen, for only having been faithful to the principles, I was taught and to which I have of course always kept. –

In your letter of May 21rst you suggest that I should relate my adventures after the escape of 76 officers of the RAF from Stalag Luft 3. Of course I will gladly do so after my return to Hermannstein very soon. Todays [sic] missive is so long already and I wish to dispatch it today, else you will consider me ungrateful indeed. And my wish is to make you feel my great gratitude for all your kindness and interest.

Please accept my wife's and my own kindest regards for yourself as well as for Mrs. Spivey, and

Believe me, dear Mr. Spivey,

Yours very sincerely,
F. von Lindeiner

F.W. von Lindeiner

>Hermannstein über Wetzlar. (16).
>Wetzlarer Strasse 194.
>Germany.
>American Zone.
>31rst of July 1948.

Colonel Air Corps Delmar T. Spivey.
Headquarters Air University.
Maxwell Field, Alabama.
U.S.A.

Dear Mr. Spivey:

I wrote to you on the 22nd of June from Hohe Mark near Oberursel some days before my return to Hermannstein. After my arrival there, I had to meet with many difficulties resulting from the devaluation of our currency. So today only I can give you the report about my adventures after the escape of 76 RAF officers of Stalag Luft 3 on March the 25th, 1944.

In the meantime I received a very kind letter from Major General William E. Hall from the OMAIS at Berlin. In consequence of your kind recommendation he offered me his valuable assistance. On the 16th of this month I made free to submit him my situation and the steps, by which he possibly could help me. So I have to thank you once more for all your goodness in aiding myself and my family.

Regarding the big escape of March 25th 1944 I can assure you that we knew weeks before that some big action was planned in the North Compound. In spite of all our precautions the tunnel No. 100 succeeded by the coincidence of several events, unlucky for us. The escape was discovered at 1.25 a.m. and within some minutes I arrived on the spot. Thanks to the well known manipulations of the POW's [sic] it became about 11 a.m. before quantity and names of the escapees could be established. In the afternoon arrived representatives of the "Air Ministry" and of the

"General-Inspektion für des Kriegegefangenen-Ministry-Wesen" as well as of Himmler's "Reichssicherheitz Hauptamt." I had to do only with the two first named. After a laborious night these two officers reported to their superiors by wire, that I was absolutely guiltless. Then they left Sagan. I did not speak to the representatives of Himmler that day, their presence in the camp only took some hours.

On the 26th of March there arrived 3 representatives of the Luftgau III Berlin (my superiors in administration affairs) with an order, that I was dispensed, that a court-martial was opened against me and that I was not allowed to leave the camp. Lt. Col. Cordes had to take my place. On the same day arrived the famous Kriminal-Kommissar Dr. Absalon in the camp with two assistants, to begin with his investigations. Everybody was interrogated except myself. Some days later a considerable number of our officers was [sic] transferred as having been too compliant to the POW's [sic] in contrast to the ruling orders. Only the removal of Major Simoleit was cancelled later on, as otherwise the lack of experienced officers would have had serious consequences.

Lt. Col. Cordes in contrast to my military superiors did his best, to make my life as torturous as possible, he and Stabszahlmeister Schmidt supplied Dr. Absalon with slanderous and absolutely untrue material against me. Eleven weeks passed before my first interrogation took place, for the first of them I had to stay in the camp Sagan, later on I was permitted to live in my wife's residence in the country-side of Sagan. After this one interrogation the examining magistrate moved the annulment of my prosecution, but he was ordered to deliver all documents to the Reich Militärgerichtshof A further enervating seventeen weeks passed, before I got any news about my destiny.

Since that time I think it is the hardest test for a living man of honour, to be prosecuted without information about his crime. Nearly all of the members of my Sagan staff and many known and unknown friends in higher offices did their best, to keep me informed about the steps taken against me. So I know, that Dr. Absalon composed a report about me, which contained no less than 122 pages of type-writing. The indignation about my treatment caused already in March very heavy cramps of my heart, but the will to fight for my honorable name against arbitrariness and falsehood gave me new force.

Finally – on the 2nd of October – I was confidentially informed that only three days later the court-martial against me should take place at Guben (halfway between Berlin and Sagan.) A great number of witnesses, experts and auditors was summoned, but I myself had not received either an accusation nor a citation. My friends convinced me not to go to Guben, but I wished to avoid a condemnation "in contumaciam " and to go personally before a court-martial which dared to accuse me.

On the 5th of October 1944 I sat in the dock at Guben, together with the Captains, Broili and Pieber. They too were accused of having trespassed against the orders for the treatment of POWs with the consequence, that by this the "German Reich" had suffered heavy disadvantages in wartime. Furthermore, I met in Guben some German soldiers who had betrayed us by selling forbodden [sic] [forbidden] things to the POWs.

On the 8th of October the public prosecutor moved a punishment against me of two years of imprisonment and degradation. The sentence was pronounced the following day with one year of confinement in a fortress. By lack of time it had been impossible for me, to procure a barrister, but the general opinion was, that I had pleaded my cause better than any barrister could have done.

In wartime any appeal against a sentence was suspended. The sentence was delivered to the condemned, who, in his turn, was permitted to hand in his view. After that the highest resort had to approve the sentence or to cancel it. In the latter case, a new court was ordered. At that time it happened often that sentences were cancelled twice or three times, till they were in accordance with the wishes of the highest resort.

In my case, everybody knew very soon, that my light punishment made Himmler furious so that he protested against it. During October nightly visitors advised me to flee as soon as possible, and I risked to be liquidated in one way or the other, when remaining in Himmler's reach. Notwithstanding all propositions I remained home, and in the case of my disappearance my wife would have been arrested. Furthermore I wished to fight for my right. – Finally my friends came with a psychiater, [sic] [psychiatrist] who ordered my transportation to a neurotic establishment. So on the 30th of October I was brought to Görlitz in a hospital, whose leading surgeon was in the plot. There I remained till January the 27th 1945, when the hospital was evacuated under the pression of the Russian advance.

In the meantime my Wehrmacht-Superiors did their best, to help me. The dispatch of my sentence was postponed till the last days of December 1944 and then I got a further four weeks for my answer. At that time I had left Görlitz and had returned to my wife's residence near Sagan. My discharge from the military service, which had been ordered earlier for the 28th of February 1945, was repealed, as Himmler often arrested officers he disliked, the day of their discharge from the military service. At that moment they were in his power and could be brought to one of his camps.

Few days after my arrival at Sagan the Russians stood before the town. My wife succeeded to leave with one of the last trains. I myself – still being a soldier – had to stay. I was wounded and escaped with a damaged light tank on the last open road to Leipzig. There I remained in hospital from February the 13th until April the 5th when I was transported to another hospital at Blankenburg am Harz. This place was taken by the USA Forces on the 20th of April and so I became a POW. On the 21s of May 1945 I was brought to the big POW-camp Immendorf near Brunswick, which some time later was taken over by the British. Some POW divisions were formed and with one of them I was dislodged to a village near Wolfenbüttel.

It was on the 7th of August 1945, that I was brought on Transport with unknown destination by a British officer and two Sergeants. On the first day we reached the concentration camp, Staumühle near Paderborn. There I was lodged in a special compound for the worst criminals without blankets, dinner-service and so on. After three days my transport was pursued till Ostende, this time manacled. On the 12th of Aught [sic] 1945 I arrived in London and well in the interrogation centre Kensington Gdns. [Gardens]. The chief officer of the War Crimes Unit, Lt. Col. Al. Scotland,[Alexander Paterson Scotland] did his utmost to make my stay there as endurable as possible, I shall always be grateful to him for it. He tried to get me repatriated but in vain. So I was transported to the POW camp. No.13 at Shap Wells (Cumberland). On the 31st of October 1946 this small camp was closed and with the other POW's I came to camp No. 18, Featherstone Park near Haltwhistle (Northumberland). The British and the German surgeons sometimes proposed my repatriation, but in consequence of the ruling embargo on senior officers I had to stay till the repeal of this order on May 1947.

On the 17th of June 1947 I left the camp No. 18 for repatriation and arrived at the first place of my destination in the British Zone on the 10th of July 1947. My treatment in the two British camps was worthy, I shall gratefully remember my three commanding officers there.

Here with my long report comes to an end and I hope, it did not bore you too much. Today again I wish to renew the assurance of my everlasting thanks. Please to give my wife's and my best compliment to Mrs. Spivey and

Believe me,

With kindest regards,

Yours sincerely,
F. von Lindeiner
[hand-written signature]

**UNITED STATES AIR FORCE
HEADQUARTERS
THE AIR UNIVERSITY
MAXWELL FIELD, ALABAMA
MONTGOMERY, ALABAMA**

14 December 1948

Colonel F.W. von Lindeiner
Hermannstein uber Wetzlar (16)
American Zone
Germany

My dear von Lindeiner,

    As Christmas draws near I recall those that I spent in your POW camp and the little things you did to make us as comfortable as possible and to afford us as much opportunity as possible to enjoy the spirit of Christmas. I have just written Group Captains Day and Kellett and reminded them of the Christmas visits during 1943 when you gave us orders that we should drink up all the homemade brew and at the same time to conduct ourselves as officers and gentlemen, and how you allowed us to visit from camp to camp. I also remember your very lenient orders during this time and how some of us disobeyed them by crawling over and under the fence and how you had given instructions to the guards not to shoot but to herd us back into our camps.

    I hope you have been able to find employment and to make an honorable living because you deserve this right to work and find happiness. I think that life will be more normal for those of you who are living in the western zone during the coming year and that you will begin to see the light of day again. I hope so.

For you and your family I wish a very happy Christmas and a healthy and prosperous New Year.

Sincerely yours,

DELMAR T. SPIVEY
Colonel, USAF
Deputy Commander for Education

F.W. von Lindeiner.

>Hermannstein über Wetzlar. -16 -.
>Amerikanische Zone.
>Deutschland.
>4 January 1949.

Colonel Air Corps Delmar T. Spivey.
United States Air Force.
The Air University Headquarters.
Maxwell Air Base.
Maxwell Field, Alabama.

Dear Colonel Spivey,

    It was my sincere wish, to send you my heartiest congratulations in time for a merry Xmas and a Happy New-Year. But some days before Christmas my wife met with a very serious accident and I hurried there to see her, passing all my time at the hospital. You don't know, what I have been through. But now the surgeon says there is no need to worry any more, all the same she'll have to stay in hospital till end of January.

    So my wishes to you are rather late, I am very sorry, I hope that 1949 will bring much luck for you and your family as well as for your work. May humanity be spared a new war, may on the contrary the world recover from the terrible wounds inflicted upon it by the last.

    In the meantime I received your nice letter of December 14 and thank you very much for your good wishes. I am so glad, you have not forgotten our mutual interests, all right people are guided by the same principles. Your interest and your help I'll never forget.

    The monetary-reform divested us of our last savings. But when things were at the worst, I found a modest position offered to me by an old German friend in Frankfurt-Höchst. 40 years ago I would have refused this proposal, now I was glad to be able, to protect my family from want. Of course it is not agreeable, to live separated from one's family but the decrees and regulations in Frankfurt for housing etc. make a removal to that city impossible, as my present position is too unimportant and too insecure.

On the 5th of September Captain William Edward Burr, II, - U.S. Army -, Marburg/Lahn, 2, Friedrichstrasse, visited us, in Hermannstein, instructed by you and Major-General E. Hall. We had a very nice conversation in the presence of my wife and daughter. He was sure that he would be able to help me to a better position, mentioned the JEIA after its fusion with the Officomex. I was and I am still willing any position. Unfortunately I didn't hear from Captain Burr since then, an inquiry from my side remained unanswered. I think he will be transferred to another place or maybe he went back to the United States. I confess that this result was a deception for me, especially as some of my former co-operators found new positions as far as I know.

I never heard anything of the Group Captains Day and Kellett, it is the same with the other officers of the RAF.

When comparing the present situation in Germany to that of three years ago, a great progress is visible. This is in the first place due to the help of the U.S. and her citicens p[sic], it may never be forgotten. And so let me thank you once more for everything you did for me and mine. Perhaps there will be still a positive result of Captain Burr's mission. In this case I will report to you immediately.

I want to repeat my best wishes for 1949 for you and Mrs. Spivey and remain

Yours,

Sincerely,
[hand-written signature]

20 December 1950

My dear Von Lindeiner:

This year as Christmas approaches I feel there is a great necessity for people who have faith in God and love freedom to draw closer together. There never has been such a need for Christian principles in our complex world affairs. I hope and pray that the holiday season may be celebrated by you and your family with good cheer. Let us all hope that the New Year will bring peace in the world and that all of us may live normal lives once more.

I shall never forget the three Christmases I spent in Germany as a prisoner of war. To my great surprise and happiness I found that there existed a common understanding of the spirit of Christmas between the German people and ourselves. I hope this understanding continues in the future.

Since last writing you, I have been ordered to the Far East and I am no longer with my family.

I shall be happy to hear from you when you have an opportunity to write.

Sincerely,

DELMAR T. SPIVEY
Brigadier General
United States Air Force

Col. F.W Von Lindeiner
Hermannstein uber Wetzlar (16)
American Zone, Germany

3 April 1951

My dear von Lindeiner:

I was distressed to learn that your health had not been so good and that it was necessary for you to go to a health resort near bad Homburg. Your daughter Elizabeth wrote me a very fine note explaining why you had not written.

I was hoping that I would be ordered to Europe instead of the Far East but such was not the case. The war in Korea moves back and forth and at best the whole situation is not good. Having been a professional soldier almost all your life, you will understand that those of us who are fighting the war over here are carrying out our duties to the best of our ability.

I am glad to learn that the North Atlantic Treaty Organization is beginning to show strength and I hope before long your own country, Germany, will be a full part in it. From the reports I read, the economic situation in Europe is much better than it was two or three years ago.

If you have an opportunity to give my regards to Dr. Simoleit or Fritz von Schilling, please do so for me.

Please thank your daughter Elizabeth for the kind note she wrote to me. Best personal regards.

Sincerely,

DELMAR T. SPIVEY
Brigadier General
United States Air Force

Col. F.W. von Lindeiner
Hermannstein uber Wetzlar (1)
American Zone, Germany

12 December 1951

Mr. F.W. von Lindeiner
Frankfurt A. Main
Seehofstrasse 18
Deutschland

My dear von Lindeiner:

It would be impossible for me to let Christmas pass without remembering you and your efforts to inject a little Christmas spirit into our drab POW life. I am still very grateful to you for the way that you treated us while we were in your camp.

I hope that you and your family have been well during the past year, and I wish for all of you a Merry Christmas and a Happy New Year.

If you have time, I would like to hear from you.

Sincerely,

Delmar T. Spivey
Brigadier General
United States Air Force

Brigadier General Delmar T. Spivey.
United States Air Forces.
Headquarters 314th Air Forces.
Office of the Commanding General.
Apo 710
c/o Postmaster San Francisco, Cal.

Dear General,

Your letter of 12 December 1951 was a very great xmas present for me, I thank you sincerely for it. I would have liked so much to send you my best wishes for the beginning of the New Year, but I dared not do so in the uncerainity [sic] of your present address. I could not take for granted, that you were still in the same place as a year ago. So I beg you to accept my best wishes for a good year 1952 still to-day. [sic] I hope that it may bring you a successful issue of your activities in the Far East and a happy return to your family.-

With my letter of 19 May 1951 I told you of the heavy attacks of illness, caused by my numerous old wounds. Later on I made a second long cure in Bad Homburg and staid [sic] some time with my wife's family in the Netherlands. In the meantime I had to fight a lengthy struggle to get my retired pay. So as you probably know I have been condemned by a German court-martial in 1944 to 12 months confinement in a fortress and people, who have been punished with prison or penal servitude, lose their title to any official payment. Finally I succeeded in convincing the German authorities that my case resulted from more or less political reasons.-

In England there is now published the fourth book treating P.o.W-Life in German airforce [sic] camps. They pretend that I was condemned for active participation in black-market operations. This is absolutely untrue and injurious for me. I have been sentenced only for disobedience against directions given in reference to the treatment of P.o.W.'s, [sic] as I thought them in contradiction to the Geneva Convention. I protested against the author's assertion, a rectification was promised but up till now I heard nothing.-

My family and I myself are living in the moderate circumstances caused by the great change of our lives during the last seven years. I am thankful that my state of health enables me to follow the world's great events, but it is not so easy to be idle after having been active in responsible positions during such a long time. –

Closing I wish you to repeat my thanks for your kind writing and my good wishes for a Happy New Year. I hope to hear furthermore from you from time to time, giving me always news about your continuous good health. I remain, dear General,

Sincerely, yours,
[hand-written signature]

8 December 1952

Col. F.W. von Lindeiner
Seehofstrasse 18
Frankfurt am Main, Germany

Dear Colonel von Lindeiner:

I hope that you and your family have a very happy Christmas and that the New year [sic] will be a good one for all of you.

This Christmas will be my third one in Japan and I hope that I will be returning to the States shortly. This has been a very busy and exasperating tour of duty. When I came over, I was in hopes that the Korean war would end shortly and we would be assured of peace in the Far East. As you well know, this has not happened and it seems to me that we are not much closer to a settlement than we were last year this time.

I have seen much progress made by the Japanese in rehabilitating their country and establishing a stable economy. Much still remains to be done but they are an industrious, energetic and capable people, who will find a way to establish their country as a leader provided the Communists are prevented by the United Nations from overrunning their nation. I have learned much from them concerning their way of life and their approach to problems. It is my belief that their greatest weakness lies in the fact that they are not willing to assume responsibilities which their newly found freedoms impose upon them. They seem to take all of them for granted and that they will remain with them without any effort on their part to guard them. I am sure that you Germans realize that this cannot be done.

It will please me much if I could hear from you and get your ideas concerning the situation in Europe, especially that which relates to Germany. Your last letter was much appreciated and I hope that you have received my answer. If perchance you see any of my German friends, please give them my best regards and tell them that Mrs. Spivey, my son and I are well and happy, and that I will be back in the States sometime around the first of 1953.

Sincerely,

DELMAR T. SPIVEY
Major General, USAF
Commanding

F.W. von Lindeiner-Wildau.

> Frankfurt am Main.
> Seehofstrasse 18.
> 22, December 1952.

Major General, USAF, Delmar T. Spivey
Headquarters.
Japan Air Defence Force.
Office of the Commanding General.
Apo 710

Dear Major General Spivey:

I thank you sincerely for your kind and interesting letter of the 8th inst. with its good wishes for xmas and the year 1953. I reply to these hearty, [sic] hoping, that the new year brings a return to the States for you.

I really was astonished to find you still always in the Far East but take it as a token of your good health and the highly distinguishing appreciation of your activities by your superiors. From your letter's head and your signature I learn, that you have been promoted and entrusted with a high command. I congratulate you herewith and am sure, that officers as well as other ranks under your command will be very happy with their commanding officer. The experience gained from a long service and especially from three wars convinced me, that the personality of the commander in chief is of the most important influence on the activities of his troops. –

Everything you write about Japan and the Japanese is very interesting for me, as I became a liaison-officer of the German Air Forces to the representatives of the Japanese Air Forces, when Japan entered the war in 1941. I had to deal then with Admiral Nomura, General Bansai, Colonel Izima and Captain Toyoda. But after being transferred from the General Staff to the P.o.W.-camps I never heard anything about their fate.-

I did my best to get through to the mentality of the Japanese race but found it very difficult, much more than to that of the Russians. In any way they were brave soldiers, ready to die for their Tenno [emperor] and their country.- My personal opinion is, that the enormous increase of the frugal population conducts to increased industrialisation and immigration with the fervent desire to conquer the market of China and South-East-Asia.- Furthermore I think that on the long run they always will remain Asiates, unreliable when they have to choose between "White" and "Coloured". But you surely will see things much better than I ever could do.-

You were so kind to ask me about my ideas concerning the situation Europe and especially that which relates to Germany. I will do that with the greatest pleasure as far as my modest abilities permit:

The world seems to be reigned by two fundamental questions: being the socialism and the nationalism, represented by Russia plus satellites and the coloured people all around the world, fighting for absolute independence from white masters and white man's influence. The doctrine of Karl Marx logically developed to Spartacism, Leninism, Trotzkiism and Stalinism. Every socialist party

[next page]

F.W. von Lindeiner-Wildau.
    to
Major General Delmar T. Spivey.   22, December 1952.

II

will produce a left wing which can lead their members gradually to communism. Therefore, I never could be a member of "Socialdemocracy" although as a Christian I will ever fight for the dignity of man. I got the impression that Stalin recently intends to strengthen the Communism by supporting the nationalism in his own ranks as well as abroad. The Russians are ardent nationalists since long but the intention is to awake a Slavic or Communist Socialism in the Satellite-States too. In Eastern Germany a new generation grows up in communist ideologies and locked up from foreign news and influences. Obstinate and old people are removed, if they try to escape to Western Germany they may do so. Besides that he supports all movements of independence in other countries whether in Africa or in Asia.- In any way I am convinced that he will avoid every violent encounter with his opponents, foreseeing that time is his best ally. His greatest danger at this moment seems to be a loss of Mao-China's partnership.-

The representatives of Communism or Nacionalism know that only one remarkable adversary is standing in their way…..the United States. This country and his [sic] governors realize the enormous danger from Stalins [sic] side and do their utmost to collect all forces, ready to fight the rigorous violence against humanity, freedom and justice. But while on Stalins [sic] side we find the united power of one iron will, rigorously annihilating the slightest indifference or opposition, on the other side rules a regrettable multiplicity of interests. One gets the impression, that some of the so-called free nations do not or will not see the joint danger. They attend to their special interests, awaiting concessions from their neighbours or calculating new collisions with them.- As long as they all do not fully work for the general aim, the general danger is increasing.

Germany is mutilated, half of his territory under hostile mastery. The consequences of two great wars produced a frame of mind "No more war." This mood seems at least partially stronger than the fear of a possible agression [sic] from the East. The aversion against military service within the youth is remarkable. Formerly men grew up in the conviction, that this service was a most honourable duty against their ruler, their country and their people, now they say, where are they. Formerly the boys were proud of their troop, their second home. Even in second world-war the soldier was convinced to fight for his home and his family. He had a [sic] "idea" and they must have an idea, if they will be ready to die. Last not least there must be trustful and camponianable [sic] relations between superiors and subordinates. All these psychical [sic] moments were the strength of the old German army. The military unit was really a second home for officers and other ranks, the honour of their troop was their own. Even now, 44 years after the first world-war, the remaining members of my old regiment meet each other eventually. One finds there royalties, princes, counts, junkers, peasants and many simple workmen, sitting together as equals.-

All these moments have been fundamentally destroyed by the degradation of the German soldier in 1945. It is very difficult to convince the youth, that this belongs to the past. The sufferings of many years produced a very materialist [sic] mood, a youth lacking ideals. If one tells them that things have changed they answer: "Well, but if we take arms to defend the remainder of our mutilated country, what within about ten years? Shall we be once more expelled from the human community as criminals?

[next page]

F.W. von Lindeiner-Wildau
    to
Major General Delmar t. Spivey.   22, December 1952

III

Shall we once more be prohibited to visit High Schools or to earn our living as workmen? Shall we for a second time be forced to work on the Black Market or to take service in the Russian Forces? It is difficult to answer these questions, one can only say: "We are not on this earth for our own pleasure but we have to fulfill a duty." Reply: "And our family?"

Dear General, I gave you my opinion. Germany is no more what it was. Prussia, the strong building against nihilism and communism is disappeared, notwithstanding it opposed Hitler much longer than any other part of the Reich. The so-called upper-classes, hated and pursued by Hitler more than anyone else, are dead or evacuated and empoverished, [sic] in every way without any influence. There runs a gap through the population of the Bundesrepublik, embodied by the names Adenauer and Ollenhauer. It will be possible to create German Forces, sufficiently in number and excellently equipped, but this is not a force, ready to stay and to die. Such a förce [sic] must have an ideal and must be led by officers and corporals, educated in ideals.-

I could tell you a lot about an officers [sic] education to dutiful self-denial and to comradeship with his subordinates in former days, but I am afraid to have written already too much. It is not without risk here, to give one's ideas openly nowadays. One will not be sent to a concentration-camp or hanged so as eight years ago, but one can be stamped as a neofaschist [sic] or a communist, with all its consequences.

I hope, you know me sufficiently. I hate vigour and cruelty, I stand for the ideals of humanity. I hope that your country will succeed in collecting the well-minded world against the powers of evil.-

And now you will be more than tired by my endless writing. Please excuse my many mistakes in writing, but I am my own and very defective secretary. Let me close with renewed best wishes for a happy new Year [sic] for you and your family as well as a lucky return to your country. You know, that I appreciate every news from your side excedingly. [sic] So I remain, Dear General,

Sincerely yours,

[hand-written signature]

8 December 1953

My dear Herr Von Lindeiner,

It has been a year to the day since my last letter to you. This one finds our little family together back in the states and very happily situated. Our tour in Korea and Japan was rather hectic in that we were separated for the three years less six months. Moreover, my wife lost her father during that period. I got back from Japan in February and had a delightful vacation in Florida. From the vacation I came to my present assignment which has kept me extremely busy ever since. As you will guess, I am in the air defense business and have the responsibility for almost 26 of our central states. It is not a very encouraging job since we have so little to accomplish so much; however, we are making progress, but as you will so well recall, the best of defenses as you had in Germany during the last war do not keep aircraft from coming in and going out. I am sure it would be the same way if we were attacked by the Russians. The only difference is the great contrast between the type of weapons now available and those we had during the last war. We have so much electronics gear in our present Air Force that we are having difficulty getting proficient personnel to man it. Our fighters are literally flying laboratories which are extremely hard to maintain.

Your last letter has been read and reread, and I must admit that I enjoy it every time I read it because it is so full of good, sound logic. We follow your progress in West Germany from day to day and constantly hope that it will be possible, before too long, to unite your country under one government. The hope, which we discussed while I was a prisoner-of-war in Germany, that Europe could be united into a kind of United States of Europe seems closer than ever before. It is significant to me that people so varied in nationality and national interest can, in the face of danger, combine their efforts and forget their differences in order to survive a menace which is the worst that our western civilization has ever known. I have great hopes that the union will become a reality, politically as well as economically, before too long. I notice that you Germans are taking the lead in this respect. Our own President has offered you much encouragement and most Americans are fully back of him although one wouldn't judge so because of the loud noises made by a small minority. We ourselves are becoming stronger day by day, and I think this applies not only to the military but to our nation as well. Our spiritual faith has grown immeasurably; the great majority of people seem to have settled down to the realization that this is a long, drawn-out struggle which will require both material and spiritual endurance. We still have great faith in NATO, our own strength, and the strength of our other allies to prevent a catastrophic war which would result if one broke out between Russia and the UN forces. I don't agree with you that the Korean struggle proved UN's inability to settle a dispute by an expeditionary force; to the contrary, I think our show of force and our ability to hold the Red tide several thousand miles away from our shores has demonstrated to the Russians and to the Red Chinese our will to prevent their overrunning Western democracies. I am sure that had we not checked that first move by force, you would no longer be in the western zone of Germany nor would the rest of western Europe be free to exist as independent nations. I think we would have seen Polands and Czechoslovakias all over the continent. I also believe that because of this show of force we have prevented a third World War provided we keep our moral and physical strength growing as it is now.

Christmas never comes but I remember 1943 and 1944 when I spent them as your guest in Sagan. When I tell people the way you conducted our prisoner-of-war camp they are incredulous and think I am slightly crazy, but to me our relationship was in the best tradition of real military services and an example which others might well follow. In 1943 when you called the senior officers into your office and reminded us that we should dispose of our forbidden, homemade brews and distilled spirits by drinking them during the holidays instead of your ordering them destroyed, you won a place in my heart which will always be held in high esteem. Although I had none of these in my camp (not having been in it long enough for our officers to make the spirits), I fully appreciated your spirit in letting the other camps enjoy themselves during the holidays. I never shall forget the good comradeship enjoyed by everyone, including your guards, during Christmas and New Year's days when we not only had a drink ourselves but gave you [sic] men one, also I hope this Christmas you and your family are well and will enjoy the holiday and that you will continue in good health and happiness during the new year. Mrs. Spivey and I send our best regards to you and your family.

Sincerely

DELMAR T. SPIVEY
Major General, USAF

F.W. von Lindeiner-Wildau
Seehofstrasse 18
Frankfurt am Main, Germany

F.W. von Lindeiner-Wildau.   Frankfurt am Main.
Liebig Strasse 18.
25th of January 1954.

Major General USAF. Delmar T. Spivey.
Central Air Defense Force.
Office of the Commander.
P.O. Box 528
Kansas City, Mo.

My dear Major General Spivey,

Your letter of December the 8th gave me great pleasure and I want to thank you most heartily for it. Had I had the necessary quiet and rest, I would have written long ago. But now at last I can do so and begin by sending you and yours my wifes [sic] as well as my own very best wishes for 1954. May it fulfill all your desires and may great happiness be in store for you all. May your health and strength enable you to accomplish your heavy, responsible and interesting task.-

As you will see we have moved into another appartement. [sic] The one we inhabited till now with our daughter and her three children, growing up, was much too small in the long run and so we were very grateful, that after years of great economy we were at last able to acquire this larger flat. Our moving with all its vicissitudes and my long absence from Frankfurt must be my excuse for writing so late and I sincerely hope you will understand this. My wife and I both hope you will visit West Germany once more and that you will give us the benefit of your visit. Even now we have heard nothing about our son-in-law, who is missed since January 1945. He was colonel in the general staff. It is difficult for the young wife as they were very happily married.-

You will surely be very glad to be reunited in your country after 2 ½ years of absence, although I think your task as officer in the Far East was most interesting as well as honourable. I only in the summer of 1938 came in contact with Air Force affairs and also than [sic] with studies about the economic potential of the Western powers, but my interest for aircraft and defense against it remained lively. I try to follow their enormous development as far as it is possible for a German civilian. But even so I Hope [sic] to realize the enormous progress especially of the technical science within so short a time. Doing so I think to understand the great importance of your present task. The air-defense of the population, the industrial establishments, the communications, the transmission of communicatios [sic] and – last not least – the instruction and dislocation of the intercepting air-forces will require not only a seldom knowledge, but also a fabulous amount of funds. I think furthermore that the claims on health, physical training, moral [sic] and instruction of the flying personal [sic] will be increased greatly. With interest I saw, that for your budget of 1954 increased funds have been disposed of for the aircraft.-

Your letter of December the 8th shows me, that I evidently have expressed myself unclearly concerning the intervening of the United Nations under the authoritative leadership of the United States against Noth [sic] Koreaan [sic] and Chinese aggression I can only say, that this proceeding was a blessing for the free world and a rescue of Western Europe. We always must and will be very thankful for the heavy sacrifices broughy [sic] especially by your country during these last years in the far East. My intention has only been to consider, whether in the long run the Japanese would join in the cry "Asia to the Asiatics." May be that I am influenced by my relations with Indonesia during many years. You have been recently 2 ½ years in these regions and nobody can criticise the circumstances out there better than you.-

You will understand, that we follow the development of the imminent Berlin-conference with the greatest interest. Generally the expectations are not very high in the conviction, that the Russians surely never will open a warm war, but that they wish to keep things more or less on the present level. They pretend, that in the long run they will conquer the world by their doctrines. Very possible they will make some easier conditions at present to diminish the hatred roused during the last years by their behavior in their zone. But I am not a prophet! I hope, that living-conditions for my two sisters in the Russian zone will become better and that still once as long as I live I may get the possibility, to visit the place in Silesia, where my parents and many generations of my ancestors were buried.-

I was very glad to read your remarks over Stalag Luft 3. Really, we did our best to make things there as bearable as possible under the ruling conditions in Germany at that time. I used to instruct my subordinates, to respect the Geneva Convention strictly and to behave themselves in a way, that the once freed P.o.W.'s [sic] could say: "Well, these Germans were harsh, but correct and chivalrous." I wrote to you five years ago about the consequences of my behavior: Court martial and loss of all belongings.-

Closing this long letter I repeat my best wishes for a very good year for youself [sic] and your family. And if you ever come to Germany, please do not forget us, but do not wait too long, as I am growing old. My wife and I send our best regards to you and to Mrs. Spivey.-

Sincerely,

[hand-written signature]

F.W. von Lindeiner- Wildau.   Frankfurt am Main, Liebigstrasse 18.

18 December 1955

To

Major General U.S.A.F.

<u>Delmar T. Spivey.</u>

Commandant Air War College.
Maxwell Air Force Base, Alabama.

Dear Major General Spivey:

    I am very sad that I was not able to write to you sooner. Your letter of September 29th reached me on October the 3rd, just before I left for Holland on the morning of the 5th. Unluckely [sic] I could not possibly put off my journey, as we had to assist the last conferences concerning our capital in Holland, which is confiscated since 1945. A positive decision is not so important for my wife and myself, as it is for our daughter and our grandchildren. Not only I but my wife too was very disappointed that circumstances kept us away from Francfort [sic] the few days you were in the neighbourhood, for she had hoped to make your acquaintance. As much to my regret I have no relations to the United States Forces in Germany I was at sea, what to do, not being able to reach you in time and explain my unremittable absence. Therefore I gave your letter to my here living daughter, together with the address of Professor Dr. Simoleit, hoping she might help you with the latter. His address is: München 25. Krümer Strasse 68. I am glad I can give you good news about him, for after several years of misery and mortification he now has a satisfactory job and is reunited with his family. I had hped [sic] my daughter might have you informed already to the like.-

    Before continuing this writing I first of all want to thank you very heartely [sic] for the above mentioned letter and the kindness in sending me that box of cigars, which token of friendship touched me greatly. I need hardly repeat my very deep regret at having missed your proposed visit, rejoicing the foresight of it all the the [sic], years, as you wrote me about your intention to come to Germany once. It would have been such a very great pleasure to have met you again after nearly 11 years. How much has happened in this lapse of time and how many interesting periods your life has given you. Your letter mentioned bad illness last year, for which I am very sorry and I sincerely hope you hace [sic] quite recovered and do not feel any bad cosequences, [sic] so that you may still devote your your [sic] energy and your service to the great cause. Without being able to judge exactly your work I am sure, that as Commander of the Air War College you will have an enormous influence on the future of the U.S.A.F.-

[next page]

F.W. von Lindeiner- Wildau.   Frankfurt am Main, Liebigstrasse 18.

To

Major General U.S.A.F. Delmar T. Spivey. 18 December 1955

After a long sojourn in Holland I was far from well for a long time, else I would of course have written to you long ago. But I may not complain, being 75 years since a short time. My head is quite strong still, but the limbs won't always keep up time with all I wish to do. This may not [be] surprising after taking part in 3 wars, getting 17 wounds and during living the dreadful years since 1938. My remaining strength is devoted to the fight against the communistic system, being convinced of the enormous danger involved by its very skilful [sic] infiltration in the neibourd [sic] Western Germany. Long ago I was convinced too, the Kremlin would not try to extend its world-domination with arms. Lenin as well as Stalin have declared the communist theories would conquer the world through peaceful penetration. And this is very imminent now especially regarding some assertions here of the socialist party and other

[sic] people, who reckon themselves to the "intellectuals". No one than myself can wish more ardently the reunion of my dismembered country as well as the return to Germany of those provinces, where my ancestors were living since nearly 800 years, but not to the price of mental slavery. We have experienced that in Hither's [sic] time.-

Will you please remember me as well as my wife to Mrs. Spivey and also to your son. It is a pity that the distance makes the possibility of making their acquaintance so very uncertain. I hope your son will tread in your footsteps and continue your work. You will understand my great interest in the mounting of new German forces, notwithstanding my being an absolute outsider in this concern. May one succeed in building a real good corps of officers, educated as strictly as we were, when I was an [sic] youngster. Than [sic] the most important priciples [sic] were: Absolute faithfullness [sic] to a governement [sic] established on the legal way, Unselfish performance of one's duties, Obedience to the orders of the superiors unless they offend against God's commandments or one's own honour. Inspiration of the inferiors with a mutual confidence, which made them trust their officers in every situation, in peace and in war. With pleasure I still look back upon those years, when I lived before 1918 in Potsdam with my dear fellow soldiers. I always enjoy our yearly meetings with the survivors feeling the bond of friendship and trust not being lossened [sic] since then.-

Closing this letter I make free to send you my wife's and my own best wishs [sic] for a happy Xmas and a very New Year, asking you to bring these wishes to Mrs. Spivey and to your son too. We hope ardently that 1956 may be prosperous for you and that we will be be [sic] more lucky with your next visit to this country. With our best regards to you and your family from Mrs. von Lindeiner too I remain

Sincerely yours,

[hand-written signature]

Frankfurt a./Main, Liebig Strasse 18

21dt of December 1958.

Dear Major General Spivey:

It is with a very bad conscience, that I write this letter to you. Already a year ago I firmly intended to send Mrs. Spivey and yourself my wife's and my own greetings. But I had not got your address and all my efforts to get it were in vain for quite a long time. Having - much to my regret - no relations in the U.S. military official circles here. I tried to get the necessary information at the U.S. Consulate General here but no success. Finally I asked friends of mine to make inquiries at the U.S. Embassy at Bonn. So it was about May 1958 before I got the longed for address. But in the same month I fell ill and went into a hospital. Shortly after being dismissed there, I had an accident accompanied by a light concussion of the brains, which I got over only slowly. And then - I confess openly – I felt ashamed to write after such a long silence. I give you all these details as a proof, that my silence was most unvolantary [sic] and not due to a lack of interest for you. On the contrary, already fifteen years ago I considered you the prototype of an [sic] responsible officer, a gentleman and a leader of his younger fellow-officers.-

So I beg you to forgive my long silence and I now take the liberty to thank you very much for your kind letter of the 12th inst. My wife and I myself sincerely return the seasons [sic] greetings, sent us by you and Mrs. Spivey. We were very glad to read, that you appreciate your present place so much and - forgive me this remark – I think you personally are the right man in the right place there. I never shall forget the most valuable indirect support your personality gave me during my most difficult and dangerous task in Stalag Luft 3 at Sagan.-

I thank you very much for your consideration about our people in Western Germany. Well, people had to work hard and were lucky to find capable regents as Adenauer and Ehrhardt, but in the long run I am to my great regret not to [sic] optimistic. In the years of the so-called "Wirtschaftswunder" [German for economic miracle – the rapid reconstruction and development of the economies of West Germany and Austria after World War II] the working classes became spoiled enormously [sic] and I am anxious to see, what will happen if the economic situation changes to the worse. Materialism and Egoism grew considerably and the Communistic propaganda is very active and skilful. [sic] It is supported by many so-called "Intellectuals" and persons who hope to advance to leading political positions. I am convinced, that the left wing of the "Social-democratie" [de Social-Démocratie] grows steadily. The taking possession by the communists of the power in the German Sowjet-Zone, [sic] [Soviet] In Chechoslovakia, [sic] Poland, Roumanie [sic] etc. gives a good example, Mr. Grotewohl in Pankow was an ardent Socialdemocrat [sic] up till 1946. The boundary of communistic mastery has been shifted with nearly 400 miles to the West, till [sic] banks of Elbe and Weser. [sic] more than 12 millions of Germans were driven out of their home, where their ancestors were settled since more than 750 years and the so-called upper-ten were put aside by Hitler and the regulations after 1945.-

[next page]

21st of December 1958

II.

But my wife and I are very old, so we can hope, not to live to see the entry of Mr. Ulbricht and companions here. I am firmly convinced, that the Russians do not like a [sic] warlike explanations with the Western Powers. Stalin and his successors fought and fight for the conquest of the whole world by communism and say, that every war brings a risk, that they do not need to take. My opinion is therefore, that the future will be decidingly [sic] influenced by the firm attitude of a united free world.-

I hope, that you will consider my honest explanations with kind indulgences and finish this letter with my wife's and my own best wishes for the new year and a long only happy future for you and your next of kin. So I shall always be

Sincerely yours,

[hand-written signature]

Christmas card from von Lindeiner to Spivey

From Commandant to Captive

Translation of Message

…to you and your family from Mrs. von Lindeiner and myself. Very often and always thankfully I think of our mutual working under the most difficult circumstances. So as you see we are still in life although we are growing very old. I should be so glad to meet you once more and shall remain always

Sincerely yours,

F.W. Lindeiner
[hand-written signature]

December 12, 1962

Dear Colonel von Lindeiner:

Again I take this opportunity to wish you and your family a very Merry Christmas and a Happy New Year. May God bless you and yours and preserve you in health, happiness, and good fortune through the years.

Mrs. Spivey and I, and our son and his family, including two wonderful grandsons, are well and happy and have been bountifully blessed in many ways. We are all very busy at the professions of our choice. Our son is flying with the Strategic Air Command and is away from home a great deal, but his family understands and my son feels that he is contributing, not only to his country, but to the safety of the world.

As for me, I find my work here at the Academy more intriguing year by year. The challenge and satisfaction of working with more than 850 boys during the nine months' Winter School and more than 1650 during the two months of Summer School are unbelievably gratifying.

At this Christmas I have greater hopes for the solution of some of our great world problems than any previous year since World War II. I believe that the strength and courage demonstrated by our President, as well as the solidarity shown by NATO countries, have done much to allay some of our fears at home and abroad. If we continue to show strength and fortitude it seems to me that the NATO countries will eventually be too much for Communism.

I am also encouraged by the prospects of greater unity and understanding brought about by the common market and perhaps even political union eventually. Collectively we have great strength, but we need to identify our common cause and to show a greater concern for the safety and future of our Western Civilization. I believe that we have a greater awareness of these two needs more than ever before.

Since retiring from the Air Force I have not been able to keep up so well with our policies, our strengths, and our weaknesses. I am now seven years away from active service and I am beginning to look at the world situation through civilian eyes. Maybe this is good.

We devoutly hope that you have been well during the past year and that you have been happy watching your country recover and grow in strength and prosperity. This must be a great satisfaction to you and must give you courage to do that which is necessary politically, economically, and spiritually. I congratulate all the West German populations on their accomplishment to date.

I remember the Christmas many years ago when soldiers, although fighting one another, could still be chivalrous and gentlemen and could take the time to remember what Christmas stood for. This was because we shared the same faiths and ideals. Now we are allies and are grateful for our mutual heritage.

Mrs. Spivey and I are still planning to make a trip to Europe, but we find it difficult to get away from our duties here. Perhaps soon we shall be able to visit you. In the meantime, we would be flattered if you would write us a letter telling us of yourself and your family.

We were so pleased to receive the very excellent letter from your daughter, Mrs. Warburg. She must be a great help to you, and I wish that you would tell her how flawless is her English in every respect. Please give her and her family our warm regards, and best wishes to you all for a Merry Christmas and a Happy New Year.

Sincerely,

DELMAR T. SPIVEY
Major General USAF (Ret.)
Superintendent

S*S

Colonel F.W. von Lindeiner-Wildau
Frankfurt am Main
Liebigstrasse 18
Germany

F.W. v. LINDEINER v. WILDAU FRANKFURT A. MAIN
LIEBIGSTRASSE 18
TEL. 722493

February, 18, 1963.

Dear General Spivey:

Your so kind and warmhearted [sic] letter of December 12 deserved an Answer [sic] immediately but unluckely [sic] I have been very little well up till now and it is only now that i [sic] am beginning to feel a little stronger, which will enable me, at last to thank you personally hartelyzk [heartily] for it. My wife and i [sic] sincerely reciprocate all your good wishes for 1963, for you, Mrs. Spivey and yours. May it bring you good health and fulfill all your wishes. I also hope it will enable you to cross over to Europe once more, for I should be delighted to meet you before I am too old, to enjoy it, this time as real friends and allies.

It has given me such pleasure that notwithstanding the circumstances which brought us teogether [sic] it became a friendship which bound us for the rest of our lives and I have been very grateful for all you did to keep up the connection. How much I should like to have a chat with you about politicsetc., [politics] a topic, in which we very much seem to agree. Let us hope, that common sense will at last make people join hands to put the world in a saner and better position, but it will be very hard work, to get the better of the communists. At least they continue here to work as moles and have too much influence in an underground way, which is the most dangerous. Europe is very ill and it will take years to see the bad results of communist activity. It was a real blessing, that your president gave Chrustchew [Khrushchev] a lesson at 5 minutes to twelve in Cuba and we may hope, that Mr. Chr. has understood that there will be an end to his wish for conquest of the world. But so as you say, the Western Countries must [be] still more united so as to get the better of him in the long run. But there is no time to loose [sic] and all the different countries must put back personal wishes in the object of gaining our goal for saving civilization and – still more important – for saving Christianity. No nation can remain long without a religious ideal. That gives hope, that even the coloured continents will not be overwhelmd [sic] by the Russian and Chinese theories for even heathen people have an idea of God and what has communism? Nothing farther than life in this world. I so well understand, that you see now things more through civilian eyes, which is as you say perhaps very good, it enlarges one's horizon, seeing it from different points of view.

You kindly ask after my family. Our daughter was very flattered about your opinion of her English letter. Fortunetely [sic] she is healthy except an [sic] light attack of the wellknown [sic] "Grippe", which gets hold of most people here Thanks [sic] to the change of the weather. Her eldest daughter is employed here by the Dutch Air Line cy., [sic] she is now enjoiing [sic] a lesue [leave] in Bangkok with friends at the German embassy there. Our Grandson is since nearly two years in Beyrouth [Beirut] for a big bankconcern, [sic] he will probably returm [sic] over one year, his mother and sisters were visiting him there. The youngest granddaughter is the Reception-Secretary of the U.S. Trade Center here in Frankfurt, which has been erected some months ago. We were told, that same U.S. Center exist [sic] in London and Bankok [Bangkok] and that a third will be opened within short at Tokoo. [Tokyo] My wife ist [sic] still going strong notwithstanding her age but unfortunally [sic] became a little deaf. Her sight diminished a little too, but her energy enables her to play the piano very much, a great help to spare the eyes.

And so I remain with repeated thank [sic] for your kind letter and the best regards to Mrs. Spivey from my wife and myself ever

Yours sincerely

[hand-written signature]

[This was the last letter Spivey received from von Lindeiner. The former commandant died before Spivey got to Europe to visit him. Von Lindeiner never returned to his beloved Silesia to visit once again where his parents and ancestors were buried.]

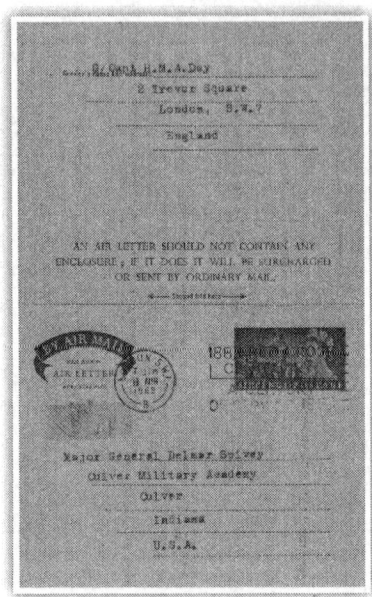

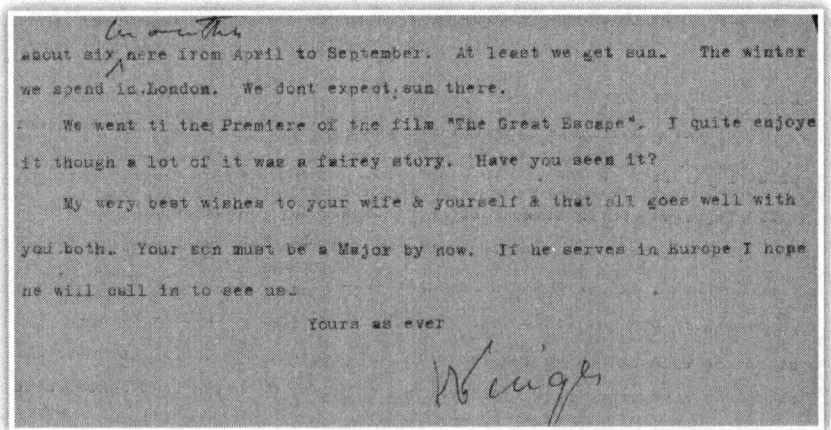

Letter from former RAF Wing Commander Harry "Wings" Day notifying Spivey of von Lindeiner's death

Monte Carlo, 14th July 1963

Dear Del,

I expect you will be interested & sorry to hear that our old Kommandant of Stalag Luft 3 is dead. His widow wrote to me & said that he had been suffering from hearts [sic] attacks for some time. The attacks became more serious & painful, which lasted a short time till he passed away on the 22nd May 1963, at his home in Frankfurt-am-Main. I suppose I had more to do with him than any other PoW. In all my dealings with him-- either stormy or calm--he always behaved with the greatest courtesy. In my opinion though an enemy, he was an "officer & a gentleman" in the best sence [sic] of the expression.

After the war when he was made a PoW in England, I visited him. Then after his release & when I retired from the RAF, I visited him three or four times at his home where I met his wife and daughter. His wife is Dutch & a very charming woman, who speaks perfect English. The last time I saw them was last year. Old Lindeiner, though still slim & straight & very much as we used to know him was definitely showing his age –he was 82 when he died.

I was very sorry indeed that von Lindeiner had passed on & wrote & expressed my sincere sympathies to his widow, from whom I got a very appreciative letter in return. I know you liked the old man & in case you feel like writing to her: a gesture I know she would value, I give you her address:- Mrs. von Lindeiner, Liebigstrasse 18,

6 Frankfurt-am-Main, M.I. Germany

My wife & I are staying in our Villa just over Monte Carlo. We spend about six months here from April to September. At least we get sun. The winter we spend in London. We don't expect sun there.

We went ti [sic] the Premiere of the film "The Great Escape". I quite enjoyed it though a lot of it was a fairey [sic] story. Have you seen it?

My very best wishes to your wife & yourself & that all goes well with you both. Your son must be a Major by now. If he serves in Europe I hope he will call in to see us.

Yours as ever

Wings
[handwritten signature]

Gott der Herr nahm heute meinen geliebten Mann, unseren lieben Vater, Schwiegervater, Großvater und Bruder im 83. Lebensjahr zu sich in sein himmlisches Reich.

FRIEDRICH-WILHELM v. LINDEINER
gen. v. WILDAU

Oberst der Luftwaffe a. D.
Inhaber beider Eiserner Kreuze von 1914 und vieler hoher Orden

Im Namen der Hinterbliebenen:

Henriette v. Lindeiner gen. v. Wildau geb. Baronesse van der Goes
Elisabeth-Charlotte v. Warburg geb. v. Lindeiner gen. v. Wildau
Albrecht v. Warburg (im Osten vermißt)
Irmgard v. Warburg
Albert v. Warburg
Alexandra v. Warburg

Frankfurt am Main, den 22. Mai 1963
Liebigstraße 18 · Seehofstraße 18 · Beyrouth / Libanon, B. P. 3246

Die Trauerfeier findet am Dienstag, dem 28. Mai 1963, um 15.30 Uhr in der Trauerhalle des Hauptfriedhofes zu Frankfurt am Main statt.

Zugedachte Blumen und Kränze direkt zum Friedhof erbeten.

Death Notice

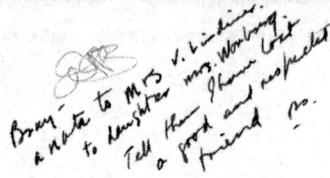

God has taken our husband, our dear father, grandfather, and brother in the 83rd year of his life.

       Friedrich-Wilhelm v. Lindeiner

          gen. v. Wildau

      Colonel (retired) of the Air Force

Possessor of both Iron Crosses of 1914 and of many high decorations

In the name of those left behind:

Henriette v. Lindeiner gen. v. Wildau geb. Baronesse van de Goes

Elisabeth-Charlotte v. Warburg   geb. v. Lindeiner gen. v. Wildau

Albrecht v. Warburg (
Irmgard v. Warburg
Albert v. Warburg
Alexandra v. Warburg

Frankfurt am Main, on May 22, 1963
Liebigstrasse 18

Funeral Tuesday, May 28, 1963 at 3:30 P.M. at the funeral home and cemetery in Frankfurt.

Flowers and wreaths to be sent directly to the cemetery.

Gen. Spivey's handwritten note on translation of death notice, asking that a note be prepared for Mrs. Lindeiner and family - "Tell them I have lost a good and respected friend."

2nd Translation

The Lord God today took my beloved, eighty-four-year-old, husband, our dear father, father-in-law, grandfather and brother to be with him in Heaven.

FRIEDRICH-WILHELM v. LINDEINER
named v. WILDAU

Colonel Luftwaffe (ret.)
Recipient of both Iron Crosses of 1914 and many higher awards

In the names of the remaining family:

Henriette v. Lindeiner named v. Wildau, nee Baronesse van der Goes
Elisabeth-Charlotte v. Warburg, nee v. Lindeiner named v. Wildau
Albrecht v. Warburg (missing on the Eastern Front)
Irmgard v. Warburg
Albert v. Warburg
Alexandra v. Warburg

Frankfurt/Main May 22, 1963
Liebigstrasse 18 Seehofstrasse 18 - Beirut /Lihaner. [Lebanon] B. F. 3246

The memorial celebration will be held on Tuesday, May 29, 1963 at 1:30 P.M. in the Hall of Mourning at the Main Cemetery in Frankfurt/Main

Flowers and wreathes are to be sent directly to the cemetery.

Signed photo of Commandant von Lindeiner
Courtesy Andrea Hatfield

Chapter 8

Final Thoughts

Severely injured in WW I, Friedrich von Lindeiner was in a unique position to observe the inner-workings of the High Command in WW II. Maintaining his "old school" principles, deeply-rooted in Prussian values, the self-confessed anti-Nazi and target of Heinrich Himmler, was determined to practice civility and humane treatment in the Luftwaffe camp. Reconciling his own beliefs, diametrically opposed to those of the High Command, he did not rule with an iron fist, but held "gentlemen's agreements" with the senior Allied officers striving to foster trust and preserve fairness.

A recurrent theme in the writings of Friedrich von Lindeiner reflects the importance he placed on treating others as he wished to be treated. That is what he aspired to do, whether they were his German contemporaries or the prisoners of war in his charge. Adhering to his own deeply ingrained personal code of conduct and value placed on honor, he frequently expressed dismay and a sense of indignation when he found that his long-held Prussian values were not always understood or respected by others in the Third Reich. According to von Lindeiner, he was unapologetic regarding his views of the Nazis, and his memoirs reveal his somewhat futile attempts to balance the needs of the prisoners with the often arbitrary dictates of the High Command, knowing missteps could mean his own life. Always under the suspicious eye of his disapproving superiors, he played a constant and potentially deadly cat and mouse game as he participated in and observed remarkable and historically-significant events during the war.

Eventually separated from his family, after losing all he owned, there is some irony and poignancy to the end of his story when he was shown benevolence by the very POWs who were formerly under his control. No sense of false pride prevented him from accepting such desperately needed help, and their willingness to give it indicates their respect for him in a reversal of roles, perhaps realizing they were treating him as they wished to be treated during their incarceration in Stalag Luft III. The admirable postwar treatment of Col. von Lindeiner is yet further testimony to the strength of character of the POWs who for years were held under his command.

See the following appendix for the story of Lisa Knüppel, Col. von Lindeiner's secretary, to gain further insight into life at Stalag Luft III and in wartime Germany.

Lisa Knüppel
Courtesy Andrea Hatfield

Appendix

Lisa Knüppel – Friedrich von Lindeiner's Secretary
A Young Woman's Life in Wartime Germany

[The following account of censor, Lisa Knüppel, is based on a 65-page interview conducted by her son, Weston Hatfield, in 1993.]

Lisa Knüppel was in school in Leipzig in 1942. If she could not pass an English exam to keep her out of conscripted labor service, she would be forced to the farms to work. With all the men gone off to war, it was expected in wartime Germany that women would work on the small farms. So she was thrilled when she passed. Next would come her oral exam.

Early on, the "Postzensur" censored the mail and books that were sent to or from all Luftwaffe prisoner of war camps. That job originally belonged to the staff at Dulag Luft where the intent had been to collect information from the mail that might be helpful in interrogating new prisoners. A Capt. von Massow, the brother of a well known Luftwaffe general, was in charge of the censoring office at Dulag Luft and remained as its chief when it was transferred to Stalag Luft III in spring 1942. At that camp, he would need lots of translators to censor the prisoners' mail.

On the day of the oral exams, von Massow, himself, and another officer sat in to listen. They interviewed the girls and then picked seven girls they felt were most fluent to serve as censors at the camp. Within a week, the girls were all at Stalag Luft III, where they would be trained. The only training they had had previously was speaking English in class.

Upon Lisa's arrival in the camp, Commandant Friedrich von Lindeiner asked censor, Alma Hauck, to show her around, and the two young women became roommates. Two barracks had been built for the forty female censors, but the buildings were completely full, so Lisa and Alma were quartered in the officers' barracks. Commandant von Lindeiner had two rooms at the end of the barrack, and Lisa and Alma were three-quarters of the way down from there. A German doctor lived next door to them, and next to him was an Austrian, Hauptman Hans Pieber, the camp adjutant, who took many of the photos in the camp. Sometimes von Lindeiner would come into the barracks and knock on their door asking, "What are you girls doing?" Lisa found he was always very cordial to them. They had the advantage of receiving the same food the officers received, while the other girls received just soup. But before too long, as the war continued, Lisa and Alma would also have only the weak cabbage soup to eat. For a time, though, Lisa was content where she was and felt grateful to be there.

Once employed at the camp, Lisa felt the relief of knowing she had bypassed laborious work on the farms. One day in the camp, she climbed a small hill and looked down from one of two towers to see women marching at 7 a.m. to go to the farms. Later, they marched back at night together. Their fates could have so easily been hers. Each year Lisa was at the camp, she was drafted again to farm service, and each year von Lindeiner wrote to the draft authorities that she was indispensable. With every reprieve, Lisa sighed with relief that she could stay.

At first, Lisa often took dictation from von Massow, whom she described as a handsome man who was kind to her and to Alma, bringing them chocolate and cloth from France when he had occasion to go there. But he was considered to be too much of an Anglophile, and some German authorities believed him to be a traitor. After about a year and a half, some Germans came looking for him. Lisa told them he had gone to Frankfurt to a seminar to gain more information on the censoring of mail and to see his wife who lived there. But later on his return, they picked him up and arrested him as a traitor, placing him in a small jail near the camp. Sometimes when he came outside Lisa spoke with him there and later directed Mrs. von Massow to the jail when she arrived. After she left, von Massow wrote small notes and gave them to Lisa to send to his wife. Von Massow once more showed up in the camp as the Russians were closing in from the East when the Germans released all German men imprisoned there to join the fight.

Each of the censors was assigned a letter of the alphabet and directed to censor the mail of all the men whose last names began with that letter. Over the months, they learned much about the POWs assigned to them. The censors could not help but notice that the POWs afforded Red Cross parcels had more to eat than they did. The camp was responsible for sending the names of the POWs to the Red Cross indicating which camps they had been assigned. Some camps failed to do so and kept personal parcels that arrived, but von Lindeiner insisted his camp play by the rules, saying, "We'll have none of that."

In von Massow's absence from the camp, von Lindeiner decided he needed a new secretary and in a room filled with others, he asked Lisa to take care of his social appointments, as he frequently invited people from other units and camps for social functions.

Lisa also worked in the commandant's office. She sat in on meetings with senior officers from the camp and translated everything said.

In her off time, she dated one of the employees in the camp. The war was not that close then, so for a short time Lisa and Alma felt their lives were idyllic. There was a Panzer unit in town for them to socialize with, and the young men in the tank regiment often invited Lisa and Alma and others to dinner. One young man taught them to play tennis. A small lake nearby was a place where they could all swim and be carefree, far from the guns of war. The war had not touched them yet, and they lived out their days as normal young people

Lisa with von Lindeiner in his office
Courtesy Andrea Hatfield

would. Sometimes von Lindeiner would have the censors driven to a movie or social event. But their carefree days were numbered.

Mrs. von Lindeiner, Baronesse Henriette van der Goes, a Dutch aristocrat, lived in a lovely country estate in Sagan called Jeschkendorf, close enough for her husband to join her on weekends.

Jeschkendorf Villa
Courtesy Marek Lazarz and Marian Swiatek

Lisa visited with the von Lindeiners there and many times spent her weekends with them. The estate was about twenty kilometers [12 miles] from the camp and belonged to a family relative. The commandant had a car, and Lisa either drove with him or rode her bicycle there. She often joined the von Lindeiners for dinner, after which the commandant's servant would drive her back to the camp. Von Lindeiner would send the servant home while they dined, "because he didn't want him to know that we could listen to the BBC there." They would listen after dinner until midnight.

"Von Lindeiner would never be a traitor, but of course, he hated Hitler," said Lisa. "One time a man came in with something in a briefcase, and he had his arm in a sling; he had been wounded at the front. And I asked who he was. Von Lindeiner said, 'It's better if you don't know.' Most of the time I was in there when he had other people coming, but this time he said, 'Lisa, I must ask you to excuse us. It will be better for your own safety not to know about what we are discussing.'"

When in July 1944, Col. Claus von Stauffenberg tried to assassinate Hitler, Lisa recognized him as the man who had visited that day. Von

Lindeiner had asked her to be quiet about his having been there, and she mentioned the visit to no one.

One day, von Lindeiner had a nice surprise for Lisa. He approached her saying, "Here Lisa, I've got something for you," and he reached into the big pocket of his coat and pulled out a very little animal that looked like a rat. "What is it?" she asked. "It's a puppy. Its mother won't feed it, and I told the lady I had another mother who would take care of it," replied the commandant, who well knew Lisa's love of animals. Then he put his hand in his other pocket, and she said, "Not another one!" He smiled and said, "Oh, I thought you might like another one." But he was just teasing her. She accepted the little rat of a pup and named it Nikki. The dog slept in her room in the camp and learned to eat the same food she did, cabbage and all.

Later, Lisa was to gain one more dog in a most unusual way when a British flier was shot down and arrived at the camp with a sling holding his arm. Tucked inside the sling was his crew's mascot that had flown that day. It was a small, white, whippet-like dog that had managed to parachute down with the flier and make it through interrogation and transfer to the camp. Her name was Kino. The flier was adamant about keeping the dog, and the Germans, who summoned him to their office, were just as adamant that he must give it up. In obvious great distress, the flier held the dog tightly. Lisa, who had been translating for the Germans, stepped forward and offered to take the dog much to the flier's relief. She kept it with her and Nikki in the barrack.

Kino adjusted to POW life well. She was fast and agile, and she could run anywhere. In fact, she became an expert at going under the wire to find her former master and share in his Red Cross parcel treats rather than eat the cabbage that Lisa and Nikki ate. Von Lindeiner loved watching her

Lisa with Kino and Nikki
Courtesy Andrea Hatfield

zip so gracefully around the barracks and the Vorlager but could not have suspected she was a spy who liked to slip through the barbed wire and visit with the prisoners and deliver messages to Lisa.

One night when Kino was lying at the foot of Lisa's bed, she ran her hand down to pet the dog, and her fingers touched a small piece of paper hidden under the dog's collar, put there by the British flier. She slowly and carefully opened it. The writing seemed almost microscopic. "Thank you so much for taking care of Kino. I wish I could send you more than thank yous." Other notes followed, and Lisa read them all, but she could never risk answering the notes for fear of severe reprisals. "If I had been caught with those, I would not be here today," she would say in her later years.

Von Lindeiner and Lisa often took the two dogs for walks just outside the barbed wire surrounding the prisoners' barracks. On one occasion, they discussed a party that the commandant was planning for all the panzer troops stationed in Sagan because they were being transferred to the Eastern Front. He knew what their fate would be. He told Lisa that they should at least be given a nice evening before they had to go into the fire. The party was scheduled for the day after the Great Escape would take place. But even before that fateful night, Von Lindeiner had sensed something was brewing.

"You know, there is something going on in the camp," he said to Lisa with great concern. "They were all waving to us, and when we were walking near the fence with the dogs, they were singing when we waved back. I think they have something. There is something going on."

"But you just put the guards and dogs in there," Lisa countered. How could there be anything else, because they already discovered a tunnel?" [Tunnel Tom was discovered September 1943.]

Von Lindeiner was not sure. As Lisa planned the party, von Lindeiner was still restless.

"I think we haven't gotten it all. I just have a feeling there is more going on. They have something in mind, or there is another tunnel."

Lisa asked how they could do it.

"There are very smart young men in there. We will have to think about that. I hope you have made arrangements for all of this," von Lindeiner said to Lisa, asking about the proposed party, and Lisa said that she had.

Alma and others had helped her. Lisa knew a lot of the young men in the panzer unit, and she particularly liked one of them. Sadly, she later found that he was shot almost immediately when he went to the Front. His parents sent her the letter he had written to her that he had in his pocket when he died. Due to the Great Escape and its immediate aftermath, it is unknown if the party ever took place for that young man and the others to attend.

Lisa drew closer to the von Lindeiners, and they depended upon her in many ways. One of their young granddaughters, Alexandra, was staying at their estate, but she grew so homesick that the commandant asked Lisa to help escort her to Frankfurt where her mother was (The girl's father was fighting in Leningrad.). Lisa went with the young girl as far as Berlin where she handed Alexandra over to another trusted helper for the continued journey to Frankfurt. Afterwards, Lisa went home to Hamburg for a little while to see her father.

As a girl living at home in Hamburg, before she went to school in Leipzig, Lisa remembered the air raids. Huge spotlights illuminated the sky searching for enemy planes and when a plane was shot down, she watched the stricken airmen coming down in parachutes. The Germans kept them in the spotlights so they could find them on the ground. "I always had this terrible feeling, I hope they don't get you, I hope they don't get you," Lisa remembered thinking. She and her brother, Eilert, three years older than she, stood on the balcony and watched the air battles. He was later taken prisoner by the Russians. Hamburg had become a town of nightly bombings where men went away and never came home.

In July 1943, Hamburg was bombed again, and 44,000 people were killed that night. Lisa heard of the bombing on the radio. The commandant tried to get through using military channels but could not learn anything of Lisa's father, who was alone there in their big family house near the river. With no telephone service, Lisa felt she needed to go to Hamburg to find him. Von Lindeiner sent her off with Unteroffizier Walters, whose family was also in Hamburg. Together Lisa and Walters took a jeep out of the camp and soon passed the destruction of bombed out Berlin. When they got to Hamburg, they tried for two days to get through all the rubble left in the wake of the raid. The Germans there were not letting anyone in without papers. Walters showed the papers that von Lindeiner had given to him, saying that they were on a mission to see some Air Force people in Hamburg. That got them in, but once past the guards, they could drive no further. They had tried to enter on the most heavily damaged side of Hamburg but having no luck, they decided to drive around to try another section. It was very hot with flames still crackling and licking the broken and crumbling foundations, a strong odor of death pervading the smoke and haze. Even in the daytime, the city was dark from so much smoke allowing no sunlight to penetrate the black pall that hung over the city. Then a tremendous windstorm arose, causing tongues of flame to skip from one house to another, burning and sparing at random, capricious in its path.

The original plan was to have Walters bring Lisa home and then go back to find his family. But finally they had to leave the car outside the city. Together, they crawled over broken rocks and jagged stones only to find streets blocked. The fire department could not get to the interior of the city, so the fire continued to burn. With agonizing effort, the two clawed their way over the mountains of rubble, and Lisa's fingers soon became raw from the effort. Former homes and well-known buildings were grotesquely misshapen and almost unrecognizable. Lisa and Walters could hardly breathe. The stench of decaying bodies became unbearable, and rats scurried around at every turn. When they could not continue, due to the smoke and the heat, they returned to the jeep and drove further around the city, where they got out and proceeded once more on foot. Lisa was then closer to where she had lived near the Alster River and could recognize what remained of the area. Getting her that far, Walters left to find his own family.

With mounting trepidation, Lisa walked along on what she remembered to be her street and cautuiously moved towards her house, locating it by noting vacant smoking holes where neighboring houses had previously stood. Families and homes were completely gone. On some lots, splintered frames and broken chimneys stood stark like broken teeth, jagged and deformed. Ahead, she saw her own house still standing and ran toward it eagerly hoping and praying that her father was there and alive. She looked up and saw him on the roof frantically jabbing at flames with a mop. The night before, the British had firebombed the city lighting roofs on fire as the deadly bombs hit. Her father had carried sandbags up there, and Lisa watched as he tried desperately to tamp down the scattered sparks.

"Oh, Papa, Papa! Be careful!" Lisa cried.

She had not seen her father in approximately a year, but there was no time for a loving reunion.

"Daughter! Come up here! Come up here quickly! Bring me some sand!"

Lisa ran through the house and up to the attic to fetch more sandbags and carry them to the roof. She and her weary father worked together to save their home.

Living in the bombed town was nearly impossible. Citizens could not drink the water, could not cook anything, and had no electricity. A soup kitchen was set up, but it took an hour and a half to receive any food there. Lisa and her father slept in the bunk beds in the basement of their home at night and sat on the front porch and watched the skies by day. A few nights later there was another attack. Lisa had been sitting in a comfortable chair in the basement when the bombs hit the house across the street. With the blast and the cacophony that followed, she flew through the air in the chair. Every window in the house was knocked out, and glass shattered in all directions. The doors were blown open, and a gaping hole opened up in the roof. Thankfully, Lisa and her father could get out of the basement. Across the street sat what remained of a bombed out home, and the rest of the street did not look much better.

Two weeks passed. Lisa and her father had remained in the damaged home until most of the rubble was cleared away. After the bombings, Lisa returned to Sagan, reluctantly leaving her father and terrified of what the future would bring. Before too long, there would be more trauma when Stalag Luft III was evacuated. "The time in Hamburg and the time when we were leaving Sagan were the worst times of the war for me," she said decades later.

Eight months passed after Lisa returned to the camp before one of the most dramatic and profound events occurred—The Great Escape—when 80 men emerged in the night from Tunnel Harry. Four were stopped at the entrance, and 76 dispersed into the nearby woods. Only three made a successful escape, and fifty were murdered by the Gestapo in the weeks that followed. On the night of the Great Escape, Lisa had gone to a movie with the young tank commander about to leave for the Front, the one who was immediately shot when he arrived there. In order to get back to the camp, they had to go down some steps at the railroad station and then walk over the tracks. The camp was below. At the station they saw more people in the station than were normally there.

"Look at all these people," she said, "Who are they?"

"Oh I think they are just Russian civilian workers," her date said. "They didn't want to go back to Russia because Stalin said that anyone who lets themselves be caught is going to lose his head if he comes home."

Her reassurance was short lived when he took her back to the barrack where Alma was anxiously waiting for her.

"It's kind of restless in camp," Alma observed.

"Von Lindeiner is restless, too, but I think he is too worried," Lisa responded.

Not fully understanding what was ahead Alma and Lisa went to sleep. At 5:00 a.m. a loud knocking on her window woke her up.

"Report to the commandant's office immediately!" the excited voice screamed.

"Now?" Lisa asked in her confusion.

"Massive outbreak, massive outbreak!" came the stunning words.

Lisa got dressed and ran over to von Lindeiner's office. He was in a great state of distress.

"Lisa, what are we going to do? What are they going to do to those people when they catch them? I have no reach as long as that, because I have to stay here! My orders are to stay here. I just don't know if they have a chance if they get caught," he continued. "Why would they do this to me? I've tried to be as good to them as I possibly could. They might hang me! The Abwehr [security] might hang me!" he said.

"Well if it had been you, you probably would have tried to do the same thing," Lisa replied.

"I know it, but I still can't believe it," came the resigned response.

Later, upon hearing the men were caught, von Lindeiner said, "These are not SS people. These are people who are supposed to be under my jurisdiction. I'm responsible, and I demand that they be brought back to our camp!"

At first, the SS brought some of the escapers back, and von Lindeiner was glad. He addressed the returning prisoners: "Now fellows, you are causing all of us, especially yourselves, a lot of trouble, and we are sorry about this, but we will try to keep you here with us as long as the war is on."

One officer in the camp, who was a real Nazi, mocked the commandant when he spoke that way confronting him and snapping to attention with a "Heil Hitler!" salute. But the worst was yet to come. Right after the Great Escape, the Abwehr descended upon the camp. The SS had accused von Lindeiner of allowing the prisoners to escape, and he protested strongly.

"I'm here to keep them here, to keep them well-treated. They were treated according to the Geneva Convention."

But his protests fell on deaf ears, and the coming days were increasingly difficult for him. Lisa remained loyal to the commandant throughout his ordeal.

"Yes, I remember going down when they got him. Von Lindeiner, with head high, so majestically walking along," said Lisa. "He walked down--they had two officers on each side. I was behind them. He turned around suddenly and tossed me his keys. He said, 'See to it that my wife gets out before the Russians come; try to see if you can get her to go to Frankfurt.'"*

[*] [There is often some confusion as to the time frame of events regarding von Lindeiner's departure from the camp. According to Col. Art Durand, author of *The Great Escape—The Secret Story,"* on March 26, von Lindeiner was ordered to stay in the camp until his court martial

was scheduled. He was handed a writ by Luftgau Command III that day when Deputy Judge Advocate General, Dr. Garbe, visiting the camp, relieved him of his command. On March 29th, von Lindeiner collapsed in the camp and returned to his estate to recuperate. He stayed there for the next eleven weeks before he was officially questioned, as were some employees of the camp. It was on Sept. 16th, late one night, that one of his employees knocked on his door to warn him of his upcoming court martial, suggesting he leave Sagan. But on Oct. 2nd he was still there and proceeded to the court martial Oct. 25th to testify. In late October, after von Lindeiner returned to Sagan after the court martial to await sentencing, a medical commission arrived and ordered him to Reserve Lazarett I at Görlitz, where he stayed until the Russians closed in from the east in January 1944. He was dismissed from the medical facility just two days before the Germans evacuated Stalag Luft III. Von Lindeiner was back in Sagan fifteen hours later to rejoin the fighting there. He was injured Feb. 12, 1945, arriving at Reserve Lazarett IV G in Leipzig, and then transferred to the Reserve Lazarett at Blankenburg in the Harz, where he became a prisoner of the Americans and then the British. Lisa's description of von Lindeiner being escorted out of the camp most likely occurred when he was first taken to Görlitz.]

And then he was gone. Greatly alarmed at the circumstances that were unfolding, Lisa went out to the estate on her bicycle to find Mrs. von Lindeiner.

"At first we didn't think it was necessary to leave," said Lisa. "I told her what he had told me. Then, when we heard that the Mongolians were coming and that the war was going badly, I went out there again and said, 'You've got to leave or you won't get out.'"

"I can't leave all my things," Mrs. von Lindeiner said.

"I had the hardest time persuading her that she had to leave. I tried to get her to pack up her clothes, and she would say, 'but this I can't leave, and this I can't leave.'

She didn't want to leave her things. I couldn't blame her; she had so many beautiful things, but I just finally talked her into putting everything into an empty water tower, or maybe it was a silo, and locking it in there."

After they hid Mrs. von Lindeiner's belongings, Lisa got her to the train station and put her on the train, telling her that maybe later she could go back and claim her belongings. [Eventually, the Russians took over Jeschkendorf, and Mrs. von Lindeiner never returned to retrieve her possessions. For years after the war, before she was reunited with her husband, the then impoverished Duchess taught piano lessons to make ends meet. Her husband later remarked how proud he was of his wife that she had managed to make it on her own.]

Back in Sagan, Lisa was called in for questioning by the SS and held in a hotel in Sagan, where she was threatened with jail time in Breslau if she didn't tell them everything she knew about von Lindeiner's alleged complicity in the escape plot.

"They said they were going to cut my hair; I had really thick, blond hair at that point, and long."

"You know, as soon as you get to the jail for women, they'll shear you, shave your head off because of the fleas and lice," the SS interrogator said.

"And I wondered what my father would think if someone told him that his daughter was in jail in Breslau….. he would wonder what in the world I could have done."

The focus of her interrogation centered on whether von Lindeiner had done certain things or not. Lisa's questioners didn't mistreat her, but they left her in a room on about the 7th floor for long hours at a time. She looked to see if she could get out if she climbed down, but decided it was too dangerous.

The hours passed slowly while she was confined. The SS fed Lisa well, but she had nothing to read and nothing to do. Interrogation broke the monotony for her and interrupted the boredom, but she continued to fear what could happen to her. One of the men who interrogated her, whom she remarked was "rather attractive," was called Absalon. [Krimilalkommissar Dr. Gunther Absalon had spent weeks in Sagan investigating the escape and collecting evidence. He chaired the German enquiry into the escape.]

Lisa said he would bring her a glass of wine and say, "Let's have a little talk. What about so and so and so and so?" he asked about all the people whom he suspected.

"Oh he's a really nice man," Lisa would reply. "He wouldn't do that."

"I don't want to know if he is a nice man; I want to know if he worked with the prisoners. Do you know if he helped the prisoners?"

"Oh no, he never would have done that."

The interrogation continued in the same vein without Lisa giving away any information.

"Several people had collaborated, but they got away," said Lisa, years later. "Several of the German soldiers would go in and out of the camp, and some of them gave the prisoners their passes so they could duplicate them. But as far as I know, none of them actually helped the prisoners escape. These were von Lindeiner's soldiers, but he didn't know about it."

With so little to eat, some Germans were tempted to trade their passes for food from the prisoners' Red Cross parcels. Walters was one of them because he always brought Alma and Lisa goodies he got from the prisoners such as coffee and chocolate. Absalon asked about others, including Walters, but mainly he wanted to know about the commandant.

"Does he listen to the foreign radio?"

Lisa knew that was forbidden and claimed she did not know.

"I don't think he even has a radio," she said.

Later, Absalon said to her, "Your commandant had a visitor not long ago, didn't he?"

Lisa knew he was referring to Col. von Stauffenberg, but she claimed she did not know and so the Abwehr could not pin any charges on von Lindeiner in connection with the assassination attempt on Hitler. After the attempt, Hitler was killing all the older officers he suspected of being involved—the old guard. Von Lindeiner was sixty-two so quite vulnerable.

After a week, Absalon could not get any information from Lisa or the others held there before her. She had been there two days and one night. She asked Absalon to tell her father that she was jailed for not telling lies and requested that he take her to the camp to get her toothbrush and other items she would need while she was confined. Absalom took Lisa to his car and started driving, passing the entrance to the camp as though he was taking her to Breslau, and she became very fearful. After ten minutes in silence he said, "I can't get anything out of you, can I?"

"There is nothing to get out of me; I don't get into the prisoners' compound. I can't tell you anything," said Lisa. So Absalon turned the car around and soon let her out at the camp with a warning. "I shouldn't do this, but I just can't take you there to that awful place. Just be careful, lady."

After her ordeal, Lisa soon returned to work. By then, a new commandant, Col. Franz Braune, had replaced von Lindeiner. He was SS, and Lisa did not want to work for him.

"It was a matter of honor with von Lindeiner to treat these people right according to the Geneva Convention. Well, the SS didn't feel that way. The Abwehr had planned to blow up the camp in case the war would go badly. Von Lindeiner would have only to push a button and blow it up, but he would not do it and that made the officers for Abwehr angry."

The war continued to go badly for the Germans, and the prisoners as well as the Germans in the camp knew the end was near. British and Russians were both approaching from different directions, and the Germans hoped the British would get there first. When that proved unlikely, there was renewed urgency to evacuate the camp. Lisa and the others had heard von Lindeiner was back in the area to fight, and Lisa could scarcely believe a man his age, who still limped from his wounds from the First World War, was in that position.

At midnight, shortly after the last POWs left the camp, Lisa and Alma and the other young women at the camp were awakened and told to be ready to leave the camp in an hour. After quickly packing what they could, including Red Cross parcels that departing prisoners had abandoned, Alma and Lisa put their things on a sled. They had given the Dachshund, Nikki the "rat dog," to Lilo Walters, a friend who was staying in Sagan. Lilo had a baby and elderly parents and felt it would be too difficult for them to travel. Her friends urged her to leave before the Russians got there, but she felt she could safely hide from them. Unfortunately, six Russians did find her, raped her, knocked out her teeth and beat her. It is unclear what happened to Nikki. When the war was over and Lisa was finally able to return to Hamburg, Lilo visited her there, having endured a long hospitalization and reconstructive surgery.

Lisa and the other censors trekked through the snow towards the train station in the freezing night after the camp had been emptied of all its prisoners but the sick, who would fall into the hands of the Russians. Much to the chagrin of some of the censors, Lisa brought Kino along, who was pregnant again after already having one litter at Stalag Luft III. But the dog proved its worth in the cold box cars later on when all the young women argued about who would get to cuddle with her for warmth.

"We took everything that we could from the camp to the train station on a sled and left the sled. It was so cold."

During the coldest winter in fifty years in Germany, Lisa stood at the Sagan train station, knowing her life was about to change dramatically and wondering where she was going or if she would ever see her father again. She looked down to see a long track of people in the snow, old men and woman and young children, many pulled in carts by oxen, puffs of bluish breath in the frigid air emitted from the exhausted animals. Some refugees fleeing from the Russians rode in covered wagons with wooden wheels clattering along the icy road, the wheels frequently freezing solid. No one had gasoline, so they could only retreat by foot and by wagons pulled by emaciated animals. The snow fell from the sky as the long undulating line slowly snaked its way forward. Refugees desperately tried to climb onto the train. It was the last train out, and some of the terrified refugees, knowing of the Russians' reputation for brutality, climbed up on the tops of the frosted cars.

"The prisoners had left the camp--marched out, and the guards marched with them. They had gone before we left and after we had been on the train half an hour, we saw them on the side of the road. You could see that they were so tired. It was cold, and they would huddle together. I can remember that sometimes the prisoners would carry the guns because many of the guards were so weak and were limping, so they helped each other. It got to be that they became friends on the march out. The British and American prisoners did not want to fall into the hands of those Russian troops either."

On that last train out, forty girls shivered in the cold. An inadequate pot belly stove sat in the center of their car, and straw covered the floor. The car only grew colder as the train steamed its way through the black frigid night. Sometimes during the night the women would hear the screams of those who had fallen off the top of the train. Badly injured German soldiers moaned inconsolably in the wagon in front of the censors' wagon. No one could guess their fate. The train started and repeatedly stopped, and the moaning continued.

When the train did stop, the women tried to get water for the soldiers and help at local Red Cross stations. At one of those stations, an exhausted woman left Lisa with her little boy. The woman had five children, including a baby, and she said, "My little boy is so tired. Can I leave him here? I think we have relatives in this town, and I will pick him up later on."

Lisa said they could make the child a little bed on a bench, but she could not guarantee she would be there later, nor could the woman from the Red Cross. Still the mother insisted on leaving her son. The little boy went to sleep right away; when he awoke a few hours later, Lisa realized that he was not normal.

He said, "Where's my mommy? Are you my mommy?"

"Our train was coming, but we couldn't just leave him there. Alma said, 'You're crazy to do this,' but you could see the hospital. It was up the hill maybe a few blocks. One other woman from the Red Cross was with me, and we ran up there to the hospital and pushed the boy in the door. She stayed with him. She was going to watch him, and I ran back, and I just got there in time. I saw the train coming, and boy I could run!"

Days later, the hissing steam engine, carrying its miserable lot, pulled into Dresden. Ambulances met the train, and workers took the wounded soldiers to the hospital. It had taken several days to get there due to sirens sounding and all the lights going out. When the sirens screamed, signaling an air raid, the train would screech to a slow stop, and the censors would jump out of the train and hold their wash basins over their heads to protect them from shrapnel. When it was over, they filed back onto the train calling, "Kino! Kino!" and the dog always came running back. Dresden and the hospital were bombed three days later, so the women knew all the injured soldiers had been killed there.

The groaning train finally delivered the censors to Nuremberg, where they were put in a camp filled with Russian prisoners. After three days they left, much relieved, as they felt that if a bomb fell on that camp, the Russian prisoners would break out and come after them. They moved on to Roth, a town near Nuremberg, initially staying in a freezing castle before being moved to an empty building that had some heat. From the top floor, they could see fighter planes coming in, and they watched bombs fall on the town. With much dismay, Lisa saw two fighter pilots shoot at grazing cows, "just to see the poor cattle run like crazy. One of the planes was flying so low that it stuck in the ground."

For safety, the women were moved to a medical institute in Roth where research was conducted on diseases and immunizations, particularly typhoid. The scientific lab was full of mice, rats, guinea pigs, and incubators full of eggs with chicks hatching every day. A week later, the Americans arrived and arrested the German military personnel working at the institute. The women were not allowed to leave the area without a permit, so the censors found themselves caring for all the lab animals, feeding them, and counting how many chicks hatched during the night. At first they were fearful of the mice, picking them up by their tails with tweezers, but in time they came to be more comfortable with them, and Lisa found the white rats to be very tame and "very nice." Lisa moved the chicks in the kitchen as it had gotten cold again, keeping them in a round container. One day some American soldiers came in, "a really rough group," and tried to persuade the women to go out with them. When the women refused, the Americans' leader got furious, and as the girls huddled together for safety, he took a kettle of hot water and poured it over the chicks. Lisa was so angry she began to cry and picked up something to hit him, screaming, "You beast!" Fortunately, the other girls held her back.

The censors knew the war was over, yet according to Lisa, "idiot German officers" continued to blow up bridges. Ironically, the POWs' mail followed the censors from the camp. The letters had been loaded on a truck during the evacuation and given to the women when they first arrived at the castle in Roth. In the chaos of the time, the personal messages of love and encouragement from families were left behind in the cold fortress when the censors moved on.

While in Roth, Kino had her puppies. She emerged from under the bed one day, bringing a puppy to place at Lisa's feet. Soon, she brought out four more. Some friendly American soldiers adopted them as pets.

The American government soon set up headquarters in Anspach, Germany. They were looking for people to work there and would provide free transportation by jeep. No trains or buses were available at that time as all modes of transportation had been destroyed. Alma and Lisa decided to go. Not knowing what their living arrangement would be, sadly Lisa finally had to leave Kino behind. A nice girl, whose home was nearby, promised to care for her. She did not know Kino was pregnant again.

That was the last Lisa saw of her beloved Kino. After the war, the Englishman who had brought Kino into Stalag Luft III traced Lisa to Hamburg and came to pick up his dog. "I was sick, I wasn't feeling well, this other fellow was in the house, and suddenly our dog barked like wild, and there came these four British officers," said Lisa. "Well, the whole neighborhood looked at me as though I was a traitor to even talk to them. But I didn't let them stay long. I just told them where they could find the dog."

As Lisa and Alma were leaving Roth to go to Anspach, the prisoners from Stalag Luft III were only about two weeks from liberation. Lisa and Alma heard on the radio that President Roosevelt had died and that Harry Truman had taken over. Lisa felt Roosevelt was a great man. The prisoners in their camps and marching along the roads towards freedom in a nearly defeated Germany heard the same news.

In order to work in Anspach, Lisa and Alma had a lot of paperwork to fill out declaring that they had not belonged to the Nazi party. A new American lieutenant just arriving there helped them with the paperwork. He asked Lisa if she had ever belonged to a youth group. She said she had but when she refused to do the Heil Hitler salute, they threw her out. Later, Alma and Lisa agreed the officer was charming and had a good sense of humor. "It might be fun to be married to someone like that,"

Alma speculated. Lisa agreed. Six months passed, and Lisa ran into the lieutenant one day on the steps of a large office building, and they exchanged pleasantries. She was working for the German Public Health Dept. and the American Public Health Division as an interpreter. The lieutenant, Weston Hatfield, asked her if she was celebrating Bastille Day, as she was wearing a dress someone had made her from the remains of an old German Nazi Party flag, one of her two sheets, and a blue piece of cloth. Lisa liked his humor.

Lisa's job as an interpreter entailed travelling with an American doctor and a German doctor to various camps, hospitals, mental hospitals, and slaughterhouses. She was able to stay at nice hotels, where she finally had her own towels and soap, which had been luxuries

Weston Hatfield and Lisa
Courtesy Andrea Hatfield

during the war. There was a tremendous shortage of German doctors at that time, not because they did not exist, but because after the war they lost their licenses to practice if they had belonged to the Nazi party. The irony was that during the Nazi era many were not permitted to graduate from medical school unless they had joined the party. When Lisa and her employers visited mental hospitals, in particular, where there were no doctors and no medicine, she shuddered at what she saw there. Children who could not be treated due to the lack of pediatricians were kept in small cages. Lisa and her colleagues argued with American authorities to let the German doctors practice. It was a slow process, but finally they saw some relief for the suffering people, who were being neglected, as German doctors were allowed to again help in the humanitarian effort.

At one point, Lisa's travels took her to Frankfurt, and she visited with von Massow's wife there. Von Massow has been taken away his wife said. In the chaos of war, Lisa had lost track of him, but after her visit she received a letter from his wife saying he had committed suicide, responding to the pressure of other Germans accusing of him of betraying the Third Reich.

Lisa's path continued to cross with that of the young Lt. Hatfield when she had to go and pick up physicians' licenses. An aide to Hatfield once asked her what she would think about dating the boss. "Not much," Lisa said, and explained she would not consider dating Americans until all the German POWs were home from the United States. Not long afterward, Lt. Hatfield was transferred to Bremen and then back to the United States. Before he left, Lisa came to know him better and through many letters after he got home their relationship grew. Three years would pass before they were to meet again. Eventually, Weston asked Lisa to come to the United States. He sold his car to buy her a plane ticket as German money had been devalued and was worthless.

Before leaving for the United States, Lisa decided to go to Graz, Austria, to see her sister Gerda, knowing full well that travel was dangerous and often nearly impossible, especially with no official papers. She made her way south from Hamburg to Munich, aware that there were people there who, for a small sum, could get her across the border to Austria. Once in Austria, dressed in a peasant-style dirndl skirt with a loaf of bread stuck into her backpack like a farmer's daughter, she made her way to Graz, traveling first by foot, sometimes hiding to avoid patrols on the road, and then by hitching rides on an ox cart and on the back of a motorcycle, relying on strangers for help and directions and advice on how to avoid the authorities.

The final leg of the journey was by train. Just as she was disembarking, exhausted but overjoyed, a loud piercing whistle screamed its alarm. Two people had escaped from prison, and the authorities were searching for them in the train station. Nobody could leave. All papers needed to be checked, and Lisa had none. In a panic, she fled to the ladies' room and hid there. When she felt it was safe, she cautiously peered from a window and realized that if she could get to the other side of the station, she could get away. With all the courage she could muster, she raced across the station and into the street, where she managed to catch a bus to an apartment where relatives of her sister lived. Safely there, Lisa sat down and cried. She learned that Gerda had taken her two boys and gone to their family's mountain house. After yet one more train ride and long walk, Lisa finally saw Gerda walking with her children and a little deer they had found that had lost its mother. She fell into her sister's arms. After a visit that she knew could be her last, Lisa borrowed her sister's papers to get back to Germany, later returning them by mail.

Her mind made up to fly to the United States to visit Weston, Lisa made her way through Hamburg at Christmas, seeing twinkling Christmas trees and candles flickering in windows, sights seldom observed in the dark years of the war. She went to Frankfurt by train to board her plane. It was cold and from the train's frosted widow she could see children going through garbage cans, a tragic aftermath of Hitler's failed Third Reich. The madness had touched them all. And now it was time for her to leave. She arrived in New York, and before her visa ran out she would become Mrs. Weston Hatfield. She and her husband would eventually have four children and a long and happy marriage.

After the war and after his years as a prisoner of war held by the British, von Lindeiner went to Hamburg to visit Lisa, who had temporarily returned from the States to introduce her infant daughter to her family in Germany. The commandant had been reunited with his wife and lived very modestly in Frankfurt, and far from his days in Sagan, he had become a broken man. That was the last time Lisa saw her friend and former boss. But in the years that followed, she corresponded with him and his wife until the day he died. He shared with her the fact that officers and former POWs from the camp were in touch with him and sent him packages, and he was grateful for their attentions. Germany's recovery was very slow, and those like Col. von Lindeiner, the censors, and the prisoners of war, whose lives crossed at Stalag Luft III, would forever retain the experience.

From the Director

It is hard for me to daily pass the cold, white, sculptured stone memorial erected by POWs in 1944 to remember the fifty RAF POWs who were murdered by the Gestapo after the mass escape known as the Great Escape without thinking of the aftermath of that horrid event for prisoners and Germans alike. For one man, the former commandant of the camp, Col. Friedrich von Lindeiner, the escape would mean his removal from the camp in disgrace and his eventual court martial. With all the books written on the Great Escape, his is a story that has remained in the background of the war's tales. With the discovery of his memoirs, we can now analyze his assessment of events in the camp. It is clear that the unexpected murder of the fifty traumatized him greatly, and fourteen years after the event he wrote of his feelings. The stone monument tells the story of the fifty. This book tells the story of von Lindeiner.

As director of the POW Camps Muzeum in Zagan, Poland, where the Great Escape took place, I would like to thank Marilyn Walton and Mike Eberhardt for their second book (like their first book) that will benefit the muzeum so that we in Poland can continue to pay tribute to the Allied airmen who were imprisoned here.

Cześć ich pamięci! (We will remember them!)

Marek Lazarz
Director
Muzeum Obozów Jenieckich (POW Camps Museum)
Zagan, Poland

Authors' Biographies

Marilyn Jeffers Walton is a graduate of The Ohio State University, an editor and author of six children's books and World War II nonfiction. This collaborative endeavor is her eleventh book and second with Michael Eberhardt after completing, *From Interrogation to Liberation - A Photographic Journey - Stalag Luft III – The Road to Freedom*. She has written two non-fiction books about police K9s and numerous magazine articles for World War II and Police K9 publications. As a World War II researcher and historian, she has visited Stalag Luft III and together with other "kriegie kids," re-enacted her father's 52-mile winter evacuation march to Spremberg, Germany. Previously, she had located her father's crash site, meeting the woman who watched him bail out of his B-24, "Rhapsody in Junk." That experience was the impetus for her book, *Rhapsody in Junk—A Daughter's Return to Germany to Finish Her Father's Story*. She is the mother of three sons and lives in Columbus, Ohio, with her retired university professor husband.

Michael C. Eberhardt is a lawyer in private practice, having previously worked for the U.S. Department of Justice, U.S. House and Senate Committees, and the Department of Defense. As co-author of *From Interrogation to Liberation – A Photographic Journey - Stalag Luft III – The Road to Freedom,* he next initiated the effort to publish the von Lindeiner memoirs. He is married with two children and resides in Dallas, Texas. His interest in the subject of this book stems from a 2011 trip to Stalag Luft III, where his father was held as a POW, as well as meetings and correspondence with ex-POWs, surviving crew members from his father's B-17, and descendants of German camp personnel. He has researched and visited his father's crash site near Munich, Germany, meeting eyewitnesses who are helping him document the experience of the crew of B-17, "Little Audrey."

Marilyn and Michael both remain active in supporting the Museum in Zagan, Poland, and its efforts to preserve the history of Stalag Luft III.